plant sciences

plant sciences

VOLUME **1**
Ab–Cl

Richard Robinson, Editor in Chief

Macmillan Reference USA

imprint of the Gale Group

San Francisco • London • Boston • Woodbridge, CT

Macmillan Reference USA
1633 Broadway
New York, NY 10019

Gale Group
27500 Drake Rd.
Farmington Hills, MI 48331-3535

Printed in Canada
1 2 3 4 5 6 7 8 9 10

Library of Congress Cataloging-in-Publication Data
Plant sciences / Richard Robinson, editor in chief.
    p.   cm.
Includes bibliographical references (p.   ).
ISBN 0-02-865434–X (hardcover : set) — ISBN 0-02–865430-7 (vol. 1) —
ISBN 0-02-865431-5 (vol. 2) — ISBN 0-02-865432-3 (vol. 3) —
ISBN 0-02-865433-1 (vol. 4)
    1. Botany—Juvenile literature.   2. Plants—Juvenile literature. [1.
    Botany—Encyclopedias.] I. Robinson, Richard, 1956-
QK49.P52 2000
580—dc21
00—046064

Preface

Someone once said that if you want to find an alien life form, just go into your backyard and grab the first green thing you see. Although plants evolved on Earth along with the rest of us, they really are about as different and strange and wonderful a group of creatures as one is likely to find anywhere in the universe.

The World of Plants

Consider for a minute just how different plants are. They have no mouths, no eyes or ears, no brain, no muscles. They stand still for their entire lives, planted in the soil like enormous drinking straws wicking gallon after gallon of water from the earth to the atmosphere. Plants live on little more than water, air, and sunshine and have mastered the trick of transmuting these simple things into almost everything they (and we) need. In this encyclopedia, readers will find out how plants accomplish this photosynthetic alchemy and learn about the extraordinary variety of form and function within the plant kingdom. In addition, readers will be able to trace their 450-million-year history and diversification, from the very first primitive land plants to the more than 250,000 species living today.

✳Explore further in Photosynthesis, Light Reactions and Evolution of Plants

All animals ultimately depend on photosynthesis for their food, and humans are no exception. Over the past ten thousand years, we have cultivated such an intimate relationship with a few species of grains that it is hardly an exaggeration to say, in the words of one scientist, that "humans domesticated wheat, and vice versa." With the help of agriculture, humans were transformed from a nomadic, hunting and gathering species numbering in the low millions, into the most dominant species on the planet, with a population that currently exceeds six billion. Agriculture has shaped human culture profoundly, and together the two have reshaped the planet. In this encyclopedia, readers can explore the history of agriculture, learn how it is practiced today, both conventionally and organically, and what the impact of it and other human activities has been on the land, the atmosphere, and the other creatures who share the planet with us.

✳Explore further in Agriculture, Modern and Human Impacts

Throughout history—even before the development of the modern scientific method—humans experimented with plants, finding the ones that provided the best meal, the strongest fiber, or the sweetest wine. Naming a thing is such a basic and powerful way of knowing it that all cultures have created some type of taxonomy for the plants they use. The scientific understanding of plants through experimentation, and the development of ra-

⭒Explore further in Ecology, History of; Biodiversity; and Phylogeny

⭒Explore further in Curator of a Botanical Garden and Landscape Architect

tional classification schemes based on evolution, has a rich history that is explored in detail in this encyclopedia. There are biographies of more than two dozen botanists who shaped our modern understanding, and essays on the history of physiology, ecology, taxonomy, and evolution. Across the spectrum of the botanical sciences, progress has accelerated in the last two decades, and a range of entries describe the still-changing understanding of evolutionary relationships, genetic control, and biodiversity.

With the development of our modern scientific society, a wide range of new careers has opened up for people interested in plant sciences, many of which are described in this encyclopedia. Most of these jobs require a college degree, and the better-paying ones often require advanced training. While all are centered around plants, they draw on skills that range from envisioning a landscape in one's imagination (landscape architect) to solving differential equations (an ecological modeler) to budgeting and personnel management (curator of a botanical garden).

Organization of the Material

Each of the 280 entries in *Plant Sciences* has been newly commissioned for this work. Our contributors are drawn from academic and research institutions, industry, and nonprofit organizations throughout North America. In many cases, the authors literally "wrote the book" on their subject, and all have brought their expertise to bear in writing authoritative, up-to-date entries that are nonetheless accessible to high school students. Almost every entry is illustrated and there are numerous photos, tables, boxes, and sidebars to enhance understanding. Unfamiliar terms are highlighted and defined in the margin. Most entries are followed by a list of related articles and a short reading list for readers seeking more information. Front and back matter include a geologic timescale, a topic outline that groups entries thematically, and a glossary. Each volume has its own index, and volume 4 contains a cumulative index covering the entire encyclopedia.

Acknowledgments and Thanks

I wish to thank the many people at Macmillan Reference USA and the Gale Group for their leadership in bringing this work to fruition, and their assiduous attention to the many details that make such a work possible. In particular, thanks to Hélène Potter, Brian Kinsey, Betz Des Chenes, and Diane Sawinski. The editorial board members—Robert Evans, Wendy Mechaber, and Robert Wallace—were outstanding, providing invaluable expertise and extraordinary hard work. Wendy is also my wife, and I wish to thank her for her support and encouragement throughout this project. My own love of plants began with three outstanding biology teachers, Marjorie Holland, James Howell, and Walt Tulecke, and I am in their debt. My many students at the Commonwealth School in Boston were also great teachers— their enthusiastic questions over the years deepened my own understanding and appreciation of the mysteries of the plant world. I hope that a new generation of students can discover some of the excitement and mystery of this world in *Plant Sciences*.

Richard Robinson
Editor in Chief

Geologic Timescale

ERA	PERIOD			EPOCH	STARTED (millions of years ago)
Cenozoic: 66.4 millions of years ago–present time	**Quaternary**			Holocene	0.01
				Pleistocene	1.6
	Tertiary	**Neogene**		Pliocene	5.3
				Miocene	23.7
		Paleogene		Oligocene	36.6
				Eocene	57.8
				Paleocene	66.4
Mesozoic: 245–66.4 millions of years ago	**Cretaceous**			Late	97.5
				Early	144
	Jurassic			Late	163
				Middle	187
				Early	208
	Triassic			Late	230
				Middle	240
				Early	245
Paleozoic: 570–245 millions of years ago	**Permian**			Late	258
				Early	286
	Carboniferous	**Pennsylvanian**		Late	320
		Mississippian		Early	360
	Devonian			Late	374
				Middle	387
				Early	408
	Silurian			Late	421
				Early	438
	Ordovician			Late	458
				Middle	478
				Early	505
	Cambrian			Late	523
				Middle	540
				Early	570
Precambrian time: 4500–570 millions of years ago					4500

Contributors

Miguel Altieri
University of California, Berkeley

Sherwin Toshio Amimoto
Redondo Beach, CA

Edward F. Anderson
Desert Botanical Garden, Phoenix, AZ

Gregory J. Anderson
University of Connecticut

Mary Anne Andrei
Minneapolis, MN

Wendy L. Applequist
Iowa State University

Rebecca Baker
Cotati, CA

Peter S. Bakwin
National Oceanic and Atmospheric Administration

Jo Ann Banks
Purdue University

Theodore M. Barkley
Botanical Research Institute of Texas

Ronald D. Barnett
University of Florida

Patricia A. Batchelor
Milwaukee Public Museum

Hank W. Bass
Florida State University

Yves Basset
Smithsonian Tropical Research Institute

Stuart F. Baum
University of California, Davis

Gabriel Bernardello
University of Connecticut

Paul E. Berry
University of Wisconsin-Madison

Paul C. Bethke
University of California, Berkeley

J. Derek Bewley
University of Guelph

Christopher J. Biermann
Philomath, OR

Franco Biondi
University of Nevada

Richard E. Bir
North Carolina State University

Jane H. Bock
University of Colorado

Hans Bohnert
Nara Institute of Science and Technology

Brian M. Boom
New York Botanical Garden

David E. Boufford
Harvard University Herbaria

John L. Bowman
University of California, Davis

James R. Boyle
Oregon State University

James M. Bradeen
University of Wisconsin-Madison

Irwin M. Brodo
Canadian Museum of Nature

Robert C. Brown
Iowa State University

Leo P. Bruederle
University of Colorado, Denver

Robert Buchsbaum
Massachusetts Audubon Society

Stephen C. Bunting
University of Idaho

John M. Burke
Indiana University

Charles A. Butterworth
Iowa State University

Christian E. Butzke
University of California, Davis

Kenneth M. Cameron
New York Botanical Garden

Deborah K. Canington
University of California, Davis

Vernon B. Cardwell
American Society of Agronomy

Don Cawthon
Texas A & M University

Russell L. Chapman
Louisiana State University

Arthur H. Chappelka
Auburn University

Lynn G. Clark
Iowa State University

W. Dean Cocking
James Madison University

James T. Colbert
Iowa State University

Daniel J. Cosgrove
Pennsylvania State University

Barbara Crandall-Stotler
Southern Illinois University

Donald L. Crawford
University of Idaho

Thomas B. Croat
Missouri Botanical Garden

Lawrence J. Crockett
Pace University

Sunburst Shell Crockett
Society of American Foresters

Richard Cronn
Iowa State University

Anne Fernald Cross
Oklahoma State University

Rodney Croteau
Washington State University

Judith G. Croxdale
University of Wisconsin

Peter J. Davies
Cornell University

Jerrold I. Davis
Cornell University

Elizabeth L. Davison
University of Arizona

Ira W. Deep
Ohio State University

Nancy G. Dengler
University of Toronto

Steven L. Dickie
Iowa State University

David L. Dilcher
University of Florida

Rebecca W. Doerge
Purdue University

Susan A. Dunford
University of Cincinnati

Frank A. Einhellig
Southwest Missouri State University

George S. Ellmore
Tufts University

Roland Ennos
University of Manchester

Emanuel Epstein
University of California, Davis

M. Susan Erich
University of Maine

Robert C. Evans
Rutgers University

Donald R. Farrar
Iowa State University

Charles B. Fenster
Botanisk Institutt

Manfred A. Fischer
University of Vienna, Austria

Theodore H. Fleming
Tuscon, AZ

Dennis Francis
Cardiff University

Arthur W. Galston
Yale University

Grace Gershuny
St. Johnsbury, VT

Peter Gerstenberger
National Arborist Association, Inc.

Stephen R. Gliessman
University of California, Santa Cruz

J. Peter Gogarten
University of Connecticut

Govindjee
University of Illinois, Urbana-Champaign

Linda E. Graham
University of Wisconsin, Madison

Peter H. Graham
University of Minnesota

Michael A. Grusak
U.S. Department of Agriculture, Children's Nutrition Research Center

Gerald F. Guala
Fairchild Tropical Garden, Miami

Robert Gutman
Athens, GA

Charles J. Gwo
University of New Mexico

Ardell D. Halvorson
U.S. Department of Agriculture, Agricultural Research Service

Earl G. Hammond
Iowa State University

Jeffrey B. Harborne
University of Reading

Elizabeth M. Harris
Ohio State University Herbarium

Frederick V. Hebard
American Chestnut Foundation

Steven R. Hill
Center for Biodiversity

J. Kenneth Hoober
Arizona State University

Roger F. Horton
University of Guelph

D. Michael Jackson
U.S. Department of Agriculture, Agricultural Research Service

William P. Jacobs
Princeton, NJ

David M. Jarzen
University of Florida

Roger V. Jean
University of Quebec

Philip D. Jenkins
University of Arizona

Russell L. Jones
University of California, Berkeley

Lee B. Kass
Cornell University

George B. Kauffman
California State University, Fresno

Jon E. Keeley
National Park Service

Dean G. Kelch
University of California, Berkeley

Nancy M. Kerk
Yale University

Alan K. Knapp
Kansas State University

Erich Kombrink
Max-Planck-Institut für Züchtungsforschung

Ross E. Koning
Eastern Connecticut State University

Thomas G. Lammers
University of Wisconsin, Oshkosh

Mark A. Largent
University of Minnesota

Donald W. Larson
Columbus, OH

Matthew Lavin
Montana State University

Roger H. Lawson
Columbia, MD

Michael Lee
Iowa State University

Michael J. Lewis
University of California, Davis

Walter H. Lewis
Washington University

Douglas T. Linde
Delaware Valley College

Bradford Carlton Lister
Rensselaer Polytechnic Institute

Margaret D. Lowman
Marie Selby Botanical Gardens, Sarasota, FL

Peter J. Lumsden
University of Central Lancashire

Lynn Margulis
University of Massachusetts, Amherst

Wendy Mechaber
University of Arizona

Alan W. Meerow
U.S. Department of Agriculture, Agricultural Research Service

T. Lawrence Mellichamp
University of North Carolina, Charlotte

Scott Merkle
University of Georgia

Jan E. Mikesell
Gettysburg College

Orson K. Miller Jr.
Virginia Polytechnic Institute

Thomas Minney
The New Forests Project

Thomas S. Moore
Louisiana State University

David R. Morgan
Western Washington University

Gisèle Muller-Parker
Western Washington University

Suzanne C. Nelson
Native Seeds/SEARCH

Robert Newgarden
Brooklyn Botanic Gardens

Daniel L. Nickrent
Southern Illinois University

John S. Niederhauser
Tucson, AZ

David O. Norris
University of Colorado

Lorraine Olendzenski
University of Connecticut

Micheal D. K. Owen
Iowa State University

James C. Parks
Millersville University

Wayne Parrott
University of Georgia

Andrew H. Paterson
University of Georgia

Jessica P. Penney
Allston, MA

Terry L. Peppard
Warren, NJ

John H. Perkins
The Evergreen State College

Kim Moreau Peterson
University of Alaska, Anchorage

Peter A. Peterson
Iowa State University

Richard B. Peterson
Connecticut Agricultural Experiment Station

D. Mason Pharr
North Carolina State University

Bobby J. Phipps
Delta Research Center

Janet M. Pine
Iowa State University

Ghillean T. Prance
The Old Vicarage, Dorset, UK

Robert A. Price
University of Georgia

Richard B. Primack
Boston University

V. Raghavan
Ohio State University

James A. Rasmussen
Southern Arkansas University

Linda A. Raubeson
Central Washington University

A. S. N. Reddy
Colorado State University

Robert A. Rice
Smithsonian Migratory Bird Center

Loren H. Rieseberg
Indiana University

Richard Robinson
Tuscon, AZ

Curt R. Rom
University of Arkansas

Thomas L. Rost
University of California, Davis

Sabine J. Rundle
Western Carolina University

Scott D. Russell
University of Oklahoma

J. Neil Rutger
U.S. Department of Agriculture, Dale Bumpers National Rice Research Center

Fred D. Sack
Ohio State University

Dorion Sagan
Amherst, MA

Ann K. Sakai
University of California-Irvine

Frank B. Salisbury
Utah State University

Mark A. Schneegurt
Witchita State University

Randy Scholl
Ohio State University

Jack C. Schultz
Pennsylvania State University

Hanna Rose Shell
New Haven, CT

Timothy W. Short
Queens College of the City University of New York

Philipp W. Simon
University of Wisconsin-Madison

Garry A. Smith
Canon City, CO

James F. Smith
Boise State University

Vassiliki Betty Smocovitis
University of Florida

Doug Soltis
Washington State University

Pam Soltis
Washington State University

Paul C. Spector
The Holden Arboretum, Kirtland, OH

David M. Spooner
University of Wisconsin

Helen A. Stafford
Reed College

Craig Steely
Elm Research Institute

Taylor A. Steeves
University of Saskatchewan

Hans K. Stenoien
Botanisk Institutt

Peter F. Stevens
University of Missouri, St. Louis

Ian M. Sussex
Yale University

Charlotte A. Tancin
Carnegie Mellon University

Edith L. Taylor
University of Kansas

Thomas N. Taylor
University of Kansas

W. Carl Taylor
Milwaukee Public Museum

Mark Tebbitt
Brooklyn Botanical Gardens

Barbara M. Thiers
New York Botanical Garden

Sean C. Thomas
University of Toronto

Sue A. Thompson
Pittsburgh, PA

Barbara N. Timmermann
University of Arizona

Ward M. Tingey
Cornell University

Alyson K. Tobin
University of St. Andrews

Dwight T. Tomes
Johnston, IA

Nancy J. Turner
University of Victoria

Sarah E. Turner
University of Victoria

Miguel L. Vasquez
Northern Arizona University

Robert S. Wallace
Iowa State University

Debra A. Waters
Louisiana State University

Elizabeth Fortson Wells
George Washington University

Molly M. Welsh
U.S. Department of Agriculture, Agricultural Research Service

James J. White
Carnegie Mellon University

Michael A. White
University of Montana

John Whitmarsh
University of Illinois, Urbana-Champaign

Garrison Wilkes
University of Massachusetts, Boston

John D. Williamson
North Carolina State University

Thomas Wirth
Thomas Wirth Associates, Inc., Sherborn, MA

Jianguo Wu
Arizona State University

Table of Contents

plant sciences

Absorption *See Water Movement.*

Acid Rain

Acid rain can be defined as rain that has a **pH** less than 5.6, formed primarily through the chemical transformation of sulfur and nitrogen **compounds** emitted by **anthropogenic** sources. In addition, acidic compounds can be deposited as aerosols and particulates (dry deposition), and mists, fogs, snow, and clouds (wet deposition). Most scientists agree that the phrase *acidic deposition* is more appropriate when characterizing the overall problem, but acid rain is the most widely used term.

Robert Angus Smith (1817–1884), a Scottish chemist, first used the expression "acid rain" in 1872 when describing the acidic nature of rain deposited around Manchester, England. The problem was believed to be localized and confined to urban areas until reports appeared during the 1970s and 1980s describing widespread acidification of lakes in the northeastern United States, eastern Canada, and Europe. Additional reports surfaced regarding declines in growth and vigor of forested **ecosystems** throughout the world, with acid rain as the possible culprit. These findings resulted in several large research initiatives, including the U.S. government-funded National Atmospheric Precipitation Assessment Program.

Results indicated that pH in rainfall, mists, clouds, snow, and fog in the United States, especially the East, was generally below normal, and was due to an increase in industrial emissions of sulfur and nitrogen compounds transported to rural areas. Some lakes and streams were acidified and their productivity reduced by acid rain. Most lakes and streams that were acidified were located in the northeastern United States. The majority of forested and agricultural ecosystems were found not to be directly affected by acid rain. Certain high-elevation systems, such as red spruce in the northeastern United States, were reported as possibly being affected by acid rain, but many other factors were involved. Research findings resulted in increased environmental legislation, including the 1990 Clean Air Act Amendments enacted by the U.S. Congress to significantly reduce sulfur emissions.

Since 1990, sulfur dioxide emissions have decreased 25 percent, resulting in a significant reduction in **sulfate** in rain and surface waters in some

pH a measure of acidity or alkalinity; the pH scale ranges from 0 to 14, with 7 being neutral; low pH numbers indicate high acidity; high numbers indicate alkalinity

compound a substance formed from two or more elements

anthropogenic human-made

ecosystem an ecological community together with its environment

sulfate a negatively charged particle combining sulfur and oxygen

1

A branch from a tree in Germany's Black Forest showing needle loss and yellowed boughs from acid rain (top) compared to a branch from a healthy tree (bottom).

saturated containing as much dissolved substance as possible

cations positively charged particles

areas of the United States. Nitrogen compounds, however, have not decreased. The role nitrogen plays in acidification is currently of concern to the scientific community. Several forested ecosystems have been found to be nitrogen **saturated**. Also, it is hypothesized that acid rain has caused a depletion in base **cations**, mainly calcium, potassium, and magnesium, in the soils of several forested ecosystems making uptake of these essential minerals more difficult. Research is underway to investigate the effects of these problems on ecosystem function. SEE ALSO ATMOSPHERE AND PLANTS.

Arthur H. Chappelka

Bibliography

Irving, P. M. "Acid Deposition: State of Science and Technology." In *National Acid Precipitation Assessment Program, 1990 Integrated Assessment Report*. Washington, DC: 1991.

Krupa, S. V. *Air Pollution, People, and Plants: An Introduction*. St. Paul, MN: American Phytopathological Society Press, 1997.

NAPAP Biennial Report to Congress: An Integrated Assessment. Washington, DC: National Science and Technology Council, 1998.

Wellburn, A. *Air Pollution and Acid Rain: The Biological Impact.* New York: John Wiley & Sons, 1988.

Agricultural Ecosystems

An agricultural ecosystem, which is also known as an agroecosystem, is a place where agricultural production—a farm, for example—is understood as an **ecosystem**. When something like a farm field is examined from an ecosystem viewpoint, food production can be understood as part of a whole, including the complex kinds of materials entering the system, or inputs, and the materials leaving the system, or outputs. At the same time, the ways that all of the parts of the system are interconnected and interact are of great importance.

Humans alter and manipulate ecosystems for the purpose of establishing agricultural production, and in the process, can make the resulting agroecosystem very different from a natural ecosystem. At the same time, however, by understanding how ecosystem processes, structures, and characteristics are modified, management of an agricultural system can become more stable, less dependent on inputs brought in from outside the system, and more protective of the natural resources with which it may interact.

Scientists who study agricultural systems as ecosystems are known as agroecologists, and the field they work in is known as agroecology. An agroecologist applies the concepts and principles of ecology to the design and management of sustainable agroecosystems. Sustainability refers to the ability to preserve the productivity of agricultural land over the long term, protect the natural resources upon which that productivity depends, provide farming communities with a fair and prosperous way of life, and produce a secure and healthy food supply for people who do not live on the farms. The challenge these scientists face is developing agroecosystems that achieve natural ecosystem-like characteristics while maintaining a harvest output. With a goal of sustainability, a farm manager strives as much as possible to use the ecosystem concept in designing and managing the agroecosystem. In doing so, the following four key traits of ecosystems are included.

Energy Flow

Energy flows into an ecosystem as a result of the capture of solar energy from the Sun by plants, and most of this energy is stored as **biomass** or used to maintain the internal processes of the system. But removing energy-rich biomass from the system causes changes. Human energy (considered renewable) as labor, and industrial energy (considered nonrenewable) from fossil fuels, become necessary. Agroecologists look for ways to increase the efficiency of the capture of energy from the Sun and increase the use of renewable energy, achieving a better balance between the energy needed to maintain internal processes and that which is needed for harvest export.

Nutrient Cycling

Many nutrients are cycled through ecosystems. Biomass is made up of organic **compounds** manufactured from these nutrients, and as organisms

ecosystem an ecological community together with its environment

biomass the total dry weight of an organism or group of organisms

compound a substance formed from two or more elements

Adjacent fields of rice and wheat in California's Sacramento Valley.

die and decompose, the nutrients return to the soil or the atmosphere to be recycled and reused again. Agricultural ecosystems lose nutrients with harvest removal, and because of their more simplified ecological structure, lose a greater proportion of nutrients to the air or by leaching in rain and irrigation water. Humans must return these nutrients in some form. In a well-designed agroecosystem, the farmer strives to keep nutrient cycles as closed as possible, reducing nutrient losses while searching for sustainable ways of returning exported nutrients to the farm.

Regulation of Populations

mutualism a symbiosis between two organisms in which both benefit

Complex interactions between organisms regulate their numbers in natural ecosystems. Competition, **mutualisms**, and other types of interactions are promoted by the organization and structure of the system. Growing one or very few crops in modern agriculture eliminates many of these interactions, often removing natural control mechanisms and allowing pest outbreaks. An agroecological alternative seeks to reintroduce more complex structures and species arrangements, often including both crop and noncrop species, in order to reduce the use of pesticides and enhance natural controls.

System Stability and Change

Ecosystems maintain themselves over time and have the ability to recover from natural disturbances such as a fire or a hurricane. In agricultural ecosystems, disturbance from cultivation, weeding, harvest, and other agricultural activities is much more intense and frequent. It is difficult to maintain any equilibrium in the system with this disturbance, requiring constant outside interference in the form of human labor and external human inputs. By incorporating ecosystem qualities such as diversity, stability, recovery, and balance, the maintenance of an ecological foundation for long-term sustainability can be established.

Agroecologists use the idea of an agricultural ecosystem as a focus for the study of farming systems that are converting from single crops and synthetic inputs to ecologically based design and management. Ecological concepts and principles are applied for the development of alternative practices and inputs. A good example is research done by Sean Swezey and his colleagues on apples in California. After three years of using organic farming techniques, an apple orchard had begun to show a reduction in the use of fossil fuel energy. Nutrients were supplied from compost and annual cover crops planted in the rows between the trees during the winter season. Nutrient recycling and storage in leaves and branches within the apple agroecosystem improved soil conditions, reduced the need for fertilizer, and even led to increased yields. Insect pests normally controlled by synthetic pesticides were reduced instead by beneficial predatory insects that were attracted to the organic orchard by mustard and fava-bean flowers in the rows between apple trees. Cover crop species smothered weeds so that herbicides were not needed. In the spring when the cover crop was mowed and cultivated into the soil, microorganism abundance and diversity increased, acting as a biological barrier to the outbreak of diseases in the soil. As the use of external human inputs for the control of the ecological processes in the apple system was reduced, a shift to the use of natural ecosystem processes and interactions and locally derived materials took place. Such an ecological foundation is an important way of determining the sustainability of the agricultural ecosystems of the future. SEE ALSO AGRICULTURE, MODERN; AGRICULTURE, ORGANIC; ECOSYSTEM.

Stephen R. Gliessman

Bibliography

Altieri, Miguel A. *Agroecology: The Science of Sustainable Agriculture.* Boulder, CO: Westview Press, 1995.

Gliessman, Stephen R. *Agroecology: Ecological Processes in Sustainable Agriculture.* Chelsea, MI: Ann Arbor Press, 1998.

Lowrance, Richard, Ben R. Stinner, and Gar J. House. *Agricultural Ecosystems: Unifying Concepts.* New York: John Wiley & Sons, 1984.

National Research Council. *Alternative Agriculture.* Washington, DC: National Academy Press, 1989.

Odum, Eugene P. *Ecology: A Bridge Between Science and Society.* Sunderland, MA: Sinauer Associates.

Swezey, Sean L., Jim Rider, Matthew Werner, Marc Buchanan, Jan Allison, and Stephen R. Gliessman. "Granny Smith Conversions to Organic Show Early Success." *California Agriculture* 48 (1994): 36–44.

Agriculture, History of

The history of agriculture (the production of food by plant cultivation and animal husbandry and control of productivity) can be organized around

An ancient Egyptian fresco depicting a man harvesting wheat.

several themes (such as time, productivity, environmental impact, and genetic diversity). The most obvious is time and the sequence of events from gathering wild plants for food to crop plant **domestication**, to yield-enhanced **hybrid** seed.

domesticate to tame an organism to live with and to be of use to humans

hybrid a mix of two species

Origins of Agriculture

The origin of agriculture was around ten thousand years ago or approximately four hundred human generations back in time and prehistory, before written records were kept. What is known is based on evidence gathered from archaeological sites. Agriculture started independently in at least three places in the world, each with a distinctive cluster of plants drawn from the local flora: Mesoamerica (Mexico/Guatemala: corn, beans, squash, papaya, tomatoes, chili, peppers), the Fertile Crescent (Middle East from the Nile Valley to the Tigris and Euphrates Rivers: wheat, barley, grapes, apples, figs, melons, lentils, dates), and north China (mid-reaches of the three-thousand-mile-long Yellow River: rice, soybeans, peaches, Chinese cabbages such as bok choy). From these regions and possibly others, notably Africa (sorghum, cowpeas, yams, oil palm), South America (potatoes, sweet potatoes, cassava, peanuts, pineapples), and a broad band of tropical southeast Asia (oranges, mangoes, bananas, coconuts, sugarcane), the invention of agricultures spread to encompass the entire world by two thousand years ago.

legumes beans and other members of the Fabaceae family

monoculture a large stand of a single crop species

propagate to create more of through sexual or asexual reproduction

polyculture mixed species

ecosystem an ecological community together with its environment

The history of agriculture is not that of a single technology to produce food, but of an array of methodologies. Planting seed broadcast across plowed fields typifies most cereals (50 percent of human calories). Vegetables, **legumes**, and corn are planted from seed in rows separated by furrows. Seed agriculture usually consists of annuals that are typically planted as genetically uniform **monocultures**. Agriculture of the humid tropics has been more vegeculture than seed-based. These vegetatively **propagated** crops are usually perennials, productive over the entire year and found in **polycultures** that tend to mimic the forest **ecosystem**.

The earliest agriculture of southeast Asia was typically based on roots and tubers such as yams and taro, tree crops such as coconut and banana, and perennials such as sugarcane. In the Americas, vegeculture developed with cassava, sweet potatoes, arrowroot, and peanuts, and moved up the eastern slopes of the Andes, ultimately domesticating the potato. These crops spread quickly throughout the world after European contact. Potatoes displaced wheat and barley in cold soils of northern Europe and bananas became the fruit of choice in the New World tropics.

Seed agriculture dominates where either a pronounced dry season or a frost results in a single crop per year. In south China rice is the summer crop, sweet potato the winter crop. In India rice is the monsoon crop, wheat the winter crop. Sometimes intercropping (different crops in alternate rows) and relay planting (starting the next crop before the previous one is harvested) are part of the multiple-crops-per-year cycle. Sequential cropping is where one crop follows another without seasonal fallowing, sometimes in double-cropping but more often in triple-cropping.

Fallowing is an important technology perfected in the Middle Ages as part of the **crop rotation** pattern. The first year a legume is planted and the soil is enriched by the nitrogen-fixing crop; the next year a cereal is planted. The third year the land is rested to regain soil moisture and restore soil health. This pattern approximates a natural ecosystem and is more sustainable over the long term than continuous cropping. The fallow crop rotation system maximizes resources but is not elastic enough to accommodate an increasing human population that has come to rely on continuous cropping or heavy use of inputs (such as fertilizer, pesticides, and irrigation) in single crop per year monocultures.

crop rotation alternating crops from year to year in a particular field

Ecologic Effects

Another theme is to measure the displacement of natural ecosystems of forest and grasslands by plowed cropland that supports an increasing human population. Only about five million people existed worldwide preagriculture, subsisting on hunting and gathering of wild animals and plants. Humans existed like any other wild animals in the biological world. Postagriculture, the human population grew slowly, but as people's mastery of food production technology developed (such as irrigation, weed control by hoe and plow, and planting crops in monocultures) and the number of crop plants increased, the world population climbed to an estimated 130 million people by the time of Christ, a twenty-five-fold increase from the Paleolithic pre-agriculture estimate. By 1650 the world population had reached a half billion, and half of these people were in settled urbanized villages, towns, and cities and not engaged in agriculture to produce their own food. All of the major food crops and domestic farm animals known today were known and used worldwide. The only significant crops added since 1650 are industrial crops such as rubber.

Since the middle of the nineteenth century the population has increased from one billion to six billion, an increase that would not have been possible without increases in agricultural yields. Through breeding, plus the use of fossil fuels to plant, fertilize, and protect crops, the average yield of all plants and productivity per unit area has increased ten- to fiftyfold. At present humans produce and consume over a twenty-year period as much food as was produced in the eight thousand years between the development of agriculture and the sixteenth century. Nonetheless, of the six billion people in the world, over one billion are estimated to be malnourished, and half of these are seriously underfed, mostly due to poverty and the diminished affordability of agricultural products. An estimated fifty thousand to eighty thousand starve to death or are fatally compromised each day—a majority are children, in part because they are growing rapidly and do not get enough essential materials such as vitamin A or quality protein.

Loss of Diversity

Another theme is to realize how few crops currently feed the human population, considering that preagriculture humankind subsisted on a list of approximately five thousand wild edible plants. The agricultural crop list is short. One-half of the plant calories people consume come from three grasses: rice, wheat, and corn.

arable able to be cultivated for crops

Just over two dozen food plants account for 75 percent of all plant calories and 90 percent of **arable** land cultivated. This list includes six grasses: rice, wheat, corn, barley, oats, and sorghum; four legumes: soybeans, peanuts, common beans, and peas; two sugar crops: sugarcane and sugar beets; two tropical tree crops: bananas and coconuts; four starchy roots: potatoes, sweet potatoes, cassava, and yams; five fruits: tomatoes, grapes, apples, oranges, and mangoes; and two vegetables: cabbages and onions. These twenty-five crops literally stand between subsistence and starvation for the human population. This is an agricultural calorie list and does not recognize the extremely rich vitamin and mineral sources found in low-calorie vegetables and fruits. Also this list does not recognize the important regional foods of the world. For instance, the native American crop cranberries is extremely important to Americans at Thanksgiving but is insignificant on the world calorie chart (less than one-millionth of 1 percent).

Selection and Breeding

progenitors parents or ancestors

A dominant theme in the history of agriculture has been crop improvement and yield advancement through selection and exploitation of genetic diversity within the species and its close relatives. And now, there is bioengineering where a gene can come from anywhere in the biological world (genetically modified crops). The earliest stages of domesticated crops were probably not much more productive than the wild **progenitors**, but the act of cultivation and saving the seed to replant was a radical break with the past. Human selection (artificial selection) was replacing natural selection in shaping the plant. Traits associated with the domestication process are seeds and fruits that remain attached to the plant (nonbrittle rachis and nondehiscent fruits) and do not self sow. Another trait is larger fruits and seeds and less nondigestible fiber in seed coats and woody fibers (cellulose) in the fruits. This increases the palatability of these structures but leaves the plant less protected to insect or rodent **predation**, so that humans had to take greater care in postharvest storage. When humans planted the seed, they set in motion many selection forces that characterize domesticated plants: simultaneous and immediate germination on being sown in the ground; rapid and uniform growth; and a trend toward annuality if biennial/perennial. Additionally, a shortened vegetative phase often resulted in

predation the act of preying upon; consuming for food

increased reproductive effort, thus increasing yield and uniform flowering and ripening. Most of these traits would be harmful for a wild plant.

Once domesticated plants began to travel through human migration and conquest beyond their local area of genetic adaptation, a large amount of genetic variation was released by chance **hybridization** of diverse forms or freedom from constraints (such as pests, **pathogens**, frost, and day length) of the old habitat. Citrus, for instance, was brought from East India to Spain by the Arabs, then taken to the West Indies by Europeans after Columbus. One mutant form gave rise to grapefruit, while a mutant orange in Brazil was the origin of the familiar navel orange.

The Columbian Exchange (New World plants to the Old World and vice versa) in the sixteenth century was the single most dramatic migration and acclimatization of crops throughout the world. Coupled with hybridization between dissimilar species, introductions of a tremendous number of new forms were generated. Examples are the potato from Peru, which conquered north Europe as a food plant displacing wheat/barley and turnips/peas; and tomatoes from Mexico, which were embraced in Italian cooking.

Recent yield improvement traces back to the rediscovery of Austrian botanist Gregor Mendel's (1822–1884) classic experiments on the heredity of garden peas. For the first time the plant breeding community had a set of principles by which to proceed with the crop improvement process. Products of this era are hybrid corn, changes in the **photoperiod** response of soybeans, and the dwarf-stature wheat from the International Center for the Improvement of Wheat and Corn (in Mexico) and rice from the International Rice Research Institute (in the Philippines). These late 1960s Green Revolution cereals and the genes they hold (dwarf stature and fertilizer responsive) now enter the food supply of three billion plus people and are directly responsible for feeding more than eight hundred million people by their increased yield alone. Never in world history had there been such a dramatic yield take-off as the Green Revolution. The hope is that the new and developing biotechnologies will have a comparable favorable outcome for global agriculture.

The irony of using elite improved varieties and commercial seed is that they have a tendency to eliminate the resources upon which they are based and from which they have been derived. Current elite varieties yield better than their parents and they displace them from farmers' fields. Once a displaced variety is no longer planted, its genes are lost to future generations unless it is conserved, usually in a seed bank collection or as a heirloom variety. The saving of old folk varieties, farmer **landraces** and garden seed passed down through a family, maintaining them in home gardens, has become increasingly widespread. Many of these heirloom varieties taste better, cook better, or possess other unique characteristics that set them apart, but they lack the productivity mechanized farming demands in modern agriculture. SEE ALSO AGRICULTURE, MODERN; AGRICULTURE, ORGANIC; AGRONOMIST; GREEN REVOLUTION; SEED PRESERVATION; SEEDS; VAVILOV, N. I.

Garrison Wilkes

Bibliography

Harlan, Jack R. *The Living Fields: Our Agricultural Heritage*. Cambridge, UK: Cambridge University Press, 1995.

hybridization formation of a new individual from parents of different species or varieties

pathogen disease-causing organism

photoperiod the period in which an organism is exposed to light, or is sensitive to light exposure, causing flowering or other light-sensitive changes

landrace a variety or breed of plant

Hybrid corn, a product of twentieth-century crop improvement processes.

Harris, Donald, and G. C. Hillman, eds. *Foraging and Farming: The Evolution of Plant Exploitation.* London: Unwin Hyman, 1989.

Heiser, Charles B., Jr. *Seeds to Civilization: The Story of Food.* Cambridge, MA: Harvard University Press, 1990.

Janick, Jules, Robert Schery, Frank W. Woods, and Vernon W. Ruttan. *Plant Science: Growth, Development and Utilization of Cultivated Plants.* San Francisco: W. H. Freeman, 1981.

Agriculture, Modern

During the latter half of the twentieth century, what is known today as modern agriculture was very successful in meeting a growing demand for food by the world's population. Yields of primary crops such as rice and wheat increased dramatically, the price of food declined, the rate of increase in crop yields generally kept pace with population growth, and the number of people who consistently go hungry was slightly reduced. This boost in food production has been due mainly to scientific advances and new technologies, including the development of new crop varieties, the use of pesticides and fertilizers, and the construction of large irrigation systems.

Basic Practices of Modern Agricultural Systems

Modern agricultural systems have been developed with two related goals in mind: to obtain the highest yields possible and to get the highest economic profit possible. In pursuit of these goals, six basic practices have come to form the backbone of production: intensive tillage, **monoculture**, application of inorganic fertilizer, irrigation, chemical pest control, and genetic manipulation of crop plants. Each practice is used for its individual contribution to productivity, but when they are all combined in a farming system each depends on the others and reinforces the need for using the others. The work of agronomists, specialists in agricultural production, has been key to the development of these practices.

Intensive Tillage. The soil is cultivated deeply, completely, and regularly in most modern agricultural systems, and a vast array of tractors and farm implements have been developed to facilitate this practice. The soil is loosened, water drains better, roots grow faster, and seeds can be planted more easily. Cultivation is also used to control weeds and work dead plant matter into the soil.

Monoculture. When one crop is grown alone in a field, it is called a monoculture. Monoculture makes it easier to cultivate, sow seed, control weeds, and harvest, as well as expand the size of the farm operation and improve aspects of profitability and cost. At the same time, monocultures tend to promote the use of the other five basic practices of modern agriculture.

Use of Synthetic Fertilizers. Very dramatic yield increases occur with the application of synthetic chemical fertilizers. Relatively easy to manufacture or mine, to transport, and to apply, fertilizer use has increased from five to ten times what it was at the end of World War II (1939–45). Applied in either liquid or granular form, fertilizer can supply crops with readily available and uniform amounts of several essential plant nutrients.

monoculture a large stand of a single crop species

Fertilizer being applied to a rice field.

Irrigation Technologies. By supplying water to crops during times of dry weather or in places of the world where natural rainfall is not sufficient for growing most crops, irrigation has greatly boosted the food supply. Drawing water from underground wells, building reservoirs and distribution canals, and diverting rivers have improved yields and increased the area of available farm land. Special sprinklers, pumps, and drip systems have greatly improved the efficiency of water application as well.

Chemical Pest Control. In the large monoculture fields of much of modern agriculture, pests include such organisms as insects that eat plants, weeds that interfere with crop growth, and diseases that slow plant and animal development or even cause death. When used properly, synthetic chemicals have provided an effective, relatively easy way to provide such control. Chemical sprays can quickly respond to pest outbreaks.

Genetic Manipulation. Farmers have been choosing among crop plants and animals for specific characteristics for thousands of years. But modern agriculture has taken advantage of several more recent crop breeding techniques. The development of hybrid seed, where two or more strains of a crop are combined to produce a more productive offspring, has been one of the most significant strategies. Genetic engineering has begun to develop molecular techniques that selectively introduce genetic information from one organism to another, often times from very unrelated organisms, with a goal of capitalizing on specific useful traits.

But for almost every benefit of modern agriculture, there are usually problems. Excessive tillage led to soil degradation, the loss of organic matter, soil erosion by water and wind, and soil **compaction**. Large monocultures are especially prone to devastating pest outbreaks that often occur when pests encounter a large, uniform area of one crop species, requiring the continued and excessive use of chemical sprays. When used excessively, chemical fertilizers can be easily leached out of the soil into nearby streams and lakes, or even down into underground water supplies. Farmers can become dependent on chemical pest and weed control. Modern farm systems lack the natural control agents needed for biological pest management, and

compaction compacting of soil, leading to loss of air spaces

larger amounts of sprays must be used as pests rapidly evolve resistance. People also worry about chemical pollution of the environment by sprays and fertilizers, and the possible contamination of food supplies. Modern agriculture has become such a large user of water resources that overuse, depletion, saltwater contamination, salt buildup in soil, fertilizer leaching, and soil erosion have become all too common. Agricultural water users compete with urban and industrial use, and wildlife as well. Hybrid seed has contributed greatly to the loss of genetic diversity and increased risk of massive crop failure, as well as an increased dependence on synthetic and nonrenewable inputs needed for maintaining high yield. Genetically engineered crops have the same negative potential, especially as the selection process takes place less and less in the hands of farmers working in their own fields, but rather in far away laboratories.

In the future, in order to take advantage of new technologies and practices, farming systems will need to be viewed as **ecosystems**, or agricultural ecosystems. By monitoring both the positive and negative impacts of modern farming practices, ecologically based alternatives can be developed that protect the health of the soil, air, and water on farms and nearby areas, lower the economic costs of production, and promote **viable** farming communities around the world. Organic agriculture, conservation tillage, integrated pest management (IPM), and the use of appropriate genetic techniques that enhance local adaptation and variety performance are a few of the possible ways of ensuring the sustainability of future generations of farmers. SEE ALSO AGRICULTURAL ECOSYSTEMS; AGRICULTURE, HISTORY OF; AGRICULTURE, ORGANIC; AGRONOMIST; BREEDER; BREEDING; FERTILIZER; HERBICIDES.

Stephen R. Gliessman

ecosystem an ecological community together with its environment

viable able to live or to function

Bibliography

Brown, Lester R. "Struggling to Raise Cropland Productivity." In *State of the World: 1998*, eds. Lester Brown, Christopher Flavin, and Hilary French. New York: W.W. Norton and Company, 1998.

Gliessman, Stephen R. *Agroecology: Ecological Processes in Sustainable Agriculture.* Chelsea, MI: Ann Arbor Press, 1998.

Agriculture, Organic

Organic farming is a production system that sustains agricultural productivity while avoiding or largely excluding synthetic fertilizers and pesticides. Whenever possible, external resources, such as commercially purchased chemicals and fuels, are replaced by resources found on or near the farm. These internal resources include solar or wind energy, biological pest controls, and biologically fixed nitrogen and other nutrients released from organic matter or from soil reserves. Thus organic farmers rely heavily on the use of **crop rotations**, crop residues, animal manures, compost, **legumes**, **green manures,** off-farm organic wastes, mechanical cultivation, mineral-bearing rocks, and aspects of biological pest control to maintain soil productivity and **tilth,** to supply plant nutrients, and to control insect pests, weeds, and diseases. In essence, organic farming aims to promote soil health as the key to sustaining productivity, and most organic practices are designed to improve the ability of the soil to support plant and microorganism life.

In contrast, conventional farming is characterized by **monoculture** systems that are heavily dependent on the use of synthetic fertilizers and pes-

crop rotation alternating crops from year to year in a particular field

legumes beans and other members of the Fabaceae family

green manure crop planted to be plowed under, to nourish the soil, especially with nitrogen

tilth soil structure characterized by open air spaces and high water storage capacity, due to high levels of organic matter

monoculture a large stand of a single crop species

ticides. Although such systems are productive and able to furnish low-cost food, they also often bring a variety of environmental effects such as pesticide pollution, soil erosion, water depletion, and biodiversity reduction. Increasingly, scientists, farmers, and the public in general have questioned the sustainability of modern agrochemically based agriculture. A large number of organic farmers do use modern machinery, recommended crop varieties, certified seed, sound livestock management, recommended soil and water conservation practices, and innovative methods of organic waste recycling and residue management. Clearly, though, there are sharp contrasts between organic and conventional agriculture.

Most management systems used by organic farmers feature legume-based rotations, the application of compost, and several diversified cropping systems, including crop-livestock mixtures. Through the adoption of such practices, organic farmers aim at:

- building up soil organic matter and soil **biota**

- minimizing pest, disease, and weed damage

- conserving soil, water, and biodiversity resources

- long-term agricultural productivity

- optimal nutritional value and quality of produce

- creating an aesthetically pleasing environment.

biota the sum total of living organisms in a region of a given size

Features of Organic Farming

Organic farming is widespread throughout the world and is growing rapidly. In Germany alone there are about eight thousand organic farms occupying about 2 percent of the total **arable** land. In Italy organic farms number around eighteen thousand, and in Austria about twenty thousand organic farms account for 10 percent of total agricultural output. In 1980 the U.S. Department of Agriculture (USDA) estimated that there were at least eleven thousand organic farms in the United States and at least twenty-four thousand farms that use some organic techniques. In California, organic foods are one of the fastest-growing segments of the agricultural economy, with retail sales growing at 20 percent to 25 percent per year. Cuba was the only country undergoing a massive conversion to organic farming, promoted by the drop of fertilizer, pesticide, and petroleum imports after the collapse of trade relations with the Soviet bloc in 1990.

arable able to be cultivated for crops

Given new market opportunities, farmers grow all kinds of crops, including field, horticultural, and specialty crops, as well as fruits and animals such as cattle, pigs, poultry, and sheep.

Although research on organic farming systems was very limited until the early 1980s, pioneering studies of R. C. Oelhaf (1978), the USDA (1980), W. Lockeretz and others (1981), D. Pimentel and others (1983), and the National Research Council (1984) on organic farming in the United States provide the most comprehensive assessments of organic agricultural systems. These studies concluded the following:

1. As farmers convert to organic farming, initially crop yields are lower than those achieved in conventional farms. In the corn belt, corn yields were about 10 percent less and soybean yields were about 5 percent less on organic farms than on paired conventional farms. Un-

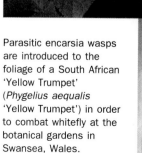

Parasitic encarsia wasps are introduced to the foliage of a South African 'Yellow Trumpet' (*Phygelius aequalis* 'Yellow Trumpet') in order to combat whitefly at the botanical gardens in Swansea, Wales.

DISTINGUISHING CHARACTERISTICS OF CONVENTIONAL AND ORGANIC FARMING

Characteristics	Conventional	Organic
Petroleum dependency	High	Medium
Labor requirements	Low, hired	Medium, family or hired
Management intensity	High	Low–medium
Intensity of tillage	High	Medium
Plant diversity	Low	Medium
Crop varieties	Hybrids	Hybrid or open pollinated
Source of seeds	All purchased	Purchased, some saved
Integration of crops and livestock	None	Little (use of manure)
Insect pests	Very unpredictable	Unpredictable
Insect management	Chemical	Integrated pest management, biopesticides, some biocontrol
Weed management	Chemical, tillage	Cultural control
Disease management	Chemical, vertical resistance	Antagonists, horizontal resistance, multiline cultivars
Plant nutrition	Chemical, fertilizers applied in pulses, open systems	Microbial biofertilizers, organic fertilizers, semi-open systems
Water management	Large-scale irrigation	Sprinkler and drip irrigation

der highly favorable growing conditions, conventional yields were considerably greater than those on the organic farms. Under drier conditions, however, the organic farmers did as well or better than their conventional neighbors. Beyond the third or fourth year after conversion and after crop rotations became established, organic farm yields began to increase, so that their yields approached those obtained by conventional methods.

2. Conventional farms consumed considerably more energy than organic farms largely because they used more petrochemicals. Also, organic farms were considerably more energy-efficient than conventional farms. Between 1974 and 1978 the energy consumed to produce a dollar's worth of crop on organic farms was only about 40 percent as great as on conventional farms.

3. Studies conducted in the Midwest between 1974 and 1977 found that the average net returns of organic and conventional farms were within 4 percent of each other. Organic farms had a lower gross income by 6 percent to 13 percent, but their operating costs were less by a similar amount.

4. The USDA formulated Midwest farm budgets in order to compare crop rotations on organic farms with continuous conventional crop practices. The analysis assumed that yields on organic farms were 10 percent lower. In addition, rotations tie up part of the cropland with forage legumes, such as alfalfa; on conventional farms this land would be producing either corn or soybeans. Since corn and soybeans command a higher price, potential income is reduced in proportion to the amount of land tied up in forage legumes. In essence, organic farmers are turning part of their potential income into renewal of the soil (by adding organic matter) in order to assure sustainability of future crop production. The conventional system maximizes present income and is not as concerned about viewing soil as a long-term investment. In conclusion, although initially yields are likely to be lower in organic farms, variable costs are likely to be much lower. With lit-

tle or no expenditure on agrochemicals, and the availability of premium prices for certain crops, the net result may be similar or higher gross margins for organic farmers.

5. Many organic farms are highly mechanized and use only slightly more labor than conventional farms. When based on the value of the crop produced, however, 11 percent more labor was required on the organic farms because the crop output was lower. The labor requirements of organic farmers in this study were similar to those of conventional farmers for corn and small grains, but higher for soybeans because more hand weeding was necessary. A number of other studies indicated that organic farms generally require more labor than conventional farms, but such needs can be kept to a minimum if hand weeding or handpicking of insects is not used. The labor required to farm organically is a major limitation to the expansion of some organic farms and an important deterrent for conventional farmers who might consider shifting to organic methods.

In many ways, organic farming conserves natural resources and protects the environment more than conventional farming. Research shows that soil erosion rates are lower in organic farms, and that levels of biodiversity are higher in organic farming systems than in conventional ones. In addition, organic farming techniques tend to conserve nitrogen in the soil/plant system, often resulting in a buildup of soil organic nitrogen. Organically managed soils have more soil microorganisms and enhanced levels of potentially available soil nitrogen.

Conversion to Organic Farming

In order for farmers to become certified organic producers, they must complete a certification procedure. The United States and most European countries have created regulations that apply to the production and sale of organically grown produce. All organic produce must carry a quality mark authorized by the government and provided to farmers by legal organizations that conduct strong verification systems with on-site annual inspections. Farmers willing to convert to organic farming must adhere to specific production standards and can be certified as organic only after three years of strictly following such standards.

From a management perspective, the process of conversion from a high-input conventional management to a low-input (or low-external input) management is a transitional process with four marked phases:

1. Progressive chemical withdrawal

2. Rationalization of agrochemical use through integrated pest management (IPM) and integrated nutrient management

3. Input substitution, using alternative, low-energy inputs

4. Redesign of diversified farming systems with an optimal crop/animal assemblage so that the system can support its own soil fertility, natural pest regulation, and crop productivity.

During the four phases, management is guided in order to ensure the following processes:

1. Increasing biodiversity both in the soil and aboveground

2. Increasing **biomass** production and soil organic matter content

3. Decreasing levels of pesticide residues and losses of nutrients and water

4. Establishment of functional relationships between the various farm components

5. Optimal planning of crop sequences and combinations and efficient use of locally available resources.

It is important to note that the conversion process can take anywhere from one to five years depending on the level of artificialization or degradation of the original high-input system. In addition, not all input substitution approaches are ecologically sound, as it is well established that some practices widely encouraged by some organic farming enthusiasts (such as flame-weeding and applications of broad spectrum insecticides) can have serious side effects and environmental impacts.

For scientists involved in transition research, an important outcome of these studies is the realization that the process of converting a conventional crop production system that relies heavily on synthetic, petroleum-based inputs to a legally certifiable, low-external input, organic system is not merely a process of withdrawing external inputs, with no compensatory replacement or alternative management. Considerable ecological knowledge is required to direct the array of natural flows necessary to sustain yields in a low-input system. SEE ALSO AGRICULTURAL ECOSYSTEMS; AGRICULTURE, HISTORY OF; AGRICULTURE, MODERN; AGRONOMIST; COMPOST; SOIL, CHEMISTRY OF; SOIL, PHYSICAL CHARACTERISTICS OF.

Miguel Altieri

Bibliography

Altieri, Miguel A. *Agroecology: The Science of Sustainable Agriculture.* Boulder, CO: Westview Press, 1995.

Gliessman, Stephen R. *Agroecology: Ecological Processes in Sustainable Agriculture.* Chelsea, MI: Ann Arbor Press, 1998.

Lampkin, N. *Organic Farming.* Ipswich, UK: Farming Press Books, 1990.

Lockeretz, W., G. Shearer, and D. H. Kohl. "Organic Farming in the Corn Belt." *Science* 211 (1981): 540–47.

National Research Council. *Alternative Agriculture.* Washington, DC: National Academy Press, 1984.

Oelhaf, R. C. *Organic Agriculture.* New Jersey: Allanheld, Osmon and Co. Pub., 1978.

Pimentel, D., G. Berardi, and S. Fost. "Energy Efficiency of Farming Systems: Organic and Conventional Agriculture." *Agriculture, Ecosystems and Environment* 9 (1983): 359–72.

Pretty, J. N. *Regenerating Agriculture: Policies and Practice for Sustainability and Self-reliance.* London: Earthscan, 1995.

Report and Recommendations on Organic Farming. Washington, DC: U.S. Department of Agriculture, 1980.

Youngberg, G. "Organic Farming: A Look at Opportunities and Obstacles." *Soil and Water Conservation* 35 (1980): 254–63.

Agronomist

Agronomy is the branch of agriculture and biology that explores the principles and concepts of plants and soils sciences. It also examines manage-

ment practices designed to optimize production for the benefit of humankind while protecting nature's resources. Agronomy is derived from the Greek words *agros* (field) and *nomos* (to manage).

Agronomy has been recognized as a separate and distinct branch of agriculture since the early 1900s, when departments of agriculture at **land-grant universities** were split into animal science and agronomy units. In 1900 agronomy units included crop science, soil science, farm management (agricultural economics), and agricultural engineering. In the 1920s and 1930s separate departments of agricultural economics, agricultural engineering, crop science, and soil science emerged. This trend to create specialized departments at the college or university level has resulted in less use of the term *agronomy*; however, it certainly has not diminished the meaning of or demand for resource managers charged with the responsibility of protecting and utilizing land, water, and plants for the benefit of humankind.

Diversity of Activities and Career Fields

Agronomy is an amalgamation of many narrowly defined disciplines or specializations focused on providing the practicing agronomist with the knowledge and understanding to make management decisions that increase productivity, utilize resources most efficiently, protect the environment, and serve society. Agronomy reflects a combination of laboratory, field, and processing activities.

Agronomists place a plastic greenhouse over crops that will be exposed to simulated rain with varying pH levels, allowing the scientists to assess the plants' reaction to the rain.

land-grant university a state university given land by the federal government on the condition that it offer courses in agriculture

Throughout the twentieth century shifts in member interests resulted in the emergence of new specializations or subdisciplines. Many reflect areas of research requiring advance study or graduate degrees. Agronomists have become renewable resource managers, particularly in the area of highly important commercial farming activities where optimizing production using new, cost-effective technology is key. Agronomists also manage various kinds of landscapes and the vegetation occupying them for direct use by humans, the support of livestock and wildlife, development of water resources, and for aesthetic, recreational, and military uses.

Agronomists at the bachelor's level find about 60 percent employment in the private sector and 30 percent in the public sector (10 percent pursue graduate studies). Graduate-level employment is approximately 65 percent in the public sector and 35 percent in the private sector. SEE ALSO AGRICULTURE, MODERN; AGRICULTURE, ORGANIC.

Vernon B. Cardwell

Alcoholic Beverage Industry

Wine

Wine has been made by humans for over eight thousand years. First made from wild grapes, today wine is produced from grapevines grown in cultivated vineyards. Vineyards produce not only wine grapes but fresh table grapes and raisins for eating as well. It takes the scientific knowledge and artistic craftsmanship of a well-educated vineyard manager and wine maker to create the finest wines.

The way wine smells and tastes depends on the grapes from which it is made, the alcoholic fermentation, and the processing and aging of the new wine. At harvest, wine makers have the following responsibilities: deciding when to pick the grapes, scheduling delivery to the winery, overseeing crushing and pressing, and monitoring the fermentations. After fermentation, wine makers must choose from the many options to finish a young wine. They supervise the winery staff to complete the different wine processing steps, such as the transfer of the wine to other vessels (racking), clarification (fining), filtration, blending of different-flavored wines, and bottling. They are responsible for assuring wine quality by sampling, tasting, and chemical analysis. Production and sale of alcoholic beverages is strictly regulated by the state and federal governments, and wine makers must keep accurate records of the wine produced to ensure that the winery complies with these regulations.

Vineyard managers direct the harvest operations by guiding the vineyard crew and harvest workers. The managers are responsible for making decisions about new plantings, the support structure (trellis) for new vines, as well as their pruning after harvest. The managers prepare schedules for water and fertilizer application, control vine pests and diseases, oversee vineyard experiments, and coordinate the sampling of grapes in the vineyard to determine ripeness prior to harvest.

While there is no official certification for wine makers or vineyard managers, students majoring in viticulture and enology (the science and tech-

A vintner at the Joseph Drouhin Winery in Vosne-Romanée, France, fills a wooden vat with red Burgundy grapes.

nology of grape growing and wine making) must develop both broad theoretical skills and in-depth technical knowledge, as well as excellent communication and problem-solving skills. Both prospective wine makers and vineyard managers need a comprehensive preparation in plant biology and microbiology, mathematics and statistics, chemistry, biochemistry, and physics. College course work focuses on the underlying scientific principles so that the students can understand current wine industry practices. These students are required to take an array of specialized courses on such subjects as vineyard establishment and management, grape development and composition, wine sensory evaluation and instrumental analysis, and winery design, as well as management, marketing, and economics. By taking local and overseas internships, students obtain valuable real-world experience from practicing enologists and viticulturists, and critically apply their understanding to create their own innovative styles and practices.

In the Northern Hemisphere, the grape harvest (crush) occurs usually between the end of August and the beginning of November, depending on location, grape variety, and weather. Intense, physically demanding fourteen-hour days (seven days a week) are to be expected during the peak of crush.

In the off-season, wine makers have become increasingly involved in the business aspects of the winery, which means they enjoy a significant amount of traveling to promote their wines, as well as public speaking and other marketing activities. The vineyard manager attends to the vines year-round and is in constant communication with the vineyard crew and the wine maker to ensure the best grape quality and yield.

As wine makers and vineyard managers deal with the production of an alcoholic beverage, they serve as role models to coworkers and consumers, educating them about the responsibilities and consequences associated with its consumption. Winegrowers enjoy teaching an appreciation for the challenges of growing an agricultural crop, good stewardship of their farmland, and respect for the great technical and artistic challenges to create a beverage that is highly regarded worldwide.

Today, wine grapes are grown in countries with moderate climates around the world, often in scenic places, especially along coastal valleys and major rivers. Living in a beautiful environment and being able to taste the fruit of one's labor are among the most rewarding aspects of becoming a successful, and sometimes famous, wine maker or grape grower. This greatly compensates for the intense seasonal workload during harvesttime and a relatively modest starting salary. The annual salary depends a lot on the size of the winery. In 1999 the average salary was $28,000 to $64,000 for assistant wine makers, $49,000 to $112,000 for wine makers, and $37,000 to $64,000 for vineyard managers. Starting salaries were around $25,000 for qualified graduates with a bachelor's degree to $35,000 for those with a master of science degree.

Beer

Beer was probably first made by the Egyptians at least five thousand years ago, possibly as a variation of baking. There is considerable evidence of beer being used in religious rituals, for sacrifice, and also in medicines. Beer is made from malt that, in turn, is made from barley. Barley is steeped (soaked) in water and then permitted to germinate with constant turning and **aeration** for four to five days. It is then dried and heated (kilned), which imparts the delicious flavors of malt. In the brewery, malt is milled and mixed with hot water (known as mashing), which extracts the starch in the form of sugars. This "wort" is then boiled with hops to add bitterness. After cooling, yeast is added and fermentation creates alcohol and carbon dioxide and a myriad of desirable flavor **compounds**. After aging to clarify and stabilize the beer, it is packaged and pasteurized for sale.

aeration introduction of air

compound a substance formed from two or more elements

The malt beverage industry comprises three interdependent industries: brewing, malting, and hop supply. Although some brewers grow hops and make malt, the malt and hop industries are generally independent. These industries are dominated by a few giant companies who have an international reach.

The malt and hop industries employ students trained in plant sciences because these businesses grow, store, and use living plants. Employees must maintain good working relations with growers of barley and hops and advise them as well to assure that malting barley is planted and nurtured correctly. Superior barley is selected and purchased upon harvest. The storage and manufacture of malt or hop products, their analysis and processing to

Employees at the Carlsberg Brewery in Copenhagen, Denmark, use computers to monitor the beer-making process as tourists look down on the vats where the beer is made.

a final product, and research and sales, also tend to involve plant scientists although a broader range of skills, including chemistry and engineering, are required. Finally the malt and hop industries maintain cordial relations with the brewers through technical sales and services.

Professional employees of these industries are therefore in the field with farmers, in the processing plants, in the analytical laboratory, or on the road visiting customers. Good communications skills are necessary. Such employees in these industries are relatively few, and there are no large pyramidal management structures for steady upward mobility and advancement over many years. Experienced employees, however, are valued and well compensated, because they build important relationships with growers and customers. Entry salaries tend to be modest although good for the sometimes rural locations of the work.

Barley for malting tends to be grown close to the Canadian border, from Minnesota to Washington, where the malt houses (factories) for making malt are also located. Hop growing and processing is concentrated in the Pacific Northwest.

Brewing companies are much less likely to seek plant scientists for employment. They tend to seek graduates in food science, food engineering, or chemical engineering. For specific tasks of laboratory analysis, those with experience in chemistry or microbiology might be required. The reason is that by the time the malt and hop products reach the brewery they have lost their identity as plant materials and are now simply bulk **commodities** with specified properties for the process of making beer.

commodities goods that are traded, especially agricultural goods

Brewers work in large plants operating sophisticated machinery in which huge volumes of a highly perishable product are processed. Much of the work is computerized. Brewers are dedicated to following well-established operating procedures for consistent production of a high-quality product in the brew house, fermenting and aging cellars, and packaging plant, as well as using standard methods in the laboratory for analysis of the product.

There are no specific training programs for the malting and hop industries; programs in cereal science and plant science, however, are broadly applicable to the field. Similarly, training in brewing science is restricted to one university, the University of California at Davis. SEE ALSO AGRONOMIST; ALCOHOLIC BEVERAGES; ECONOMIC IMPORTANCE OF PLANTS; FOOD SCIENTIST.

Christian E. Butzke and Michael J. Lewis

Bibliography

American Journal of Enology and Viticulture. [Online] Available at http://www.ajev.com.

American Society for Enology and Viticulture. [Online] Available at http://www.asev.org.

Bamforth, Charles. *Beer: Tap into the Art and Science of Brewing.* New York: Plenum, 1998.

Boulton, Roger B., Vernon L. Singleton, Linda F. Bisson, and Ralph E. Kunkee. *The Principles and Practices of Winemaking.* Frederick, MD: Aspen Publishers, 1999.

Fetzer, Pat. "1999 Salary Survey." *Practical Winery and Vineyard* 20, no. 4 (1999): 6–15.

Hardwick, William A., ed. *Handbook of Brewing.* New York: Marcel Dekker, 1995.

Hough, James S., D. E. Briggs, R. Stevens, and T. W. Young. *Malting and Brewing Science,* 2nd ed. Frederick, MD: Aspen Publishers, 1981.

Jackson, Ron S. *Wine Science,* 2nd ed. San Diego: Academic Press, 2000.

Lewis, Michael J., and Tom W. Young. *Brewing.* Frederick, MD: Aspen Publishers 1996.

UC Davis Dept. of Viticulture and Enology. University of California at Davis. [Online] Available at http://wineserver.ucdavis.edu.

Winkler, Albert J. *General Viticulture,* 2nd ed. Berkeley, CA: University of California Press, 1975.

Alcoholic Beverages

anaerobic without oxygen

Alcoholic beverages all share the common feature of being produced through **anaerobic** fermentation of plant-derived carbohydrate materials by yeasts. Sugars are converted to alcohol (ethanol) and carbon dioxide by these fungi, which also impart characteristic flavors and aromas to the beverage. Depending upon what fermentable material is used, and the method by which the materials are processed, alcoholic beverages may be classified as being wines, beers, or spirits. Many countries in which they are produced regulate the production of most spirits, beer, and wine and carefully control taxation of these alcoholic beverages.

Wine

Wines are alcoholic beverages that have been fermented from fleshy fruits (e.g., apples, grapes, peaches, and plums), although most often from the cultivated grape *Vitis vinifera* (family Vitaceae) and related species. While the vast majority of wines are made from grapes, wines may also be made from the vegetative parts of certain plants.

Wines are made by harvesting ripened grapes from farms known as vineyards. The timing of the harvest is critical, since a balance of accumulated sugar, acids, and other grape flavor components reaches an optimal level to ultimately produce a fine wine. If the grapes are harvested too soon or too late, there is the possibility of producing a lower quality wine. Bunches of

DISTINGUISHING CHARACTERISTICS OF ALCOHOLIC BEVERAGES

Beverage	Fermented Materials	Carbonated?	Distilled?	Other Features
Beers				
Ales	Barley malt, wheat, rice	Yes	No	Warm fermented
Stout	Highly kilned (dark) malt	Yes	No	An ale using dark malts
Lagers	Barley malt	Yes	No	Cold fermented
Weizen beers	Wheat malt	Yes	No	Wheat beers of Germany
Wines				
Red	Grapes fermented with skins	No	No	Served at room temperature
White	Grapes fermented without skins	No	No	Served chilled
Port	Grapes	No	No/Yes	Fortified with alcohol/cognac
Champagne	Grapes fermented without skins	Yes	No	A sparkling wine
Sparkling wines	Grapes	Yes	No	May be blended
Spirits				
Whiskeys				
Scotch (single malt)	Barley malt, often peat-smoked	No	Yes	Aged in oak casks
Rye	Rye (at least 51 percent)	No	Yes	Maximum 80 proof
Bourbon	Corn (at least 51 percent)	No	Yes	Sour mashed with bacteria
Gin	Malt, other grains	No	Yes	Flavored with juniper cones
Rum	Sugarcane or molasses	No	Yes	Light or dark rums available
Tequila/Mescal	*Agave tequiliana* stems	No	Yes	Traditional drinks of Mexico
Vodka	Malt, grains, potatoes	No	Yes	Few additional flavors
Brandy/Cognac	Wines	No	Yes	Distilled wines
Liqueurs	Wines	No	Yes	Sweetened with added sugars
Other				
Sake	Rice	No	No	Double fermentation
Cider	Apples	Yes/No	No	May be flavored/spiced
Mead	Honey	Yes/No	No	May be flavored/spiced

grapes are removed from the vines, usually by manual labor, and are brought to the winery for production. The grapes are passed through a mechanical destemmer that removes the nonfruit portions of the bunches, and the fruits are then crushed to express the juice from the fleshy berries. The liquid obtained from the crushed grapes is termed "must." The must is placed in either open or closed fermentation vessels (typically closed vessels in modern wineries) and readied for fermentation. If red wines are being made, the skins from the pressed grapes are also added to the fermentation vessel (the grape skins contribute reddish pigments to the finished wine); for white wine production, the skins are not used and only clear must is fermented.

The must that is ready to be fermented is then inoculated with a particular strain of yeast (*Saccharomyces cerevisiae*) that has been selected for wine fermentation. There are hundreds of different strains of wine yeast, each imparting a particular flavor during the fermentation. When complete, the fermentation will produce an alcohol content of approximately 12 to 14 percent alcohol by volume. Following fermentation, any suspended particulate material (the lees) is allowed to settle, and the clear wine is siphoned (or racked) to a new storage vessel, which is usually a large barrel made from white oak wood. The wine is then conditioned in these barrels for a year or more, occasionally being racked to new oak barrels as the wine matures. Under these conditions, chemical reactions take place in the wine that add complexity to the flavor profile. Even contact with **tannins** in the walls of the barrel provides subtle and desirable flavor characteristics that lower quality wines conditioned in stainless steel vessels lack. Most wines are "still" (not carbonated), but sparkling wines are allowed to undergo another fermentation after they mature, and are bottled while this fermentation is occuring, thereby carbonating the wine. Champagne is one famous version of a sparkling (white) wine originally from the region of France known by that name.

Wines are bottled in glass containers and are usually sealed by inserting a compressed cork into the neck of the bottles. Wine is stored and further matured while laying on the side, so that the cork remains moist to maintain its airtight seal. Some wines should be consumed within a year or two of production; others need many years or decades to achieve their optimum flavor.

The wine industry is an extensive one, with major centers of production in France, California, Italy, Spain, and Germany, with additional developing centers of production in South Africa, Australia, Argentina, and Chile. Although wine is vinted around the world, certain places are favored for wine production due to optimal climates and suitable land for the establishment of vineyards. Wine grapes often need warm days and cool nights, with minimal temperature extremes seasonally. Furthermore, ample sunlight, available soil nutrients, and sufficient water are required for grape production. Due to variation in seasonal climates, growing and harvest conditions, and seasonal timing of production events, significant changes occur from year to year that make wines produced in certain years of higher or lower quality. Thus, the practice of labeling vintages of wine (the year of wine production) and the grape variety from which they were made is established so that enologists (people who study wine) can evaluate differences from year to year, as well as to ensure that enophiles (people who enjoy and collect wine) can purchase wines of known quality. Since many of the variables that go into wine production are not controllable by the wine producers, differences are bound to occur in each production cycle. The variation in wine flavors is therefore unending and the source of fascination for many who appreciate wine.

Beer

Among the oldest records of the production and use of alcoholic beverages is that of beer, which originated in Mesopotamia and the Babylonian regions of Asia at least fifty-five hundred years ago. Beer is a beverage obtained by fermenting carbohydrate-containing extracts of various grains with yeast. It is usually flavored with bittering substances to balance the sweet flavor of unfermented sugars, which are typically found in beer.

The brewing process begins by taking grains, usually barley (*Hordeum vulgare*), and producing malt. To do this, viable barley grains are steeped in water and allowed to germinate under controlled conditions. The germination process produces **enzymes** that begin to break down the complex car-

tannins compounds produced by plants that usually serve protective functions; often colored and used for "tanning" and dyeing

enzyme a protein that controls a reaction in a cell

bohydrates (starch) found in the **endosperm** of the barley grains into soluble sugars. When a specified stage of germination is reached, the enzyme concentration in the sprouted grains is maximized to an optimal level, and the entire process is halted abruptly by rapid drying (called kilning) of the grains to remove most of the water. At this stage the sprouted and dried grains are called malt. The degree of kilning of the malt determines the darkness and color of the resulting beer; for instance, malts that are highly kilned produce beers with darker color.

In order to extract a sufficient amount of fermentable sugars, the malt is crushed to expose the embryo and endosperm components; the ground malt is called grist. To begin conversion of starches and complex carbohydrates into fermentable sugars, the grist is mixed with water (the mash) and heated to a temperature of approximately 65°C (150°F). Under these conditions, the once active enzymes (amylases) are reactivated and continue to break down the carbohydrate materials. When the brewer determines that the conversion is complete, the fluid portions of the mash are removed through a process known as sparging, and the liquid (called sweet wort) is transferred to a boiling vessel.

The sweet wort is then boiled for a specific length of time, typically one to two hours, while the resinous, cone-like **inflorescences** of the hop plant (*Humulus lupulus;* family Cannabinaceae) are added to provide flavoring, aromatic, and bittering characteristics to the beer. Hops contain resins, collectively termed lupulin, which gives the beer its characteristic aroma and bitterness. Prior to the use of hops, other herbs, such as spruce, nettle, and woodruff were used for the same purpose: to balance the beer's sweetness with bitterness. The boiling process also kills microorganisms that would otherwise spoil the wort, or produce undesirable fermentation products. The liquid that has been boiled with hops is now termed bitter wort; it is rapidly cooled and passed on to a fermentation vessel.

Fermentation historically took place in open-topped fermenters, although modern commercial breweries use closed fermenters and are meticulous in their sanitary practices to ensure that fermentation is accomplished only by the yeast strain with which the brewer inoculates the cooled bitter wort. Two main kinds of yeast are used: ales are beers fermented with beer strains of the yeast *Saccharomyces cerevisiae* at temperatures of 15° to 25°C (59° to 77°F); lagers are beers fermented with strains of *S. uvarum* at temperatures of 5° to 15°C (41° to 59°F), which are further conditioned (lagered) at near-freezing temperatures for several weeks or months. The alcohol content of the majority of beers is generally around 5 percent by volume, although certain styles of beer are produced with alcohol contents ranging from 8 to 14 percent and higher.

Some beers are naturally carbonated by continued slow fermentation after they are bottled, or they are artificially carbonated prior to bottling. Beers are also packaged in kegs (traditionally in oaken barrels) or in metal cans. Although the earliest beer production took place originally in the Middle East, the origins of modern beer styles can be traced to Germany, the United Kingdom, and the Czech Republic. There are a number of indigenous beers produced by many cultures around the world, but few have had as much influence on the brewing industry as those originating from the European region.

endosperm the nutritive tissue in a seed, formed by fertilization of a diploid egg tissue by a sperm from pollen

inflorescence an arrangement of flowers on a stalk

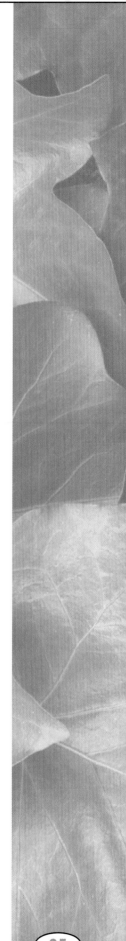

Spirits

Beverages produced from plant products that have been fermented and then distilled are considered spirits. The distillation process takes the fermented materials, often with a maximum alcohol content of 14 to 16 percent, and increases it to 40 to 75 percent alcohol by vaporizing the alcohol and many flavor components and then condensing them in specialized equipment known as stills. The concentrated alcoholic beverages resulting from this process are spirits or liquor, alluding to the condensate coming from the distillation process. Whiskeys (including Scotch or single-malt whiskey), bourbon, gin, vodka, rum, brandy, and various other liqueurs are produced through the distillation process. Each begins with a different starting material prior to fermentation and these impart different flavor characteristics in the finished spirit. Spirits are measured for alcohol content, and are then described as having a certain proof, or twice the measured alcohol content (an 86 proof whiskey has an alcohol content of 43 percent, for example). Spirits are the major component of mixed drinks.

Other Alcoholic Beverages

A variety of other alcoholic beverages exist in nearly every culture. Often they are safer to drink than local water sources, which may contain parasites, so they are widely used. Additionally, many alcoholic beverages complement different cuisines of served foods, and in some cases have been shown to improve digestion. Sake is a beerlike beverage originating in Japan that uses rice as the source of carbohydrate materials and is double fermented using yeast and a species of *Aspergillus* fungus. Cider (sometimes called hard cider) is an alcoholic beverage, popular in England, produced from yeast-fermented apple juice; it is occasionally flavored with a variety of spices. Mead, a beverage originating from medieval Europe, consists of honey that is fermented, occasionally together with other herbs or fruits, to produce a winelike drink that may be still or sparkling. The term "honeymoon" is coined from the practice of giving a gift of mead to a newly married couple: if they drank mead (honey) each night until the next moon, they would be given the gift of a new child. SEE ALSO ALCOHOLIC BEVERAGE INDUSTRY; CORK; ECONOMIC IMPORTANCE OF PLANTS; GRASSES.

Robert S. Wallace

Bibliography

Jackson, Michael. *The New World Guide to Beer*. Philadelphia, PA: Courage Books, 1988.

Johnson, H. *The World Atlas of Wine*. New York: Simon and Schuster, Inc., 1985.

Simpson, B. B., and M. C. Ogorzaly. *Economic Botany: Plants in Our World*, 2nd ed. New York: McGraw-Hill Inc., 1995.

Algae

Scientists' concepts of which organisms should be termed *algae* (alga, singular; algae, plural; algal, adjective) have changed radically over the past two centuries. The term algae originally referred to almost all aquatic, photosynthetic organisms. But, as more has been learned about the evolutionary

EUKARYOTIC ALGAE

Division	Common Name	Pigments	Habitats	General Morphology
Glaucophyta		Chlorophyll *a* Phycocyanin	Freshwater	Unicellular flagellates

Rhodophyta	Red algae	Chlorophyll *a*
		Phycoerythrin
		Phycocyanin
			Mostly marine	Unicells, filaments, thalli;
				  no flagellated stages;
				  some calcified, some mucilaginous

Cryptophyta	Cryptomonads	Chlorophyll *a* Chlorophyll *c* Phycocyanin Phycoerythrin	Marine and freshwater	Mostly unicells
Heterokontophyta (Ochrophyta)				
Chrysophyceae	Golden brown algae	Chlorophyll *a* Chlorophyll *c* Fucoxanthin	Freshwater	Mostly unicells or colonies; biflagellate

Xanthophyceae
  (Tribophyceae)
		Chlorophyll *a*
		Chlorophyll *c*
			Mostly freshwater and
			  terrestrial; some marine
				Coccoid, flagellate, or amoeboid unicells;
				  colonies, uni- and multinucleate filaments;
				  biflagellate

Eustigmatophyceae		Chlorophyll *a* Violaxanthin	Freshwater and marine	Unicells and coccoid; uni- or biflagellate
Bacillariophyceae	Diatoms	Chlorophyll *a* Chlorophyll *c* Fucoxanthin	Freshwater and marine	Unicells and colonial coccoids; no flagella
Raphidophyceae		Chlorophyll *a* Chlorophyll *c* Fucoxanthin Diadinoxanthin Vaucheriaxanthin Heteroxanthin	Freshwater and marine (Marine species only)	Unicellular biflagellates
Dictyochophyceae	Silicoflagellates	Chlorophyll *a* Chlorophyll *c* Fucoxanthin	Marine	Unicellular uniflagellates
Phaeophyceae	Brown algae	Chlorophyll *a* Chlorophyll *c* Fucoxanthin	Marine	Multicellular; reproductive cells biflagellate
Dinophyta (Pyrrhophyta)	Dinoflagellates	Chlorophyll *a* Chlorophyll *c*	Mostly marine	Mostly unicells, some coccoids and filaments; biflagellate
Haptophyta		Chlorophyll *a* Chlorophyll *c*	Mostly marine	Unicellular biflagellates
Euglenophyta	Euglenoids	Chlorophyll *a* Chlorophyll *b*	Mostly freshwater	Unicellular uniflagellates
Chlorophyta	Green algae	Chlorophyll *a* Chlorophyll *b*		
Prasinophyceae			Marine and freshwater	Unicells; 1–8 flagella

Chlorophyceae			Mostly freshwater; some
			  terrestrial and marine
				Unicellular, coccoid, or colonial flagellates;
				  multicellular or multinucleate filaments;
				  bi- or tetraflagellate

Ulvophyceae			Marine or subaerial	Uni- or multicellular or multinucleate filaments; reproductive cells bi- or tetraflagellate
Pleurastrophyceae			Subaerial	Coccoid or filament; reproductive cells biflagellate

Charophyceae	Stoneworts or
	  brittleworts;
	  desmids
			Fresh or brackish water
			  or subaerial
				Coccoid or filament, reproductive cells biflagellate
				  or with no flagella; or multinucleate cells, complex
				  thalli with biflagellate male gametes

history of algae, which spans at least five hundred million years, the definition has narrowed considerably. For instance, the assemblage of organisms traditionally called the blue-green algae will not be discussed here. These organisms are now known as **cyanobacteria**, a name that more accurately reflects their nature as **prokaryotes**. The algae are now generally considered to include only **eukaryotic** organisms.

Even after narrowing the group by excluding cyanobacteria, a succinct, precise definition of algae is not really possible. It would be accurate to say that algae are eukaryotic, photosynthetic **autotrophs** (and their colorless relatives), and that most are aquatic (there are some terrestrial species). The

cyanobacteria photosynthetic prokaryotic bacteria formerly known as blue-green algae

prokaryotes single-celled organisms without nuclei, including Eubacteria and Archaea

eukaryotic a cell with a nucleus

autotrophs "self-feeders"; any organism that uses sunlight or chemical energy

Green algae magnified fifty times their original size.

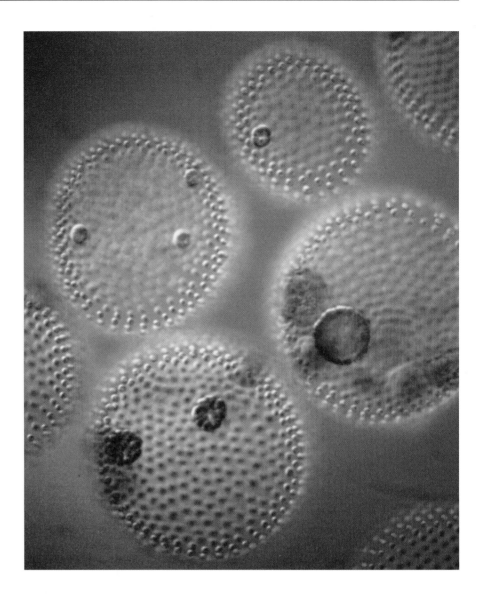

morphological related to shape

algae include organisms ranging in size from the microscopic to those reaching lengths as tall as a six-story building (e.g., the giant kelp, *Macrocystis*, which exists off the California coast), but no species of alga achieves the **morphological** complexity of true land plants; furthermore, sexual reproduction in algae is completely different than that of true land plants. Although not as beautiful to most people as roses and redwood trees, the algae are arguably the most important photosynthesizing eukaryotes on Earth.

Data analysis based on morphological, biochemical, and molecular research has led many systematists (scientists who study relationships among organisms) to conclude that traditional classification schemes for algae, and plants in general, do not reflect natural groupings and so should be abolished. It is useful, nevertheless, to have a classification system that provides a structure for comparing and discussing the various groups in terms that phycologists (scientists who study algae) and other scientists who work with algae (such as ecologists and biochemists) and students can understand. The accompanying table compares different groups of algae at the taxonomic level of division using a scheme that is generally accepted by many phycologists.

Of the eight divisions of algae in the table, only the group called the Chlorophyta is considered to be closely related to green plants. The organisms in the other groups are considered to be more closely related to **protists** than to green plants.

An ancient unicellular green alga gave rise to all algae in the Chlorophyta **lineage**. Green algae within the Chlorophyta are further split into two groups, one that contains the charophycean algae and another that consists of all other green algae. It is generally accepted among botanists (scientists who study plants) that a charophycean alga is the closest ancestor to the higher green plants.

Without the ancestral green algae, there would be no land plants, and without the algae and land plants, life as we know it would not be possible. Algae are primary producers in any aquatic environment. They are the basis of the food web, forming the very bottom of the food chain, meaning that they provide, as a byproduct of photosynthesis, a majority of the oxygen humans and animals breathe.

Some algae form **symbiotic** relationships with other organisms. Specific algae, in association with various types of fungi, form lichens of many different species, one of which is a major food source for reindeer in arctic regions. Algae can also form symbiotic relationships with animals, as evidenced by the very successful association of some reef-forming corals and the dinoflagellate algae of the species *Symbiodinium*.

Many algae are of economic importance. The fossilized remains of **diatoms**, known as diatomaceous earth, are used in cleaning products and as filtering and **inert** processing agents. Algal **polysaccharides** provide agar, used to prepare media for culturing bacteria, fungi, and plant tissues and in the purification and separation of nucleic acids and proteins. In Asia, certain algae are a major source of food. A tour through an Asian food store will turn up innumerable products made with algae, including the red alga, *Porphyra* (also known as nori or laver), which is used as a wrapper for sushi; prepared packets of dried soups featuring green algae; and several species of red and brown algae that are packaged, dried, salted, refrigerated, pickled, or frozen. The red alga *Chondrus crispus* provides carrageenan, used in the food industry as a thickener and **emulsifier** in many brands of ice cream, pudding, baby food, and chocolate milk. Brown algae provide alginates, also used as thickeners and stabilizers in numerous industries including food, paints, and cosmetics. Algal seaweeds are also collected and used as fodder for livestock in many parts of the world.

Some algae are of concern to humans because of the problems they cause. Some algae grow on the sides of buildings and on statues or other structures, forming unsightly discoloration. Rarely, and generally only in immuno-compromised individuals, certain species of green algae invade human tissues, initially gaining entry through a cut or abrasion on the skin and then proliferating. The green alga *Cephaleuros virescens* can become parasitic on the leaves of economically important plants such as coffee and tea. But, by far, the most destructive algal incidents are harmful algal blooms (HABs), the consequences of which can cost millions of dollars and cause serious health problems to livestock, fish, and even humans. HABs can occur in freshwater, contaminating watering sources for livestock and killing fish, or in marine environments. The marine HAB known as red tide is caused by

protist usually a single-celled organism with a cell nucleus, of the kingdom Protista

lineage ancestry; the line of evolutionary descent of an organism

symbiosis a relationship between two organisms from which each derives benefit

diatoms hard-shelled single-celled marine organisms

inert incapable of reaction

polysaccharide a linked chain of many sugar molecules

emulsifier a chemical used to suspend oils in water

Giant kelp growing in a sheltered bay in the Falkland Islands.

toxin a poisonous substance

certain **toxin**-producing dinoflagellates. The toxin can poison fish and shellfish, and shellfish contaminated by the toxin can cause mild to severe illness, even death, in humans who consume them. The alga *Pfiesteria* has caused toxic reactions in fish and humans in estuaries in the southeastern United States. Many HABs can be attributed to pollution, especially runoff into waterways that causes a nutrient-rich environment conducive to the rapid growth of algae.

Divisions of Algae

The type of chlorophyll and other pigments is characteristic of certain groups of algae. For instance, the Chlorophyta (and the pigmented members of the euglenoids) have both chlorophylls *a* and *b*. These pigments are contained in **chloroplasts** that are the result of endosymbiotic events; that is, during the evolutionary history of the algae, photosynthetic, prokaryotic organisms survived being ingested by their algal hosts

chloroplasts the photosynthetic organelles of plants and algae

and became an integral part of them. The main features distinguishing the algal divisions are listed in the accompanying table. Here are a few more details:

Glaucophyta. The glaucophytes are unusual unicells in which the plastids are recent endosymbionts.

Cryptophyta. The cryptomonads are unicells with phycobiliprotein pigments like the red algae, but the pigments are located in a different position within the chloroplast.

Haptophyta. The haptophytes are distinguished by the haptonema, an anterior **filament** that sometimes serves to attach the unicells to a substrate or to catch prey. The haptophytes include the coccolithophorids, the scales of which formed the white cliffs of Dover on the coast of England.

filament a threadlike extension of the cell membrane or other part of an organism

Dinophyta (or Pyrrhophyta). The dinoflagellates provide a good example of the problems in classifying algae, as many species do not have chloroplasts and, thus, live heterotrophically. As discussed above, some species are notorious for causing HABs, including red tides.

Euglenophyta. The euglenoids are **motile** unicells often found in organically enriched waters; like the dinoflagellates, some species of euglenoids are colorless heterotrophs.

motile capable of movement

Heterokontophyta (or Ochrophyta). This large division includes the brown algae (class Phaeophyceae) and the diatoms (Bacillariophyceae). Brown algae are mostly seaweeds, very diverse in form and habitat. They range in size from microscopic filaments to kelps 50 or 60 meters in length. *Sargassum* floats freely in the Sargasso Sea, but some kelp, such as *Laminaria*, have a holdfast that attaches to a substrate, leaving the stem and leafy blade to undulate in the current.

Diatoms are noted for their **siliceous** walls, which can form many intricate and beautiful shapes. Diatoms are very abundant in both freshwater and marine environments and are important primary producers.

siliceous composed of silica, a mineral

Rhodophyta. The red algae are mostly seaweeds, and they form some of the most beautiful, exotic shapes of all algae. Some species are calcified and resemble corals.

Chlorophyta. The very diverse green algae form two major lineages. The charophycean algae have complex morphologies and **ultrastructural** and genetic features that indicate they are ancestral to land plants. The other lineage comprises all other green algae, which range from unicells to large multinucleate filaments. SEE ALSO AQUATIC ECOSYSTEMS; CYANOBACTERIA; ENDOSYMBIOSIS; EVOLUTION OF PLANTS.

ultrastructural the level of structure visible with the electron microscope; very small details of structure

Russell L. Chapman and Debra A. Waters

Bibliography

Bold, Harold C., and Michael J. Wynne. *Introduction to the Algae*, 2nd ed. Upper Saddle River, NJ: Prentice-Hall, 1985.

Graham, Linda E., and Lee W. Wilcox. *Algae*. Upper Saddle River, NJ: Prentice-Hall, 2000.

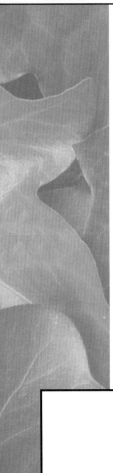

Lembi, Carole A., and J. Robert Waaland, eds. *Algae and Human Affairs*. Cambridge: Cambridge University Press, 1988.

Sze, Philip. *A Biology of the Algae*, 3rd ed. Boston: WCB McGraw-Hill, 1998.

van den Hoek, C., D. G. Mann, and H. M. Jahns. *Algae: An Introduction to Phycology*. Cambridge: Cambridge University Press, 1995.

Alkaloids

Alkaloids are natural, organic substances that are predominantly found in plants and normally contain at least one nitrogen atom in their chemical structure. Their basic (alkaline) nature has led to the term *alkaloids*. Since the identification of the first alkaloid, morphine, from the opium poppy (*Papaver somniferum*) in 1806, more than ten thousand alkaloids have been isolated from plants. Alkaloids are the active components of numerous medicinal plants or plant-derived drugs and poisons, and their structural diversity

Structures of some alkaloids, with the names of the plants that produce them.

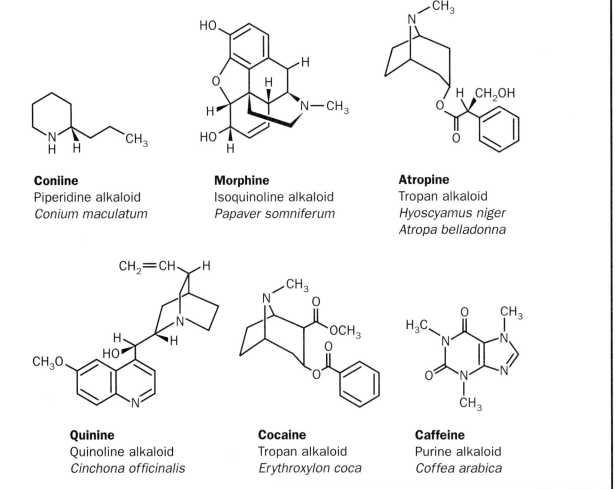

Coniine
Piperidine alkaloid
Conium maculatum

Morphine
Isoquinoline alkaloid
Papaver somniferum

Atropine
Tropan alkaloid
Hyoscyamus niger
Atropa belladonna

Quinine
Quinoline alkaloid
Cinchona officinalis

Cocaine
Tropan alkaloid
Erythroxylon coca

Caffeine
Purine alkaloid
Coffea arabica

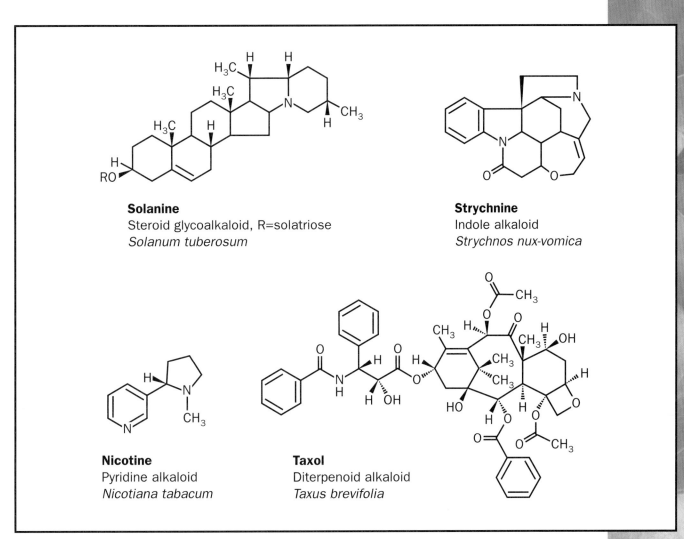

Solanine
Steroid glycoalkaloid, R=solatriose
Solanum tuberosum

Strychnine
Indole alkaloid
Strychnos nux-vomica

Nicotine
Pyridine alkaloid
Nicotiana tabacum

Taxol
Diterpenoid alkaloid
Taxus brevifolia

Structures of some alkaloids, with the names of the plants that produce them.

and different **physiological** activities are unmatched by any other group of natural products.

Although alkaloids have been detected in some animals (e.g., in the toxic secretions of fire ants, ladybugs, and toads), their major occurrence is in the flowering plants. Alkaloids are relatively stable **compounds** that accumulate as end products of different biosynthetic pathways, mostly starting from common amino acids such as lysine, ornithine, tyrosine, tryptophan, and others. Their classification is usually based on the formed **heterocyclic** ring system (e.g., piperidine in coniine, pyridine in nicotine, and quinoline in quinine). Some structures are relatively simple, whereas others are quite complex.

Alkaloids can occur in all parts of the plant but frequently, depending on the plant species, they accumulate only in particular organs (e.g., in barks, roots, leaves, and fruits), whereas at the same time other organs are alkaloid-free. In potato plants, the edible tubers are devoid of alkaloids,

physiology the biochemical processes carried out by an organism

compound a substance formed from two or more elements

heterocyclic a chemical ring structure composed of more than one type of atom, for instance carbon and nitrogen

whereas the green parts contain the poisonous solanine. The organ in which alkaloids accumulate is not always the site of their synthesis. In tobacco, nicotine is produced in the roots and translocated to the leaves where it accumulates.

The functions of alkaloids in plants are mostly unknown, and their importance in plant metabolism has been much debated. A single plant species may contain over one hundred different alkaloids, and the concentration can vary from a small fraction to as much as 10 percent of the dry weight. Breeding for plants devoid of alkaloids has also demonstrated that alkaloids are apparently not vital. Why does a plant invest so much nitrogen and energy in synthesizing such a large number and quantity of compounds? Most alkaloids are very toxic and, therefore, have the potential to function in the chemical defense arsenal of plants against attack by **herbivores** and microorganisms. For example, the nicotine present in tobacco leaves inhibits the growth of tobacco hornworm larvae; the purified compound is also applied as an effective insecticide in greenhouses. In addition, alkaloids have been suggested to serve as a storage form of nitrogen or as protectants against damage by ultraviolet light.

Alkaloids have traditionally been of great interest to humans because of their pronounced physiological and medicinal properties. From the beginning of civilization, alkaloid-containing plant extracts have been used in all cultures as potions, medicines, and poisons. Greek philosopher Socrates died in 399 B.C.E. by consumption of coniine-containing hemlock (*Conium maculatum*), and Egyptian queen Cleopatra (69–30 B.C.E.) used atropine-containing plant extracts (such as **belladonna**) to dilate her pupils. In modern times, the stimulants caffeine in coffee, tea, and cacao and nicotine in cigarettes are consumed worldwide. Alkaloids with **hallucinogenic**, narcotic, or **analgesic** properties have found medical application as pure compounds (e.g., morphine, atropine, and quinine) or served as model compounds for modern synthetic drugs, while several are abused as illegal drugs (e.g., cocaine). Other alkaloids are too toxic for any therapeutic use (e.g., coniine and strychnine), but plant constituents are still screened for new, biologically active compounds. An example is the discovery of taxol, which has **cytostatic** properties and is applied as an anticancer drug. SEE ALSO Cacao; Coca; Coffee; Defenses, Chemical; Medicinal Plants; Opium Poppy; Poisonous Plants; Potato; Tobacco.

Erich Kombrink

herbivore an organism that feeds on plant parts

belladonna the source of atropine; means "beautiful woman," and is so named because dilated pupils were thought to enhance a woman's beauty **hallucinogenic** capable of inducing hallucinations

analgesic pain-relieving

cytostatic inhibiting cell division

Bibliography

Harborne, Jeffrey B., and Herbert Baxter, eds. *Phytochemical Dictionary: A Handbook of Bioactive Compounds from Plants.* Bristol: Taylor & Francis, 1995.

Kutchan, Toni M. "Alkaloid Biosynthesis: The Basis for Metabolic Engineering of Medicinal Plants." *Plant Cell* 7 (1995): 1095–1070.

Mann, John, R. Stephen Davidson, John B. Hobbs, Derek V. Banthrope, and Jeffrey B. Harborne. *Natural Products: Their Chemistry and Biological Significance.* Essex: Longman Group, 1994.

Wink, Michael, ed. *Biochemistry of Plant Secondary Metabolism.* Sheffield, UK, and Boca Raton, FL: Sheffield Academic Press and CRC Press, 1999.

Allelopathy

Allelopathy describes those situations and events where chemicals produced by higher plants, algae, fungi, or microorganisms cause some effect, either inhibitory or stimulatory, on other members of the plant or microbial **community**. Unlike competition for a resource, the central principle in allelopathy arises from the fact that plants and microorganisms collectively produce thousands of chemicals, and many of these chemicals are released from the producing organism by leaching, **exudation**, **volatilization**, or decomposition processes. Subsequently, some of these **compounds** (known as allelochemicals) alter the growth or **physiological** functions of organisms that encounter them during growth. For example, almost pure droplets of sorgoleone (a quinone) are exuded from the roots of *Sorghum* species, and sorgoleone inhibits growth in plants that contact it by blocking photosynthesis and respiration. While the word "allelopathy" was first used in the 1930s, the phenomenon that it describes was suggested by natural philosophers more than two thousand years ago as they observed that some plants did not grow well near other kinds of plants.

Research conducted in the last half of the twentieth century demonstrated cases of growth inhibition by allelochemicals that influenced vegetational patterns, rate and sequences in plant succession, weed abundance, crop productivity, and problems in replanting fruit and other crops. Investigators have focused on identifying the producing plants and the chemicals they give off, the physiological effects on receiving species, and how climatic and soil conditions change the action of allelochemicals. Cinnamic and benzoic acids, **flavonoids**, and various terpenes are the most commonly found allelochemicals, but several hundred chemicals have been identified, including many other classes of secondary plant compounds. A few allelochemicals have been developed as herbicides and pesticides, and it may be possible to genetically engineer a crop to produce its own herbicides. SEE ALSO FLAVONOIDS; INTERACTIONS, PLANT-PLANT.

Frank A. Einhellig

community a group of organisms of different species living in a region

exudation releasing of a liquid substance; oozing

volatilization release of a gaseous substance

compound a substance formed from two or more elements

physiology the biochemical processes carried out by an organism

flavonoids aromatic compounds occurring in both seeds and young roots and involved in host-pathogen and host-symbiont interactions

Bibliography

Inderjit, K., M. M. Dakshini, and Frank A. Einhellig, eds. *Allelopathy: Organisms, Processes, and Applications.* Washington, DC: American Chemical Society, 1995.

Putnam, Alan R., and Chung-Shih Tang, eds. *The Science of Allelopathy.* New York: John Wiley & Sons, 1986.

Rice, Elroy L. *Allelopathy*, 2nd ed. Orlando, FL: Academic Press, 1984.

Alliaceae

The Alliaceae or onion family was once included in the monocot family Liliaceae, but is now recognized by many as a separate plant family. The family includes herbaceous (nonwoody) monocot plants that are generally perennial but not evergreen. Most are native to dry or moderately moist regions and other open areas. The family includes bulb or corm-forming plants as well as plants without bulbs or corms. Leaves may be round, flat, or angular in cross section and are alternately or spirally arranged. The leaves of most species in the Alliaceae are aromatic, frequently smelling like onion.

Flowers are generally organized into ball- or umbrella-shaped clusters called umbels.

Alliaceae includes several **genera**. Most genera are not commonly grown, although some species, including examples from *Tulbaghia*, *Nothoscordum*, and *Ipheion*, are occasionally grown as ornamentals. The only widely grown genus in the family is *Allium*, with approximately five hundred species that are native throughout the Northern Hemisphere. Important *Allium* species used for food include onion and shallot (*A. cepa*), garlic (*A. sativum*), leek and elephant garlic (*A. ampeloprasum*), Japanese bunching onion (*A. fistulosum*), chives (*A. schoenoprasum*), and garlic chives (*A. tuberosum*).

Many *Allium* species are also grown as ornamentals including *A. giganteum*, *A. christophii*, *A. karataviense*, *A. aflatunense*, *A. caeruleum*, the nodding onion (*A. cernuum*), the yellow-flowered *A. moly*, and the interspecific cultivar Globemaster. A few *Allium* species are also noxious weeds in some parts of the world (e.g., *A. vineale* and *A. triquetrum*). The consumption of garlic has been shown to significantly reduce both blood levels of cholesterol and the chance of coronary heart disease. Evidence also suggests that garlic has anticancer and antibiotic properties and can reduce hypertension and blood clotting. Other alliums, particularly onion, have some of the same health benefits of garlic, but effects vary widely between species. SEE ALSO ECONOMIC IMPORTANCE OF PLANTS; MONOCOTS.

James M. Bradeen

Bibliography

Brewster, James L., and Haim D. Rabinowitch, eds. *Onions and Allied Crops.* Boca Raton, FL: CRC Press, 1990.

Davies, Dilys. *Alliums: The Ornamental Onions.* Portland, OR: Timber Press, 1992.

Anatomy of Plants

The anatomy of plants relates to the internal structure and organization of the mature plant body, especially the vegetative organs of plants.

Cells

As in all other organisms, cells make up the fundamental unit of the plant body. Plant cells, whether formed in vegetative or reproductive organs, are usually bounded by a thin, mostly cellulosic wall that encloses the living **protoplast**. Young cells characteristically develop numerous membrane-bound **vesicles**, originating from the endoplasmic reticulum (ER) and **dictyosomes**. Some of these immature cells retain their ability to divide and are called meristematic. As cells age, the vesicles grow together, usually forming one relatively large water-filled **vacuole** positioned in the cell's center, which inhibits further cell division. Some older cells additionally produce a thick **lignified** cell wall located between the cellulosic wall and the protoplast. Cell walls are ordinarily considered a part of the cell's nonliving environment, but considerable research has revealed that a number of important physical and chemical events take place within cell walls.

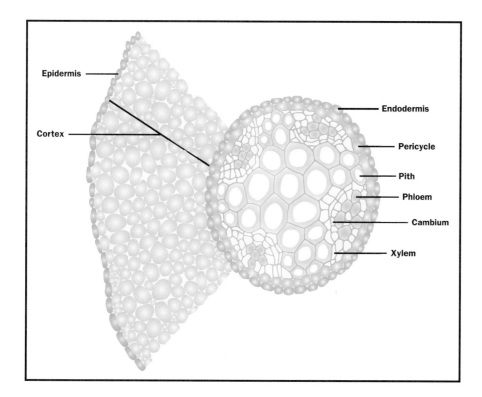

Transverse section of tissues of a dicot root. Redrawn from Van de Graaff et al., 1994.

Labels: Epidermis, Cortex, Endodermis, Pericycle, Pith, Phloem, Cambium, Xylem

Tissues

Groups of adjacent cells having similar structure and function constitute the tissues of the plant. Tissues having a structural or functional similarity comprise the plant organs. All of the cells, tissues, and organs trace their origins back to the **zygote** or embryo, which develops within the seed. Meristematic tissues within the embryo and young plant are responsible for generating new cells that ultimately result in increased plant size. **Apical** meristems develop near the ends of all stems and roots, and they contribute to the increased length of both. **Lateral** meristems (cambia), such as the **vascular** cambium and cork cambium are responsible for increased diameter, especially noticeable in long-lived tree species. The vascular cambium is initiated more internally within the plant body, producing cells both interiorly and exteriorly. Xylem tissue is produced interiorly and phloem tissue is produced exteriorly. The thick-walled secondary xylem tissue constitutes the wood, while all tissues outside of the vascular cambium, including the cork cambium, comprise the plant's bark. Tissues produced by the apical meristems result in the primary growth of the plant, while tissues resulting from cell divisions of the cambia result in secondary growth.

One way in which plant tissues are categorized is on the basis of their cell wall thickness. Parenchyma tissue is composed of evenly thin-walled cells, having cellulosic walls. Sclerenchyma tissue is composed of evenly thick-walled cells as a result of developing both cellulosic and lignified wall layers. Collenchyma tissue is an intermediate tissue type having unevenly thickened cells aggregated together. Sclerenchyma tissue functions both in support and water conduction, while parenchyma participates in food storage, cell division, and food conduction. Collenchyma is the least common tissue type among the three and may be involved in a combination of activities associated with the other two types.

zygote the egg immediately after it has been fertilized; the one-cell stage of a new individual

apical at the tip

lateral away from the center

vascular related to transport of nutrients

Plant tissues can also be characterized by their relative position within the plant organs. There are three tissue systems within the mature plant: the dermal, the vascular, and the ground tissue systems. Dermal tissues compose the outermost tissue layer, the epidermis. Xylem and phloem are prominent tissues comprising the vascular system of the plant. In the root, the vascular system (also referred to as the vascular cylinder or stele) has as its outer boundary a single layer of pericycle tissue that is immediately exterior to the xylem and phloem. The pith, composed of thin-walled cells, may develop immediately interior to the vascular tissues, more centrally located in stems and roots. Root pericycle is a common tissue of origin for the formation of lateral roots, while the pith tissue is involved in food storage. Positioned in between the dermal and vascular tissue systems is the ground system, often referred to as the cortex. The cortex of younger stems and roots may be further partitioned from outside to inside into the hypodermis, the **cortical** parenchyma, and the endodermis. The endodermis of underground roots and stems, especially, often develops waxy deposits of suberin in the cell walls. These water-impervious deposits are referred to as Casparian thickenings and are believed to prevent the diffusion of water and dissolved substances along the cell walls, directing the movement through the protoplast.

The dermal and ground tissue systems of roots and stems of older tree species may be sloughed off by the activity of the ever-increasing circumference of the vascular cambium. In these older organs another dermal tissue, the cork, is produced outwardly by the cork cambium. The enclosing cork functions not only as a protective surface layer but also as a tissue involved in water conservation.

Organs

Organs of the plant body can be classified as either vegetative or reproductive. Usually the vegetative organs are involved in procuring required nutrients for the plant. For example, the green photosynthetic leaves are responsible for the production of food, while the roots can function as excellent food storage organs, as well as obtaining water and dissolved minerals by absorption from the soil. Cellular extensions of the root epidermal cells, the root hairs, increase the absorbing surface of roots. Stem organs, developing between the leaves and the roots, produce conducting tissues (xylem and phloem) responsible for transporting food, water, and dissolved substances throughout the rest of the plant. Reproductive organs of the **angiosperms** are the flowers, fruits, and seeds. These three organs are ordinarily involved in sexual reproduction, while the vegetative organs may function in asexual reproduction.

Complete flowers are composed of the four **appendages** produced by the reproductive apical meristem of the stem: **sepals**, petals, stamens, and **carpels**. The **whorl** of petals can be quite conspicuous, attracting pollinators such as insects to the flower, where pollen can be inadvertently gathered from the stamens. The carpels together constitute the pistil, the component parts of which are the landing pad for the pollen (the stigma), the style, and the basal ovary. Ovules develop within the ovary, and following fertilization give rise to the seeds and fruit, respectively.

cortical relating to the cortex of a plant

angiosperm a flowering plant

appendages parts that are attached to a central stalk or axis

sepals the outermost whorl of flower parts; usually green and leaf-like, they protect the inner parts of the flower

carpels the innermost whorl of flower parts, including the egg-bearing ovules, plus the style and stigma attached to the ovules

whorl a ring

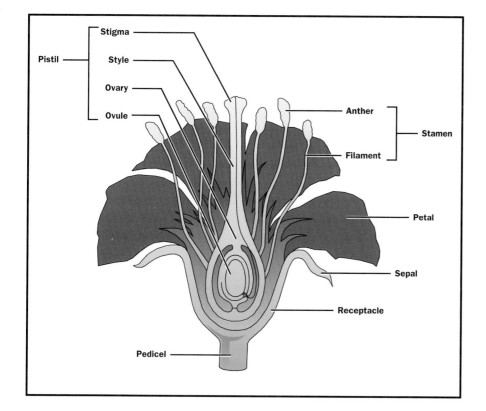

Structure of angiosperm flowers. Redrawn from Van de Graaff et al., 1994.

Organs of the embryo or young plant are used to distinguish the two large groups of flowering plants. The monocotyledonous and dicotyledonous plant groups produce one or two embryonic cotyledons, respectively. Both internal and external features of both vegetative and reproductive organs can be used to distinguish the monocots from the dicots. The more prominent leaf veins have venation patterns that are referred to as reticulate (netlike) in the dicots and parallel venation in monocots. The number of floral appendages (sepals, petals, stamens, and carpels) can also be used to identify the two angiosperm groups. Dicot species usually produce the separate floral appendages in whorls of fours or fives, while the monocots develop whorls of appendages in threes. Whole number multiples of these base numbers can similarly be used to distinguish the two groups.

Leaves

Leaves, produced as appendages or outgrowths from the vegetative stem apical meristem, have a different tissue arrangement than the stems and roots. The component tissues of the leaf are the epidermis, the mesophyll, and the vascular bundles. The epidermis is formed from the surface cell layer of the stem apical meristem. The epidermis serves a protective function.

Vascular bundles, also called veins, are cylindrical traces of xylem and phloem that diverge from the stem's central stele. The leaf's midvein is the largest medianly positioned vascular bundle. Minor leaf veins develop laterally on either side of the midvein. Both the midvein and minor veins differentiate through the stalk of the leaf (the petiole) into its flat blade.

Transverse section of a dicot leaf. Redrawn from Van de Graaff et al., 1994.

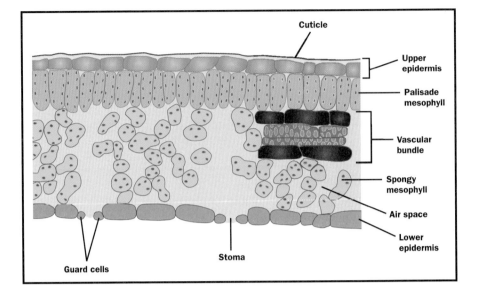

The blade is composed mostly of mesophyll tissue that develops interior to the enveloping leaf epidermis and surrounds the vascular bundles. Most leaves have two types of mesophyll cells, the palisade and spongy mesophyll. Palisade mesophyll develops near the upper epidermis and is composed of columnar-shaped cells. The spongy mesophyll cells are more spherically shaped and are characterized by the presence of numerous intercellular spaces between adjacent cells. Plants produce most of their food during photosynthesis in cells of the mesophyll tissue.

Although considerable variation in anatomy occurs in the internal leaf tissues of dicots and monocots, the differences are mostly based on environmental rather than taxonomic criteria. There is a distinct difference, however, in the leaf anatomy of certain species, both dicot and monocot, based on whether the first product produced in photosynthesis is a three-carbon or a four-carbon (C_4) **compound**. C_4 plants, best represented by tropical grasses, develop a thick-walled cell layer around each leaf vascular bundle, called the bundle sheath cells. This concentric organization of surrounding bundle sheath cells is referred to as Kranz (German for "wreath") anatomy. Additionally, the bundle sheath cells contain more **organelles** such as mitochondria and **chloroplasts**. Dicot and monocot species in which the first photosynthetic compound produced is a three-carbon compound do not exhibit Kranz anatomy.

compound a substance formed from two or more elements

organelle a membrane-bound structure within a cell

chloroplast the photosynthetic organelle of plants and algae

Stems and Roots

The arrangement of the vascular tissues within the stele not only distinguishes dicot from monocot species, but also provides a means of identifying the specific vegetative organs. Stems are partitioned into nodes and internodes. Nodes are the locations of leaf development, while the internodes are the distances between the leaves, comprising most of the stem's length. Young dicot internodes usually develop a single ring of vascular bundles when viewed in cross sections. As a result of vascular cambium activity in older woody dicots, the vascular bundles are disrupted and eventually give way to concentric rings of secondary xylem interiorly and secondary phloem exteriorly. The major secondary phloem cell type involved in food conduction is the sieve-tube element. The interiorly produced secondary xylem is composed of **tracheids** and vessel elements, the water-conducting cells, which have heavily lignified cell walls. The majority of dicot tree species are composed of these thick-walled xylem cells, which represent the wood or lumber used in commerce. A central pith, with peripheral **vascular** tissues, develops in the center of both dicot and monocot stems, as well as monocot roots. The stems of many monocot species (for example, grain crops) produce a scattered arrangement of vascular bundles that develop throughout the pith and cortex. These vascular bundles do not become disrupted in older stems, since no vascular cambium develops in monocot species. Thus, young and old monocot stems resemble each other in their anatomy. Young and old dicot roots do not develop a central pith but have xylem in their centers. Vascular bundles, so characteristic of stems and leaves, are absent throughout most of the length of roots in both angiosperm groups.

The stems and roots of flowering plants are categorized by their appearance. For example, stem structural types include bulbs, rhizomes, corms, tubers, and **stolons** that develop underground. **Cladodes**, tendrils, tillers,

tracheid a type of cell that conducts water from root to shoot

vascular related to transport of nutrients

stolons an underground stem that may form new individuals by sprouting

cladode a modified stem having the appearance and function of a leaf

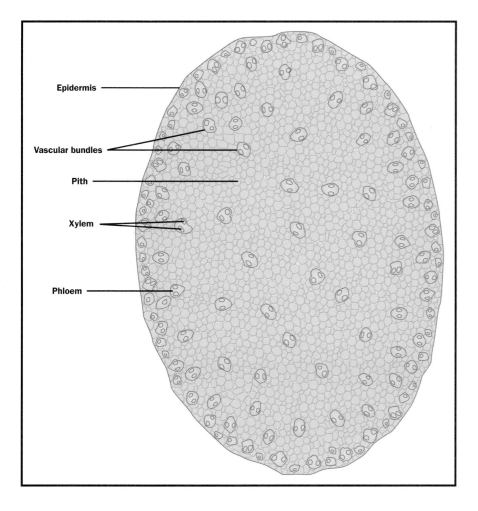

Epidermis

Vascular bundles

Pith

Xylem

Phloem

Transverse section of a monocot (*Zea mays;* corn) stem. Redrawn from Van de Graaff et al., 1994.

and thorns are types of aboveground stems. Root structural types include underground tap and fibrous roots, while buttress and prop roots occur above ground.

Bryophytes and Ferns

Two important groups of nonflowering plants include the bryophytes and the ferns. The bryophytes include the mosses, liverworts, and hornworts. They lack vascular tissues, and therefore do not develop true leaves, stems, and roots. Since bryophytes produce organs that are similar in structure and function to leaves and stems, these organ names are used, however. Being nonvascular plants, bryophytes ordinarily form a low-growing ground cover, never becoming a conspicuous part of the temperate vegetation. While most cells are thin-walled and spherical, elongated cells of conducting tissues develop within the stems of some bryophytes. Leptome and hydrome are analogous to the phloem and xylem tissues of higher plants, respectively. Leaves of bryophytes are produced spirally around the stem. Leaves contain **filaments** of cells, the photosynthetic **lamellae**.

filament a threadlike extension

lamellae thin layers or plate-like structures

Ferns are primitive vascular plants and commonly have complicated arrangements of phloem and xylem tissues within stem and root steles. Most temperate ferns develop elongated underground stems (rhizomes) from which the aboveground leaves (fronds) originate. Developing on the lower side of the rhizome are the slender roots. Fronds, on their inception, are tightly coiled into fiddleheads, termed such because of their resemblance to the carvings on the end of a violin or fiddle. One of the most conspicuous attributes of ferns is the formation of older leaves that are compound, giving them a dissected or lacy appearance. Reproductive structures commonly develop on the underside of fern fronds and are conspicuous due to their brown color in contrast to the leaf's green background. These are the sori in which spores are produced. No development of flowers, fruits, or seeds occurs in the ferns. SEE ALSO BARK; BRYOPHYTES; CELLS; CELLS, SPECIALIZED TYPES; FERNS; FLOWERS; LEAVES; MERISTEMS; ROOTS; STEMS; TISSUES.

Jan E. Mikesell

Bibliography

Cassab, Gladys I. "Plant Cell Wall Proteins." In *Annual Review of Plant Physiology and Plant Molecular Biology*, Vol. 49. Russel L. Jones, ed. Palo Alto, CA: Wadsworth, 1998.

Esau, Katherine. *Anatomy of Seed Plants*, 2nd ed. New York: John Wiley & Sons, 1977.

Fahn, Abraham. *Plant Anatomy*, 4th ed. New York: Pergamon Press, 1990.

Mauseth, James D. *Plant Anatomy*. Menlo Park, CA: Benjamin Cummings, 1987.

Moore, Randy, W. Dennis Clark, and Kingley R. Stern. *Botany*. Boston: Wm. C. Brown Publishers, 1995.

Salisbury, Frank B., and Cleon W. Ross. *Plant Physiology*, 4th ed. Belmont, CA: Wadsworth, 1992.

Van de Graaff, K. M., S. R. Rush, and J. L. Crawley. *A Photographic Atlas for the Botany Laboratory*, 2nd ed. Englewood, CO: Morton Publishing Co, 1994.

Angiosperms

The angiosperms, or flowering plants (division Anthophyta or Magnoliophyta), comprise more than 230,000 species and are thus by far the largest division of plants; they represent the dominant group of land plants today. In both vegetative and floral **morphology** the angiosperms are highly diverse. In size, for example, they range from the duckweeds (the genus *Lemna*), which are roughly one millimeter in length, to *Eucalyptus* trees, which are well over one hundred meters. Although all are characterized by the possession of flowers, these structures are also highly diverse in form and size. The smallest flowers are less than a millimeter in size (the flowers of duckweeds) while the largest flowers are approximately one meter in diameter (the flowers of *Rafflesia*). Features unique, or nearly so, to angiosperms include the flower; the presence of seeds within a closed structure (actually a modified leaf) referred to as the **carpel**; the reduction of the female **gametophyte** to eight nuclei and seven cells; double fertilization (the

morphology shape and form

carpels the innermost whorl of flower parts, including the egg-bearing ovules, plus the style and stigma attached to the ovules

gametophyte the haploid organism in the life cycle

MAJOR ANGIOSPERM GROUPS

Major Clades and Representative Families	Common Name	Number of Species in Family (approximate)
Eurosid		
Rosaceae	Rose family	3,500
Fabaceae	Pea or legume family	17,000
Brassicaceae	Mustard family	3,000
Fagaceae	Beech or oak family	1,000
Cucurbitaceae	Pumpkin or gourd family	700
Euphorbiaceae	Spurge family	5,000
Juglandaceae	Walnut or hickory family	50
Begoniacae	Begonia family	1,000
Geraniaceae	Geranium family	750
Malvaceae	Cotton family	1,000
Euasterid		
Cornaceae	Dogwood family	100
Ericaceae	Heath family	3,000
Lamiaceae	Mint family	3,000
Solanaceae	Tomato or potato family	2,500
Asteraceae	Sunflower family	25,000
Apiaceae	Parsley family	3,000
Hydrangeaceae	Hydrangea family	170
Caryophyllales		
Cactaceae	Cactus family	2,000
Caryophyllaceae	Carnation or pink family	2,000
Aizoaceae	Mesembryanthemum family	2,300
Portulacaceae	Portulaca family	500
Polygonaceae	Buckwheat or rhubarb family	750
Magnoliids*		
Magnoliaceae	Magnolia family	200
Lauraceae	Avocado or cinnamon family	2,500
Piperaceae	Pepper family	3,000
Myristicaceae	Nutmeg family	380
Annonaceae	Sweetsop family	2,000
Monocots*		
Orchidaceae	Orchid family	18,000
Poaceae	Grass family	9,000
Arecaceae	Palm family	2,800
Araceae	Arum family	2,000

* Indicates major clades that are noneudicots; other major clades are eudicots.

A magnolia in bloom. Magnolias are basal angiosperms (plants thought to have evolved first) and are ancestors to both monocots and eudicots.

zygote the egg immediately after it has been fertilized; the one-cell stage of a new individual

endosperm the nutritive tissue in a seed, formed by fertilization of a diploid egg tissue by a sperm from pollen

floristic related to plants

gymnosperm a major group of plants that includes the conifers

genera plural of genus

strobili cone-like reproductive structures

fusion of egg and sperm resulting in a **zygote** and the simultaneous fusion of the second sperm with the two polar nuclei, resulting in a triploid nucleus) and subsequent **endosperm** formation; a male or microgametophyte composed of three nuclei; stamens with two pairs of pollen sacs; and sieve tube elements and companion cells in the phloem. Nearly all angiosperms also possess vessel elements in the xylem, but vessel elements also occur in Gnetales and some ferns.

Origins of Angiosperms

Because of the sudden appearance of a diverse array of early angiosperms in the fossil record, Charles Darwin referred to the origin of the flowering plants as "an abominable mystery." Although there are reports of earlier angiosperm remains, the oldest fossils that are indisputably angiosperms are from the early Cretaceous period, about 130 million years ago. Based on fossil evidence, it is clear that angiosperms radiated rapidly after their origin, with great diversity already apparent 115 million years ago. By 90 to 100 million years ago the angiosperms had already become the dominant **floristic** element on Earth. By 75 million years ago, many modern orders and families were present.

The closest relatives and ancestor of the flowering plants have long been topics of great interest and debate. There was widespread belief during the last decades of the twentieth century that the Gnetales, a group of **gymnosperms** having three existing, highly divergent members (*Gnetum, Ephedra, Welwitschia*), were the closest living relatives of the flowering plants among existing gymnosperms. These three **genera** resemble angiosperms in having special water-conducting vessels in the wood and reproductive structures organized into compound **strobili** similar in organization to compound flower clusters. In addition, some Gnetales (the genus *Gnetum*) have angiosperm-like leaves. Gnetales also have a process that, in part, resembles double fertilization, a feature unique to angiosperms. In Gnetales, both sperm produced by the male gametophyte (in the pollen) fuse with nuclei in the female gametophyte. However, in Gnetales the second fusion produces an additional embryo and does not result in the triploid endosperm characteristic of flowering plants. Beginning in the mid-1980s, however, **phylogenetic** trees derived from gene sequence data have indicated instead a close relationship of Gnetales to conifers, with all of the living gymnosperms forming a **clade** that is the sister group to the angiosperms. The molecular evidence is compelling and indicates that Gnetales are probably not the closest living relatives of the flowering plants. Several fossil **lineages** have been suggested as close relatives of the angiosperms. These include *Pentoxylon* and Bennettitales, and these plants must be considered as possible candidates for the closest relatives of the flowering plants.

Taxonomy

Traditionally, angiosperms have been divided into two major groups or classes: dicotyledons (Magnoliopsida) and monocotyledons (Liliopsida). In recent classification schemes, each class was then divided into a number of subclasses. In this scheme, dicots were divided into six subclasses: Magnoliidae, Hamamelidae, Caryophyllidae, Rosidae, Dilleniidae, and Asteridae. The monocots were similarly divided into subclasses: Alismatidae, Arecidae, Commelinidae, Zingiberidae, and Liliidae. Although the division of angiosperms into monocots and dicots, with subsequent division into subclasses, has long been followed in classifications and textbooks, phylogenetic studies have dramatically revised views of angiosperm relationships. In fact, trees derived from deoxyribonucleic acid (DNA) sequence data have stimulated the most dramatic changes in views of angiosperm relationships during the past 150 years. As reviewed next, DNA data indicate that many of these groups do not hold together (that is, they do not form distinct clades—they are not monophyletic); hence they should not be recognized.

Until recently, the radiation of the angiosperms was thought to have occurred so rapidly that many scientists believed that it might not be possible to identify the earliest angiosperms (this is also known as Darwin's "abominable mystery"). However, a series of recent molecular systematic (DNA) studies using different genes and molecular approaches all identify the very same first branches of the angiosperm tree of life. The evidence from these studies indicates that the angiosperms, formerly grouped as dicots and monocots, are best classified as either eudicots (true dicots) or noneudicots. The noneudicots are further divided into the monocots and the basal angiosperms. This scheme reflects what is now known about angiosperm evolution: The basal angiosperms are those plants thought to have evolved first and are ancestral to both monocots and eudicots. This group is represented by the Magnoliaceae (Magnolia family), Lauraceae (Laurel family), Nymphaeaceae (water lily family), Amborella (a shrub **endemic** to New Caledonia), and a group of shrubs that include *Illicium, Schisandra, Trimenia,* and *Austrobaileya.* Many of these early diverging angiosperms possess pollen with a single groove, or aperture (line of weakness).

The monocots, which also have pollen with a single aperture, are believed to have arisen as one line of this earliest group of plants, probably more than 120 million years ago. Eudicots have pollen with three apertures. The details of their origins from basal angiosperms is less clear, but they are believed to have split off perhaps 127 million years ago.

phylogenetic related to phylogeny, the evolutionary development of a species

clade group of organisms composed of an ancestor and all of its descendants

lineage ancestry; the line of evolutionary descent of an organism

endemic belonging or native to a particular area or country

The term *dicot*, therefore, refers to plants that include both the eudicots and the basal angiosperms. Since the basal angiosperms are ancestral to the monocots as well, *dicot* cannot be meaningfully contrasted to *monocot*, and is thus not considered to be a taxonomically useful label.

Whereas *monocot* remains a useful term, *dicot* does not represent a natural group of flowering plants and should be abandoned. That there is no monocot-versus-dicot split in the angiosperms is not a total surprise—botanists have long theorized that the monocots were derived from an ancient group of dicots during the early diversification of the angiosperms, and recent phylogenetic analyses simply confirm this hypothesis.

The early branching angiosperms (or noneudicots) comprise not only the monocots, but many of those families (fewer than twenty-five) traditionally placed in the subclass Magnoliidae. Many of these families of early branching flowering plants possess oil cells that produce highly volatile oils referred to as ethereal oils. These ethereal oils are the basis of the characteristic fragrance of these plants; these **compounds** are responsible for the characteristic aroma of many spices, including sassafras, cinnamon, laurel or bay leaves, nutmeg, star anise, and black pepper. The noneudicots are also highly diverse in floral morphology. Familiar families of noneudicot or early diverging angiosperms include woody families such as the magnolia family (Magnoliaceae), the laurel or cinnamon family (Lauraceae), the nutmeg family (Myristicaceae), and the sweetsop or custard-apple family (Annonaceae). Members of these families often have relatively large flowers with numerous parts that may be spirally arranged. Other early branching angiosperms include plants often referred to as paleoherbs. As the name implies, paleoherbs are predominantly herbaceous and have small flowers with very few flower parts. The paleoherbs include the black pepper family (Piperaceae) and wild-ginger family (Aristolochiaceae).

Once the noneudicots are excluded, the remaining dicots form a well-supported clade referred to as the *eudicots*. This group contains, by far, the vast majority of angiosperm species; approximately 75 percent of all angiosperms are eudicots. Eudicots include most familiar angiosperm families. Recent phylogenetic trees demonstrate that the eudicots comprise a number of well-supported lineages that differ from traditional **circumscriptions**. The earliest branches of eudicots are members of the order Ranunculales, which include the Ranunculaceae (buttercup family), Papaveraceae (poppy family), Proteaceae (protea family), and Platanaceae (sycamore family). Following these early branching **taxa**, most remaining eudicots form a large clade (referred to as the core eudicots), comprised of three main branches and several smaller ones. The main branches of core eudicots are:

- eurosids, or true rosids (made up of members of the traditional subclasses Rosidae, Dilleniidae, and Hamamelidae)

- the euasterids, or true asterids (containing members of the traditional subclasses Asteridae, Dilleniidae, and Rosidae)

- the Caryophyllales (the traditional subclass Caryophyllidae, plus some Dilleniidae).

Importantly, there is no clade that corresponds to the traditionally recognized subclasses Dilleniidae and Hamamelidae. As noted, these subclasses

compound a substance formed from two or more elements

circumscription the definition of the boundaries surrounding an object or an idea

taxa a type of organism, or a level of classification of organisms

have members scattered throughout the eudciots—hence, they are not *natural*, or monophyletic groups. Because of the enormous insights that DNA-based studies have provided into relationships within the angiosperms, the use of long-recognized subclass names and group delineations, such as Magnoliidae, Rosidae, Asteridae, Dilleniidae, has been abandoned in recent classification schemes.

Evolution and Adapations

Based on the earliest branches of the angiosperm tree reconstructed from DNA sequence data, as well as fossil evidence, early angiosperms were likely woody shrubs with a moderate-sized flower possessing a moderate number of spirally arranged flower parts. There was no differentiation between **sepals** and petals (that is, **tepals** were present). The stamens did not exhibit well-differentiated anther and **filament** regions (these are often referred to as laminar stamens). The **carpels**, the structures that enclose the seeds, were folded and sealed by a sticky secretion rather than being fused shut, as is the typical condition in later-flowering plants. In contrast, later angiosperms (the eudicots, for example) have well-differentiated sepals and petals and flower parts in distinct **whorls**. Their stamens are well-differentiated into anther and filament regions and the carpels are fused during development.

By eighty to ninety million years ago the angiosperms were dominant floristic elements. Obvious reasons for their success include the evolution of more efficient means of pollination (the flower for the attraction of pollinators) and seed dispersal (via the mature carpel, or fruit). One important innovation was the evolution of the bisexual flower; that is, the presence of both carpels and stamens in one flower. In contrast, gymnosperms have separate male and female reproductive structures or cones. Bisexual structures may have an advantage over unisexual structures in that the pollinator can both deliver and pick up pollen at each visit to a flower. Other possible reasons for the success of flowering plants involve morphological, chemical, and anatomical attributes. These include the presence in angiosperms of more efficient means of water and carbohydrate (sugar) conduction via vessel elements and sieve tube elements/companion cells, respectively. These anatomical features may be viewed as adaptations for drought resistance. Vessel elements are found in only a few groups other than flowering plants, and the presence of the sieve tube/companion cell pair is unique to the flowering plants.

The evolution of the deciduous habit was also important in the success of the flowering plants. This feature permitted woody plants to lose their leaves and to become inactive physiologically during periods of drought and cold. Other important evolutionary innovations in angiosperms that also may have contributed to their success include a more efficient source of nutrition for the developing embryo through the production of triploid endosperm (in other seed plants the **haploid** female gametophyte tissue nourishes the young embryo) and the protection of ovules and developing seeds inside a novel, closed structure, the carpel. Compared to other plants, the angiosperms also possess enormous biochemical diversity, which includes a diverse array of chemicals that presumably act in defense against **herbivores** and **pathogens**.

sepals the outermost whorl of flower parts; usually green and leaf-like, they protect the inner parts of the flower

tepal an undifferentiated sepal or petal

filament a threadlike extension of the cell membrane or other part of an organism

carpels the innermost whorl of flower parts, including the egg-bearing ovules, plus the style and stigma attached to the ovules

whorl a ring

haploid having one set of chromosomes, versus having two (diploid)

herbivore an organism that feeds on plant parts

pathogen disease-causing organism

The first seed-producing plants (various lineages of gymnosperms) were wind-pollinated. The angiosperms, in contrast, as well as some gymnosperms (cycads and Gnetales), typically employ a more efficient system—insects feeding on pollen or nectar transfer pollen from one plant to the next. The more attractive the flower of the plant is to the insect, the more frequently the flowers will be visited and the more seed produced. The first angiosperms likely were pollinated by beetles that foraged on pollen and in so doing moved pollen from one flower to the next. Plants with flowers that provided special sources of food for pollinators, such as nectar, had a selective advantage. In this general way angiosperms and insects coevolved, or diversified. The rise and diversification of the diverse array of flower visitors we see today, such as bees, moths, and butterflies, occurred in concert with the increasing diversification of flowers. Both pollinators and angiosperms were influenced by the diversification of the other. SEE ALSO DICOTS; EVOLUTION OF PLANTS; FLOWERS; GYMNOSPERMS; MONOCOTS; PHYLOGENY; SYSTEMATICS, PLANT; TAXONOMY.

Doug Soltis and Pam Soltis

Bibliography

Cronquist, A. *An Integrated System of Flowering Plants.* New York: Columbia University Press, 1981.

Anthocyanins

Anthocyanins are a class of molecules pervasive in plants that are responsible for the showy bright purple, red, and blue colors of flowers and variegated leaves. Anthocyanins are located in the **vacuoles** of cells, and different genes control the particular shades of colors. Aside from their coloration, anthocyanin molecules are also active in plant defense mechanisms against insect and fungal attacks and in the recognition of nitrogen-fixing bacteria by leguminous plants (providing a molecule that attracts the bacteria). Approximately twenty genes are involved in the formation of the anthocyanin molecule with various **amendments**, such as **hydroxyl** groups or glucose alterations, to vary the coloration and cause the molecule to function in a particular way. In maize, there are two major types of genes, regulatory and structural,

vacuole the large fluid-filled sac that occupies most of the space in a plant cell. Used for storage and maintaining internal pressure

amendment additive

hydroxyl the chemical group -OH

Structure of anthocyanin.

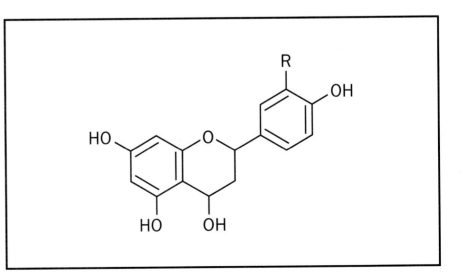

that control the formation of the anthocyanin molecule used to give the corn kernel its color. The variegated Indian corn is caused by an interruption of the color formation by an insert in one of these genes, thus releasing the gene to form color. SEE ALSO FLAVONOIDS; NITROGEN FIXATION; PIGMENTS.

Peter A. Peterson

Aquatic Ecosystems

Most of the water on our planet is in the oceans that cover 71 percent of Earth's surface. Less than 1 percent of all the water is considered freshwater, and most of that is frozen in the polar ice caps. The study of freshwater aquatic **ecosystems**, limnology, has often been separated from the study of marine systems, oceanography. Although freshwater and marine ecosystems are extremely diverse in structure, all of the plants and animals must live in or on water. The physical constraints and opportunities for life in water, and how all of these living organisms interact with each other in a liquid medium, give a unifying theme to aquatic studies.

The Influence of Water

Water is a liquid and has a greater density and viscosity than air. It can absorb a large amount of solar radiation with a small increase in temperature. Once heated, it will get cooler at a slower rate than land. Aquatic organisms are therefore somewhat buffered against massive, rapid changes in temperature. Aquatic organisms, however, may have to adapt to the water temperature in hot freshwater springs, to the hot vents in the ocean floor in volcanic areas, and to the chilling cold of the water of the polar oceans and freezing winters in the temperate zones of the world. Cold water is denser than hot water, and this may lead to massive mixing and turnover in lakes. In rivers and streams, the water depth and the water flow rate will determine the structure of the biological communities. Plants have to be attached and be highly specialized in structure to survive in fast-flowing water. In larger bodies of water, such as lakes and oceans, wind and tides will mix waters and carry sediments and organisms over large distances. Wave action will alter the physical structure and the geography of shores and coastlines and have a tremendous effect on the biological communities that can survive there.

Water is not always clear, and photosynthetic plants are limited to growing on or near the water surface, or in shallow coastal zones where they can receive sufficient sunlight. While marine habitats all have high levels of salts, the nutrient ion content and the alkalinity and acidity (pH) of freshwater habitats are variable. Plants in water need to get all of their mineral nutrients from the water or from the sediment below. They must also find sufficient oxygen and carbon dioxide to respire, photosynthesize, grow, and reproduce.

Diversity of Habitats

In both freshwater and marine ecosystems, the majority of the photosynthetic plants are algae. Most of these algae are microscopic. Huge colonies of algal cells, however, can be seen as algal blooms and colonies of **filamentous** forms are easily observed in patches on rocks and in slow-

Variegated Indian corn, whose color is controlled by genes within anthocyanin molecules.

ecosystem an ecological community together with its environment

filament a threadlike extension

moving streams. In oceans, microalgae form a major part of the plankton. This phytoplankton is pelagic, living freely in the seawater. Large plants (macrophytes) are less common in oceans, although huge mats of large, floating algae are found in the Sargasso Sea in the mid-Atlantic. Forests of large algae (seaweeds) and some flowering plants (sea grasses) are confined to shallower coastal habitats. These macrophytes are generally attached to rocks or sand on the ocean bottom: they are benthic organisms. Rivers, lakes, and other freshwater habitats contain benthic or pelagic flowering aquatic plants, ferns, mosses, and liverworts that have reinvaded the water from the land at various times during their evolution. In rivers and streams, the water depth and the water flow rate will be a key determinant of plant success. In oceans, currents and tides will carry sediments and organisms over large distances.

All of the aquatic plants are primary producers. Their ability to fix carbon dioxide into carbohydrates by their light-driven photosynthetic reactions makes them the basis of the aquatic food chain. They are grazed upon and eaten, and, when they die, their structures are degraded by a huge variety of dependent organisms in the food web. These freshwater and ma-

A variety of phytoplankton or floating algae. In both freshwater and marine ecosystems, the majority of the photosynthetic plants are algae.

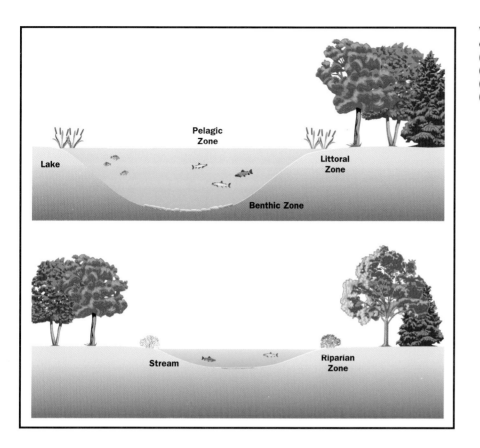

rine organisms will include fish and other strictly aquatic organisms as well as bacteria, fungi, birds, and mammals that are related to land-living forms.

Freshwater aquatic ecosystems are very diverse. They include lakes, ponds, rivers, and streams with a wide range of depth, flow rates, and water chemistry. Aquatic ecosystems include wetlands, where the water is either just below or just above the soil surface. The depth and distribution of this water may change with season. Wetlands are termed bogs, fens, swamps, and marshes. These have been extensively catalogued depending upon the position of the **water table**, the water chemistry, and the plant communities that grow in them.

Aquatic ecosystems are not isolated from the adjacent land nor from each other. The inputs and exchanges of sediments, water, and organisms are continuous. The marine shoreline—the littoral zone—is particularly rich in species and has a clearly visible **zonation** of organisms and habitats from the land into the sea. A similar habitat zonation is seen on the shore of a lake. Riverbanks—the riparian zone—will have a specialized plant **community** influenced by the amount of shading by trees on shore. These interactions between freshwater and marine ecosystems are seen both in estuaries, where rivers flow into the sea, and in coastal salt marshes.

Apart from this wide variety of natural aquatic ecosystems, humans continue to build and develop a large number of artificial aquatic ecosystems. These range from reservoirs, canals, channels for irrigation and drainage, and paddy fields for the production of rice, through lakes and ponds built for landscaping and fish culture, down to the decorative home aquarium. The understanding and management of these natural and artificial aquatic

water table level of water in the soil

zonation division into zones having different properties

community a group of organisms of different species living in a region

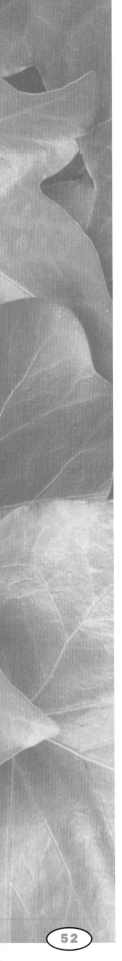

ecosystems, together with the need to slow the destruction and move to restore many of the natural areas, will continue to challenge us all. Human populations have always lived close to water. The ecosystems on seacoasts, by lakes, and in the river valleys are under tremendous pressure from **urbanization**, industrialization, and commerce. SEE ALSO ALGAE; AQUATIC PLANTS; COASTAL ECOSYSTEMS; ECOSYSTEM; WETLANDS.

Roger F. Horton

urbanization increase in size or number of cities

Bibliography

Dawes, Clinton J. *Marine Botany*, 2nd ed. New York: John Wiley & Sons, 1998.

Dobson, Mike, and Chris Frid. *Ecology of Aquatic Systems.* Harlow, England: Longman, 1998.

Giller, Paul S., and Bjorn Malmqvist. *The Biology of Streams and Rivers.* Oxford: Oxford University Press, 1998.

Wetzel, Robert G. *Limnology.* Philadelphia: W.B. Saunders, 1975.

Aquatic Plants

All land plants have evolved from aquatic ancestors. Species from nearly one hundred flowering plant families, along with some ferns, mosses, and liverworts, have reinvaded the water. Many land plants can tolerate flooding for some time. A good definition of aquatic plants is therefore difficult. The term is normally used for plants that grow completely underwater or with leaves floating on the surface. Parts of the shoot, particularly flowering stems, will often grow up above the water. Most aquatic plants live in freshwater—in lakes, ponds, reservoirs, canals, or rivers and streams. These habitats are very different in water depth, flow rates, temperature, acidity and alkalinity (**pH**), and mineral content. Some aquatic plants live in river mouths, with an ever-changing mixture of fresh- and saltwater, and a few (such as sea grasses) live completely submerged in the sea. Aquatic plants can be free-floating (e.g., water hyacinths) or rooted to the bottom of the pond or stream (e.g., water lilies). The most important grain crop in the world, rice, is an aquatic plant.

pH a measure of acidity or alkalinity; the pH scale ranges from 0 to 14, with 7 being neutral; low pH numbers indicate high acidity; high numbers indicate alkalinity

Water supply is generally not a problem for aquatic plants. They do not need waterproof **cuticles** or a lot of woody tissue to keep them erect. Life underwater, however, is a challenge. All green plants need oxygen and carbon dioxide. These gases cannot diffuse easily from the air down through the water. Most of the alterations in **physiology** and structure in water plants are adaptations to solve these gas exchange problems. Many water plants develop large internal air spaces—aerenchymatous tissues—in their roots and shoots. These air spaces make the tissues buoyant and help them float. Green leaves, photosynthesizing underwater in the light, release oxygen that can be temporarily stored in the air space and later used for cellular respiration. If the plant grows or floats to the surface, oxygen can also easily diffuse down through the air spaces. One of the water lilies, *Nuphar*, has even developed a ventilation system to circulate air from the leaves floating on the water surface down to its roots in the mud. The rapid growth of shoots to the surface—called depth accommodation growth—seen in rice seedlings and many other aquatic and amphibious species, is driven by the shoot buoyancy and a buildup of carbon dioxide and the naturally produced gas, ethylene, in the tissues under water. Plant organs in the mud at the bottom of lakes survive long periods without much oxygen.

cuticle the waxy outer coating of a leaf or other structure, providing protection against predators, infection, and water loss

physiology the biochemical processes carried out by an organism

Water hyacinths (*Eichhornia crassipes*) and floating ferns (*Salvinia auriculata*) on Lake Naivasha, Kenya.

Aquatic plants require carbon dioxide for photosynthesis. The amount of carbon dioxide dissolved in water depends on the pH and temperature. Aquatic plants may acidify their leaf surfaces. This causes carbon dioxide to be liberated from carbonate and bicarbonate salts dissolved in the water. Underwater leaves are often finely divided, with a large surface area. Unlike land plants, they may have **chloroplasts** for photosynthesis in the surface cell layer—the epidermis.

chloroplast the photosynthetic organelle of plants and algae

The amount of light available for photosynthesis declines with depth (especially in dirty water), and the light quality (the proportion of red, far-red, and blue light) is also altered. Some species (e.g., *Potamogeton, Sagittaria*) can produce underwater, floating, or emergent leaves, each with different shapes and structures all on the same plant—a phenomenon called heterophylly. This is a response to light quality and the amount of a plant hormone, abscisic acid (which is at slightly higher levels in emergent shoots).

Most aquatic plants flower and set seed. Many of them, however, can also grow rapidly and reproduce vegetatively. Aquatic plants, particularly free-floating species, can **colonize** the surface of a water body very quickly. If the water dries up, plants can produce a variety of tubers and resting buds (turions) that will persist in the mud until the water returns. These abilities make aquatic plants some of the most troublesome and persistent weeds in the world, particularly in tropical and subtropical countries. There is, understandably, considerable reluctance to put herbicides into rivers and lakes. A wide variety of control methods, including mechanical harvesting and the introduction of fish and other animals to eat them, have been attempted. The canal system of late nineteenth-century Britain was clogged with introduced *Elodea canadensis*; the water hyacinth, *Eichhornia crassipes*, has spread from tropical South America to waterways in Africa, Asia, and North America; and *Salvinia auriculata*, a free-floating aquatic fern, rapidly covered the 190-kilometer lake behind the Kariba Dam on the Zambezi River in Africa in the 1960s. The Everglades and waterways of the southeastern United

colonize to inhabit a new area

States have been repeatedly invaded by quickly spreading, alien aquatic plants.

Many aquatic habitats, and the aquatic plants that live in them, however, are under constant threat from pollution and from drainage for urban and industrial development across the globe. Aquatic plants can help remove pollutants and purify our water supplies. They are also a vital part of a fully functional aquatic **ecosystem** for fish and other wildlife. SEE ALSO AQUATIC ECOSYSTEMS; COASTAL ECOSYSTEMS; RICE.

Roger F. Horton

ecosystem an ecological community together with its environment

Bibliography

Cook, Christopher D. K., Bernardo J. Gut, E. Martyn Rix, Jacob Schneller, and Marta Seitz. *Water Plants of the World.* The Hague: Dr W. Junk b.v. Publishers, 1974.

Crawford, R. M. M. *Plant Life in Aquatic and Amphibious Habitats.* Oxford: Blackwell Scientific Publications, 1987.

Sculthorpe, C. D. *The Biology of Aquatic Vascular Plants.* London: Edward Arnold, 1967. Reprint, Konigstein: Koeltz Scientific Books, 1985.

Arboretum   *See Botanical Gardens and Arboreta.*

Arborist

Arboriculture is the care of trees, shrubs, and other woody plants. An arborist is a professional who cares for these plants. Many career opportunities are waiting for arborists in the tree care industry.

Arborists are people who like to work outdoors with their hands, enjoy helping the environment, take pride in their work, and prefer work that is physically and mentally challenging. Arborists combine physical skills, technical knowledge, and a sincere interest in trees to gain personal satisfaction and earn a good living.

Trees have enormous value. They produce oxygen, filter impurities from the air and water, and help to control erosion. They provide shade and can significantly lower heating and cooling costs. When properly selected, planted, and maintained, they greatly increase property values.

Trees are the largest and oldest living things on Earth. It may seem strange to think that trees need help to survive in urban and suburban conditions. But without regular care, they can quickly change from a valuable resource to a costly burden. That's when the skills of the professional arborist are needed.

Arboriculture involves many types of activities. Arborists select and transplant trees. Arborists prune, cable, fertilize, plant, and remove trees. They treat trees for harmful insects and diseases. In short, arborists ensure that the trees in their care grow well and remain structurally safe so that people can enjoy them for generations to come.

There are arborists who work for cities and towns, utility companies, and colleges and universities. By far, however, the largest employer of arborists in North America is the commercial tree service industry. Commercial arboriculture involves individuals, partnerships, and companies.

A tree trimmer hangs over a tree damaged by Hurricane Andrew at the Fairchild Tropical Garden on Biscayne Bay, Florida.

Commercial arborists work for homeowners, property managers, golf courses, power companies, and government agencies.

Career opportunities in commercial arboriculture across the United States are plentiful. Most employers eagerly accept applications and readily train people with the right attitude. Employers commonly provide on-the-job training for entry-level positions, which means that inexperienced employees can prepare for advancement while they earn a living. Training prepares the fledgling arborist for advancement into such positions as tree climber and crew leader. Promotions into sales or management positions are common.

Specialized training is available at technical and vocational schools and community colleges. Many four-year colleges and universities have programs in arboriculture, forestry, horticulture, plant science, pest management, and natural resources.

Wages and benefits available in arboricultural careers vary widely, depending upon the employer's size, geographic location, and other factors. The National Arborist Association conducted a survey of commercial tree service companies across the United States. It showed that in 1999 the average hourly wage paid to an entry-level employee without an advanced degree was $9.51.

As computers and new electrical tools enter the profession, the need for skilled, educated professionals will grow. Modern arboriculture demands de-

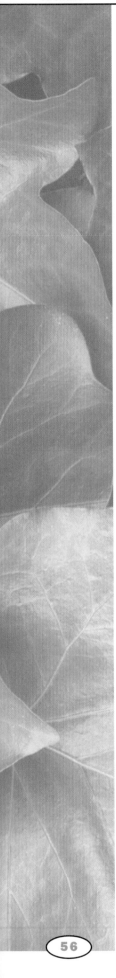

cisions and treatments based on an understanding of a tree's biological and chemical systems. Working with trees offers a unique chance to challenge oneself both physically and mentally.

The arboriculture profession has diverse employment opportunities. Where one starts depends upon attitude, education, and experience. The same opportunity for advancement is available for everyone. With a career in arboriculture, advancement opportunities and potential financial rewards are wide open. Finally, working in the field of arboriculture is stimulating, personally rewarding, and beneficial to the environment. SEE ALSO FORESTRY; TREE ARCHITECTURE; TREES.

Peter Gerstenberger

Archaea

At first glance, members of domain Archaea look very much like Bacteria in **morphology**, but biochemical and evolutionary studies have shown that they are a unique branch of life, separate from Bacteria (Eubacteria) and Eukaryotes. This was first recognized by comparing the sequences of their ribosomal deoxyribonucleic acid (DNA) and their type of cell wall to those of other organisms. Although Archaea also have a **prokaryotic** cell organization, other differences set them apart from Bacteria. While most Archaea have cell walls, they do not contain **murein** as in Bacteria, but are made of a number of different molecules, including proteins. The lipids found in their cell membranes are also different from those found in Bacteria and **eukaryotes**. Archaea can be motile by rotating **flagella**, but the proteins that make up the flagella are different from those found in Bacteria. Archaea have a number of traits that make them more similar to eukaryotes than to Bacteria. For example, in Archaea ribonucleic acid (RNA) polymerases and other proteins involved in making RNA from DNA are more similar to those in eukaryotes than those in Bacteria. Because of these and other similarities to eukaryotes, Archaea are thought to be the ancestors of the nuclear and cytoplasmic portions of eukaryotes.

Archaea include many organisms that live in extreme environments or that have unique metabolisms. These include methanogenic (methane-making) Archaea, halophilic (salt-loving) Archaea, extremely thermophilic (heat-loving) sulfur metabolizers, and thermoacidophiles, which live in acidic high-temperature environments.

Methanogens are killed in the presence of oxygen and live in **anoxic** places, such as the muds of rice fields and the guts of animals, particularly insects and cows. They produce methane, or natural gas, which is used by humans as a source of energy.

Halophiles can only live in places with very high salt concentrations, much saltier than the open oceans. They contain a pigment similar to one found in human eyes, bacteriorhodopsin, which allows them to use light energy to make adenosine triphosphate (**ATP**). Carotenoid pigments, which help shield the cells from damaging ultraviolet (UV) light, make the cells appear orange-red. High-salt aquatic areas containing many halophilic Archaea can be seen from a distance because of this red color.

Thermoacidophiles are a group of Archaea that can live in very acidic environments at elevated temperatures. They are found in hot springs such

morphology shape and form

prokaryotes single-celled organisms without nuclei, including Eubacteria and Archaea

murein a peptidoglycan, a molecule made of sugar derivatives and amino acids

eukaryotic a cell with a nucleus (*eu* means "true" and *karyo* means "nucleus"); includes protists, plants, animals, and fungi

flagella threadlike extension of the cell membrane, used for movement

anoxic without oxygen.

ATP adenosine triphosphate, a small, water-soluble molecule that acts as an energy currency in cells

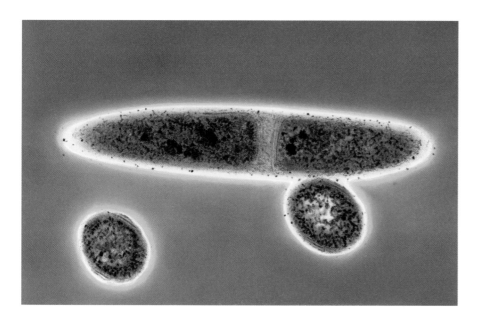

Colored transmission electron micrograph of the archaea *Methanospirillum hungatii* undergoing cell division.

as those in Yellowstone National Park, volcanoes, burning coal piles, or at undersea hydrothermal vents. Many of them use sulfur compounds for their metabolism. Some are hyperthermophiles, organisms that live at the highest temperatures known (between 80° and 113°C). They are even found living in boiling water.

Because Archaea inhabit extreme environments that were probably prevalent on the early Earth, some believe that they are an old group of organisms (hence their name) that may hold clues to the origin of life. However, extreme thermophiles have also been found among the Bacteria, and Archaea have been shown to be abundant in more moderate environments as well. Environmental studies using DNA survey techniques (PCR) show that low-temperature Archaea make up a significant portion of the prokaryotic **biomass** in terrestrial and planktonic marine environments. From these types of environmental PCR studies, which can tell us what kind of organisms are present in the environment without relying on traditional methods of culturing, we know that both Archaea and Bacteria are abundant in the biosphere, and that the majority of these organisms and their ecological role have yet to be described and understood. SEE ALSO EUBACTERIA; EVOLUTION OF PLANTS.

J. Peter Gogarten and Lorraine Olendzenski

biomass the total dry weight of an organism or group of organisms

Bibliography

Needham, Cynthia, Mahlon Hoagland, Kenneth McPherson, and Bert Dodson. *Intimate Strangers: Unseen Life on Earth.* Washington, DC: ASM Press, 2000.

Woese, C. R. "Bacterial Evolution." *Microbiological Reviews* 51 (1987): 221–71.

Arecaceae   *See Palms.*

Asteraceae

Asteraceae (or Compositae), the sunflower family, is the largest family of flowering plants, encompassing some fifteen hundred **genera** and nearly

genera plural of genus

Open faces of sunflowers in Norfolk, England.

pistil the female reproduction organ

twenty-five thousand species. Most species are herbs, but some are shrubs and a few are trees. They are of worldwide distribution and are often conspicuous in their habitats. Members of the family share a distinctive flowering structure, consisting of numerous small flowers (often called florets) that are tightly clustered into a head. The five petals of a floret are fused to form a corolla tube that encloses the stamens and **pistil**. Florets that have all evenly sized petals are called disk florets. Florets that have fused petals expanded greatly on one side into a long strap are called ray florets. A typical head consists of numerous disk florets in the center and a row of ray florets around the margin. The strap-shaped corollas of the ray florets project outward, giving the entire head the appearance of a single, large flower (e.g., sunflowers, *Helianthus annuus*). Some members of the family have heads with only disk florets (e.g., ironweeds, *Vernonia* spp.), and some have all florets with strap shaped corollas (e.g., dandelions, *Taraxacum officinale*). A few members have the florets and heads greatly reduced and are wind pollinated (e.g., ragweeds, *Ambrosia* spp.).

Despite the size of the family and its wide distribution, only a few members have become economically important crops, such as lettuce (*Lactuca serriola*), artichokes (*Cynara scolymus*), sunflowers (*Helianthus annuus*), chicory (*Cichorium intybus*), and pyrethrum (*Tanecetum cinerariifolium*, an insecticide). Some species are notable weeds (e.g., dandelions) and some, like sagebrush (several species of *Artemisia*), dominate the landscape where they occur. Many species are cultivated as garden ornamentals, and some use their generic names as common names, for example, aster, chrysanthemum, dahlia, gaillardia, and zinnia. SEE ALSO ANGIOSPERMS; DICOTS; FLOWERS; INFLORESCENCE.

Theodore M. Barkley

Bibliography

Bremer, K. *Asteraceae: Cladistics and Classification*. Portland, OR: Timber Press, 1994.

Hind, D. J. N., and H. J. Beetje, eds. *Compositae: Systematics. Proceedings from the International Compositae Conference*. Kew, UK: Royal Botanic Gardens.

Atmosphere and Plants

Plant distribution and health is controlled by properties of the atmosphere such as climate, hurricanes, lightning, and pollution. Plants also play a large role in controlling the atmosphere. In fact, the atmosphere at any one location is not only the result of global atmospheric weather patterns, it is also the end result of the type and amount of vegetation.

Effect of Plants on Climate

Over the course of a day, the bulk of energy from the Sun is used in one of two processes: raising temperatures or changing water from a liquid or solid state to vapor form. (Photosynthesis uses only about 2 percent of the Sun's energy.) If a large amount of vegetation is present and is actively conducting photosynthesis, most solar energy is used to convert liquid water in leaves to water vapor. This release of water vapor from leaves is called transpiration. If there is no vegetation, as after a logging clear-cut, evaporation can take place from the soil, but much more energy is used to increase temperatures. Therefore, clear-cutting large forests can significantly raise temperatures. In the Amazon forest in South America, the process of transpiration produces high humidity in the atmosphere, which in turn is then returned to Earth as rain. As much as half of the precipitation in the western Amazon is from this recycled moisture. In these and other ways, plants influence the climate in their region. The type of vegetation also affects the radiation budget, that is, the percent of solar radiation that is reflected back into space; for instance, sparsely vegetated areas reflect more light than densely vegetated areas.

Plants and Atmospheric Oxygen

Forests—in particular, the tropical forest—are often called the lungs of the planet. It is true that plants produce oxygen during photosynthesis, but they and the organisms living in their **ecosystems** also consume about the same amount of oxygen during respiration. Oxygen makes up 21 percent of Earth's atmosphere but annual production of oxygen by plants is only about .05 percent of the atmospheric amount. There is so much atmospheric oxygen that completely destroying all vegetation would have only a minor effect on atmospheric oxygen levels. Doubling the amount of vegetation would increase atmospheric oxygen by only .5 percent. So it is not true that plants are responsible for our global oxygen supply, at least in the short term. Other processes relating to the weathering of rocks and oceanic circulation operating at the timescale of tens of thousands of years are principally responsible for regulating oxygen levels. Plants are, however, very important in the cycling of carbon dioxide.

ecosystem an ecological community together with its environment

Plants and Volatile Organic Compounds

Easily evaporated **compounds** containing hydrogen and carbon are known as volatile organic compounds (VOCs). There are thousands of VOCs in the atmosphere, and plants produce many of them. Monoterpenes and isoprenes are the best-known plant-produced VOCs. Most monoterpenes are produced by conifers in leaves, wood, and bark. Once produced, monoterpenes stay in the plant tissue and are used by plants for defense

compound a substance formed from two or more elements

Mist shrouds plants in the rain forest near Limoncocha, Ecuador.

herbivore an organism that feeds on plant parts

against **herbivores**. Isoprene, produced by deciduous trees, spruces, and mosses, does not stay in the plant. The production of isoprene helps plants conduct photosynthesis at high temperatures that would otherwise be very damaging. Production of other VOCs gives many plants their characteristic aroma.

VOCs also react quickly in the atmosphere. In the presence of nitrogen oxides and sunlight, VOCs react to form ozone, a major component of smog. In urban areas, industrial activity and the use of cars can produce very high levels of nitrogen oxides. This, combined with the production of VOCs by plants, can be a major contributor to urban pollution. In cities with large forest populations, such as Atlanta, Georgia, plant-produced VOCs can account for a large portion of the urban smog problem. Human activities, however, are still responsible for the bulk of urban smog as well as the production of the large amounts of nitrogen oxides reacting with the VOCs. In Switzerland, a highly industrialized country, plant-produced VOCs made up only 23 percent of total VOCs. Trees should therefore not be blamed for most smog.

Air Pollution and Pollution-Tolerant Plants

Our industrial society produces large amounts of pollution. Sulfur dioxide is produced by the combustion of a variety of high sulfur fuels, especially coal. Acid rain is produced from sulfur dioxide. Aluminum and glass factories produce fluoride, a pollutant that can accumulate in plants. Ozone and peroxyacetyl nitrate, both produced in the presence of sunlight, nitrogen oxides, and VOCs, are major components of smog and together are the most serious air pollution problem faced by plants.

Pollution enters the plants through stomata, tiny pores used by leaves for gas exchange. Yellow or brown coloration along leaf edges and veins are signs of pollution damage. Cell membranes are destroyed and the biochemical reactions of photosynthesis are slowed or stopped. Air pollution itself does not usually kill plants, but it can severely reduce crop yields and makes plants more susceptible to diseases and insects. The damage created by pollution depends on the concentration of the pollutant as well as on the duration of the pollution event. For example, long-term exposure to low pollution levels may be less damaging than short, intense pollution events. Long-term processes such as acid rain, though, can damage forests by changing soil acidity over many years.

Plants vary greatly in their ability to resist pollution. In some cases, plants are resistant to sulfur dioxide, but not to ozone. In Australia, *radiata* pines are usually more resistant to sulfur dioxide than broadleaf eucalyptus trees. Yet in Sweden, broadleaf trees resist ozone better than the conifers. There is also tremendous variation in ozone resistance within the *Eucalyptus* genus. Sweeping generalizations about individual species are virtually impossible, but plants do seem to follow several patterns:

- thick leaves are pollution-resistant

- species or varieties that have high rates of stomatal conductance (the process that brings carbon dioxide and pollution into the leaf) experience more pollution damage

- plants can often adapt to high pollution over time

- older plants are more resistant than younger plants.

For most species that have been studied, botanists can develop plant varieties that are resistant to a certain pollutant or combination of pollutants. Therefore it is usually better to assess local pollution problems and to select or breed plant varieties for that situation than it is to identify universally resistant species. SEE ALSO ACID RAIN; CARBON CYCLE; DEFENSES, CHEMICAL; GLOBAL WARMING; HUMAN IMPACTS; PHOTOSYNTHESIS, CARBON FIXATION AND; TERPENES; WATER MOVEMENT.

Michael A. White

Bibliography

Cozic, Charles P., ed. *Pollution.* San Diego: Greenhaven Press, 1992.

Gay, Kathlyn. *Ozone.* New York: Franklin Watts, 1989.

Jones, Hamlyn G. *Plants and Microclimate*, 2nd ed. New York: Cambridge University Press, 1992.

Miller, Christina G., and Louise A. Berry. *Air Alert.* New York: Atheneum Books for Young Readers, 1996.

Sharkey, Thomas D., Elizabeth A. Holland, and Harold A. Mooney. *Trace Gas Emissions by Plants.* San Diego: Academic Press, 1991.

Tolbert, N. Edward, and Jack Preiss, eds. *Regulation of Atmospheric CO$_2$ and O$_2$ by Photosynthetic Carbon Metabolism.* New York: Oxford University Press, 1994.

Auxins *See Hormones.*

Bamboo

Bamboos are members of the grass family (Poaceae). Like other grasses, bamboos have jointed stems, small flowers enclosed in structures known as spikelets, a specially modified embryo within the seed, and a grainlike fruit. However, bamboos are the only major group of grasses adapted to the forest habitat, and they differ from other grasses in having highly scalloped photosynthetic cells in their leaves. Many bamboos have tall, somewhat arched stems, but others are shrubby, or slender and **twining**, and some resemble ferns. The largest bamboos reach 30 meters (100 feet) in height and 30 centimeters (12 inches) in diameter, while the smallest ones have delicate stems no more than 10 centimeters (4 inches) tall.

There are at least twelve hundred known species of bamboos worldwide, which occur from 46°N (Sakhalin Island, Russia) to 47°S (southern Chile), although most are tropical or warm temperate. Bamboos often grow at low elevations, but many species grow in mountain forests, and some range up to 4,300 meters (14,200 feet) elevation in equatorial highlands. Woody bamboos (**tribe** Bambuseae), with at least eleven hundred species, make up the bulk of bamboo diversity: these are the plants normally thought of as bamboos. The woodiness of their stems is derived entirely from primary growth, and although there are other woody grasses, the Bambuseae are the only major group of grasses characterized by woodiness. Approximately one hundred species of tropical, herbaceous, broad-leaved grasses (tribe Olyreae) are closely related to their woody cousins, and these are now also classified as bamboos. Bamboos are typically associated with Asia, but close to one-half of their diversity is native to Central and South America, and there is one species (giant cane, or switch cane) native to the southeastern United States.

Woody bamboos are ecologically important in the tropical and temperate forests where they grow. Rapid elongation of bamboo shoots, tall, hard stems, and profuse vegetative branching allow woody bamboos to compete with trees for light. Woody bamboos easily **colonize** forest edges and gaps by means of vegetative reproduction through their well-developed underground stems (rhizomes), whereas herbaceous bamboos are characteristic of the shady forest floor. The large **biomass** of bamboo stems and leaves provides an excellent habitat for a wide variety of animals, including beetles and other insects, birds, monkeys, frogs, rats, and pandas.

Woody bamboos are well known for their unusual flowering behavior, in which the members of a species grow for many years (up to eighty or more) in the vegetative condition, and then flower at the same time and die after fruiting. Other flowering behaviors are documented in bamboos, but many exhibit this periodic, gregarious type of flowering, and the effect on the forest is dramatic when it occurs. Large areas of bamboo plants die back, providing openings for recolonization by the forest while the bamboo seeds sprout and start the next generation. How bamboo plants count the passage of time, or what triggers the gregarious flowering, is unknown.

In Asia, where a bamboo culture has existed for several thousand years, bamboos are a symbol of flexible strength, and they are an integral part of daily life. Young, tender bamboo shoots are a tasty vegetable, whereas the mature stems are used in construction, scaffolding, fencing, and bas-

A bamboo grove at Haleakala National Park on Maui, Hawaii.

ketry or for paper pulp. Mature stems are also fashioned into utensils, water pipes, musical instruments, and a multitude of other items. Bamboo is an important theme in Asian artwork, and bamboos frequently are used as a material for artwork. Bamboos are also widely planted as ornamentals in many parts of the world. The utility of bamboo is exploited wherever it is cultivated or grows naturally, and there is increasing recognition of the potential of bamboo as a renewable resource, especially for reforestation and housing. SEE ALSO ECONOMIC IMPORTANCE OF PLANTS; GRASSES; MONOCOTS.

Lynn G. Clark

Bibliography

Conover, A. "A New World Comes to Life, Discovered in a Stalk of Bamboo." *Smithsonian Magazine* (October 1994): 120–129.

Farrelly, D. *The Book of Bamboo.* San Francisco: Sierra Club Books, 1984.

Judziewicz, E. J., L. G. Clark, X. Londoño, and M. J. Stern. *American Bamboos.* Washington, DC: Smithsonian Institution Press, 1999.

Recht, C., and M. F. Wetterwald. *Bamboos.* Portland, OR: Timber Press, 1992.

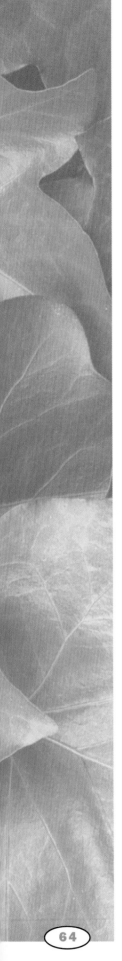

Bark

vascular related to transport of nutrients

Bark is the outer protective coating of the trunk and branches of trees and shrubs and includes all the tissues outside of the **vascular** cambium. A typical bark consists of several layers of different types of tissue. The inner bark, or bast, is living and contains the conductive tissue, called phloem, by which sugars are transported from the leaves in the crown of a tree to the roots, and from storage tissues to other parts of the plant. The outer bark is layered, with the inner layer consisting of the cork cambium, a **meristem** that produces cork cells to the outside. The cork cells are usually tightly packed and have fatty substances deposited in their thick walls. In contrast to the cork cambium, cork cells are dead and filled with air, making cork lightweight and insulating.

meristem the growing tip of a plant

The appearance of a bark depends on the type of cork cells produced by the cork cambium, the relative amount of cambial products, and the amount of secondary conducting tissue (phloem). In some species, such as the cork oak (*Quercus suber*), the cork cambium is very active and produces a thick layer of cork, which is extracted and used commercially. Other species, such as birch trees, have a papery bark because the cork cambium alternatively produces several layers of thin-walled cells. These are fragile, and the thicker layers can come off as sheets. In habitats where natural fires occur, such as tropical savannas and the pine and redwood forests of California, trees tend to have a thick, corky bark to insulate them from the heat of fires. In some arid regions many trees have chlorophyll-containing bark to continue the process of photosynthesis when the leaves are absent during long periods of drought. The varied texture and thickness of bark is often a function of the environment in which the tree grows. The variation in the structure of bark often gives a tree its characteristic appearance, for example, the hairy look of the shagbark hickory. A forester can recognize the species of trees by the differences in their bark either externally or by cutting a small slash to examine the inner structure.

Bark is used in many ways and is of considerable economic importance. Many indigenous peoples have made clothes, canoes, houses, drinking vessels, arrow poisons, and medicines from bark. Bark has also provided commercial medicines such as quinine and curare, and is also the major source of **tannins** for the leather industry and cork for wine bottles. In horticulture, bark is used for mulch. Some of our favorite flavors and spices, such as cinnamon and angostura bitters, come from bark. Bark is much more than the protective skin of trees; it is one of the most useful products of nature. SEE ALSO Stems; Tissues; Tree Architecture; Trees.

tannins compounds produced by plants that usually serve protective functions; often colored and used for "tanning" and dyeing

Ghillean T. Prance

Bibliography

Junikka, L. *Survey of English Macroscopic Bark Terminology.* Leiden, The Netherlands: Hortus Botanicus, 1994.

Prance, G. T., and A. E. Prance. *Bark: The Formation, Characteristics, and Use of Bark Around the World.* Portland, OR: Timber Press, 1993.

Bessey, Charles

American Botanist
1845–1915

Charles Edwin Bessey was a late nineteenth- and early twentieth-century American botanist who developed a modern classification system for flowering plants. Born in Ohio in 1845 the son of a school teacher, Bessey was educated at home and in small rural schools. He was able to attend the Michigan Agricultural College, where he was introduced to botany. After graduation, he helped to initiate the botany program at the Iowa Agricultural College, and began teaching students. He made advances in botany education by adding a laboratory component to his classes. He used his one microscope initially to teach his students during laboratory. Later, as he helped to start botany programs at other state colleges in the American west, he introduced microscope techniques to botany classes there as well.

In 1872 Bessey worked at Harvard in American botanist Asa Gray's (1810–1888) laboratory and became more interested in the microscopic characteristics of plants. His examinations of cell structure and organization led to the publication of several papers on plant diseases. He further contributed to American botany education by writing an American version of German plant physiologist Julius von Sachs's *Lehrbuch der Botanik* that he called *Botany for High Schools and Colleges*.

Bessey's most important publication, however, was probably *Phylogenetic Taxonomy of Flowering Plants*, published in 1915, the year of his death. This last major work of Bessey's established the phylogenetic system of organizing flowering plants that taxonomists are still building on today with the use of genetic techniques. In this publication, Bessey proposed new evolutionary relationships between plants. Previously, it was thought that plants that had flowers without petals were the most primitive. Bessey instead suggested the opposite. He believed what is still thought to be true now, that the most primitive, original flowers had many separate petals and stamens and carpels. As flowering plants evolved, these **whorls** of flower parts fused together, or were reduced or became absent in some species. This indicated that flowers such as *Ranunculus*, or buttercup flowers, were the more primitive, while tiny flowers such as those hanging in **catkin inflorescences** in some trees were more advanced. This also implied that monocotyledonous plants, such as grasses, had evolved from dicotyledonous broad-leaved plants. These ideas led to a big change in principles for plant taxonomy, and they encouraged a new wave of research into plant phylogeny.

whorl a ring

catkin a flowering structure used for wind pollination

inflorescence an arrangement of flowers on a stalk

Bessey worked in many ways to promote science and the study of plants. In addition to his great contributions to taxonomy, Bessey was also part of many scientific societies. He was a member of the American Association for the Advancement of Science, and served as its president in 1910. He participated in the Iowa Farmers' Institute, which was the first institute of its kind in the country. Bessey was also associate editor of prestigious journals, such as the *American Naturalist* and *Science*. Bessey will remain best known, however, for his contribution to a detailed and modern plant phylogenetic system. Botany students still study the branching tree diagrams of plant evolutionary relationships like those Bessey proposed in 1915. SEE ALSO Evo-

LUTION OF PLANTS; GRAY, ASA; PHYLOGENY; SACHS, JULIUS VON; TAXONO-MIST; TAXONOMY.

Jessica P. Penney

Bibliography

Ewan, Joseph. *A Short History of Botany in the United States.* New York: Hafner, 1969.

Humphrey, Harry B. *The Makers of North American Botany.* New York: Ronald Press, 1961.

Biodiversity

Biodiversity exists at three interrelated levels: species diversity, genetic diversity, and community-level diversity. When we talk about plant biodiversity, we refer to the full range of plant species, the genetic variation found within those species, and the biological communities formed by those species. For vascular plants, biodiversity includes all species of ferns, **gymnosperms**, flowering plants, and related smaller groups such as clubmosses and horsetails. The genetic variation found within **populations** and among populations arises through the mutation of individual genes or chromosomes and is rearranged by genetic recombination during the sexual process. Genetic variation is important not only for the survival and evolution of species; it is also important to people for breeding improved crop plants with higher yields.

Biological diversity also refers to all biological communities, including temperate forests, tropical forests, grasslands, shrub lands, deserts, freshwater wetlands, and marine habitats. Each of these biological communities represents an adaptation of plants to particular regimes of climate, soil, and other aspects of the environment. This adaptation involves **ecosystem** interactions of each biological community with its physical and chemical environment. For example, the ability of a forest community to absorb rain water and slowly release the water into streams and the ability of a swamp to process and detoxify polluted water are both aspects of ecosystem-level biological diversity that are of central importance to human societies.

Measuring Biodiversity

Biological diversity can be measured in various ways, each of which captures some of the overall meaning of biological diversity. The most common method of measuring biological diversity is simply to count the number of species occurring in one particular place, such as a forest or a grassland. Since it is not possible to count every species of plant, insect, fungus, and microorganism, the usual procedure is to count certain types of organisms, such as birds, butterflies, all flowering plants, or just tree species. This type of local diversity of species is usually referred to as species richness or alpha diversity. A tropical rain forest might contain three hundred or more tree species in a square of forest measuring 400 meters on a side, whereas a temperate forest of equal area might contain only forty tree species. Biological diversity can also be measured in larger areas. For example the country of Colombia has more than fifty thousand species of higher plants, in contrast to sixteen hundred species for the United Kingdom and nearly sixteen thousand for Australia. This type of regional or large-scale diversity is referred to as gamma diversity.

gymnosperm a major group of plants that includes the conifers

population a group of organisms of a single species that exist in the same region and interbreed

ecosystem an ecological community together with its environment

Another way to measure biodiversity is to consider the number or percentage of a region's species that are **endemic** to that region. For example, of the United Kingdom's fifteen-hundred native plant species, only sixteen species or 1 percent are endemic. The overwhelming majority of the United Kingdom's plants can be found in other neighboring countries, such as Ireland, France, and Germany. In contrast, 14,074 of the 15,000 plant species of Australia are endemic and found in no other country.

Individual species can also be compared for their evolutionary uniqueness. Species that are not closely related to other species are generally considered to have greater value to overall biological diversity than species that have many close relatives. For example, the maidenhair tree, *Ginkgo biloba*, is the only species in its genus, and *Ginkgo* is the only genus in the gymnosperm family Ginkgoaceae. In contrast, the common dandelion, *Taraxacum officinale*, has many related species in the same genus and is a member of a large family, the Asteraceae, with twenty-five thousand species and eleven hundred genera. Using this approach, a species that was the only member of its genus and family would have greater biodiversity value than a species that had many relatives in the same genus and belonged to a family with many genera. In contrast, a few biologists would argue that a species in a large genus has greater value because this species has the greater potential to undergo further evolution than a species with no close relatives that may be an evolutionary dead end.

Bialowieza National Park in eastern Poland displays great biodiversity of species. Covering 312,000 acres, it is the last primeval forest in Europe, with some of its trees more than 600 years old and 100 feet tall.

endemic belonging or native to a particular area or country

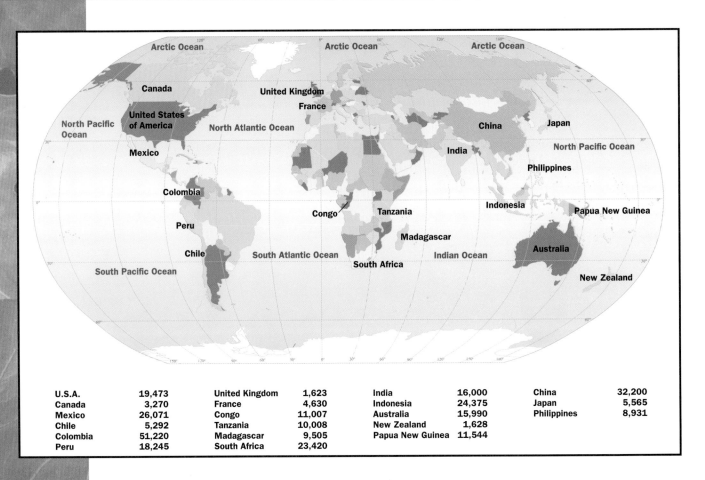

U.S.A.	19,473	United Kingdom	1,623	India	16,000	China	32,200
Canada	3,270	France	4,630	Indonesia	24,375	Japan	5,565
Mexico	26,071	Congo	11,007	Australia	15,990	Philippines	8,931
Chile	5,292	Tanzania	10,008	New Zealand	1,628		
Colombia	51,220	Madagascar	9,505	Papua New Guinea	11,544		
Peru	18,245	South Africa	23,420				

Number of species of higher plants in selected countries.

Extent of Diversity

There are around 250,000 living species of higher plants in the world today. Of these species, the overwhelming majority are flowering plants. Flowering plants are grouped into more than three hundred families, including such large and economically important families as the Poaceae, which contains the grasses and the cereal crops we depend on for food and animal fodder; the Fabaceae, which includes the beans and peas we need for protein in our diet; and the Rosaceae, which is important for fruit trees and ornamentals such as apples, pears, and roses.

Higher plants exhibit a great diversity of growth forms, leaf shapes and sizes, flower and fruit types, seed types, and particular adaptations for growing in different environments. Growth forms include trees, shrubs, annual herbs, perennial herbs, climbers, and aquatic plants.

Plant diversity is not equally distributed across the world's surface. Only a relatively few land plants are adapted to salt water, and these are found rooted in shallow waters. So the large oceanic expanses of the world are devoid of higher plants. On the land surface, the greatest diversity of plants is found in the tropical lowland and **montane** rain forests of the Americas, central Africa, and Southeast Asia. In such forests there is a great diversity of plant species in the form of trees, shrub, herbs, and climbers. There is also an abundance of **epiphytes**, in particular orchids and bromeliads, that perch on the branches of the trees. Illustrating this tropical diversity, there are only around thirty tree species in all of northern Canada, in contrast to

montane growing in a mountainous region

epiphytes plants that grow on other plants

more than one thousand tree species in just the southern countries of Central America.

There is also great species diversity in the temperate regions of the world that have mild, wet winters and dry, hot summers, such as the Mediterranean basin, the California region, central Chile, the cape region of South Africa, and southwest Australia. In such areas, many plants have adaptations to drought, such as **succulent** cacti, which store water in their stems, and annual plants that grow, reproduce, and die in one growing season.

succulent marked by fleshy, water-holding leaves or stems

Certain regions of the world are known as hot spots of biodiversity because of their high concentrations of species overall, their high percentages of species that are endemic, and the high degree of threat that those species face. In addition to rain forest areas and localities with Mediterranean climates, many of these are islands, such as the Caribbean Islands, Madagascar and nearby islands, New Caledonia, New Zealand, Sri Lanka, and the islands between New Guinea and peninsular Malaysia. Biodiversity hot spots encompass the entire range of 44 percent of the world's plant species, 25 percent of the bird species, 30 percent of the mammal species, 38 percent of the reptile species, and 54 percent of the amphibian species on only 1.4 percent of Earth's total land surface. The premier hot spot is the tropical Andes, in which 45,000 plant species, 1,666 bird species, 414 mammal species, 479 reptile species, and 830 amphibian species occur in the tropical forests and high-altitude grasslands that occupy less than 0.25 percent of Earth's land surface. This approach can also be applied to individual countries. In the United States hot spots for endangered species occur in the Hawaiian Islands, the southern Appalachian Mountains, the arid Southwest, and the coastal areas of the lower forty-eight states, particularly California, Texas, and Florida.

Threats to Biological Diversity

Biological diversity is being lost today at all levels, including genetic variation, species, and biological communities. The most serious threat is the extinction of species, because once a species is lost, it can never be regained. The loss of genetic variation is occurring in two different ways: when populations of a species are eliminated and when populations become smaller in size. This loss of populations is seen most immediately in the local extinction of species. In a study of a conservation area in Massachusetts, one-third of the native plant species present one hundred years ago could no longer be found today. They were not replaced by other native species, but there was an increase in the number of nonnative species. This park is now poorer in total species, and many species still present have fewer populations. Many species that were formerly listed as common now have only a few individuals left.

Biological diversity is most severely threatened when entire biological communities are lost. In many tropical countries of the world, the tropical rain forests that are so rich in species have been largely destroyed. Examples of countries with devastated forests are Madagascar (87 percent lost), Rwanda (84 percent), Vietnam (83 percent), and the Philippines (94 percent). With the loss of these communities comes the extinction of plant and animal species, the loss of genetic variation within remaining species, and the loss of the **ecosystem** services provided by these communities, such as

ecosystem an ecological community together with its environment

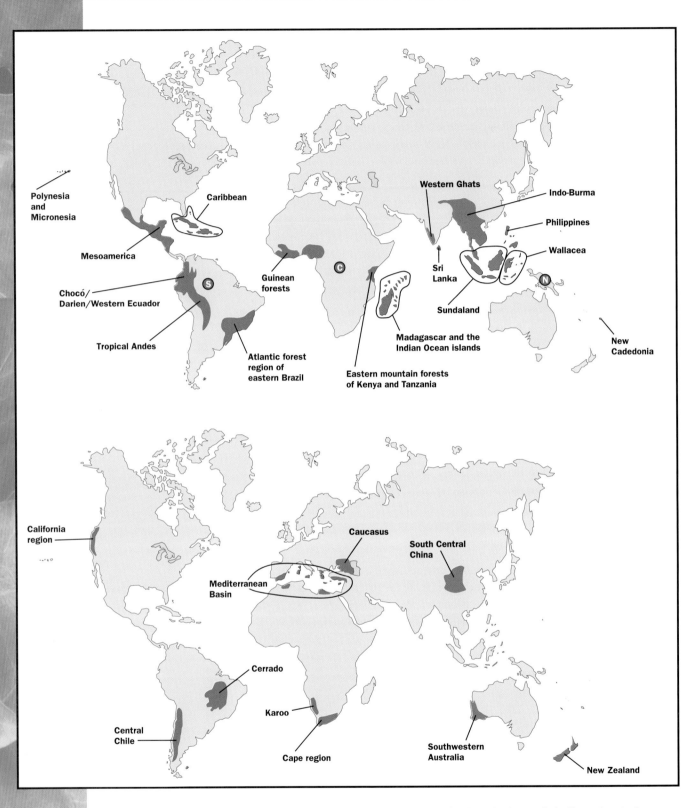

At top, fifteen tropical rain forest hot spots of high endemism and significant threat of imminent extinctions. The circled areas enclose four island hot spots: the Caribbean, Madagascar and Indian Ocean islands, and the Sundaland and Wallacea regions. The Polynesia/Micronesia region covers a large number of Pacific Ocean islands, including the Hawaiian Islands, Fiji, Samoa, French Polynesia, and the Marianas. Circled letters indicate the only three remaining tropical forest wilderness areas of any extent: S = South America, C = Congo Basin, N = New Guinea. The bottom map indicates ten hot spots in other ecosystems. The circled area encloses the Mediterranean Basin. Redrawn from Primack, 2000.

flood control, soil erosion protection, and the production of wood and food. Other habitats almost completely destroyed include tropical deciduous forests, of which more than 98 percent have been destroyed in Central America, and temperate grasslands, which are readily converted to agriculture and ranching. In the United States, only around 560 acres of the tallgrass prairie of Illinois and Indiana remains undisturbed, only about one ten-thousandth of the original area. Wetlands including swamps, bogs, floodplains, and **vernal** pools are similarly suffering devastation. As these habitats are damaged by human activity and converted to other uses, the species they contain decline in abundance and eventually become extinct. Habitats that are restricted in area and contain high concentrations of endemic species are particularly vulnerable, such as the rain forests of Hawaii and isolated mountain peaks in the southwestern United States.

vernal related to the spring season

In general, the rate of extinction for plants has been lower than that for animals. To date, there are recorded extinctions of around four hundred plant species, about 0.2 percent of the total in contrast with around 2.1 percent of mammals and 1.3 percent of birds already extinct. The lower percentages of plants that are extinct are related in part to our ability to protect small populations of plants in nature reserves. In contrast, many animals have a greater need to migrate and have often been extensively exploited. At the turn of the twenty-first century, around 9 percent of plant species are in danger of extinction, a figure only slightly lower than that for birds (11 percent) and mammals (11 percent). The extinction rates for certain groups of plants are much higher than this average value. For example, 32 percent of gymnosperms and 33 percent of palms are threatened with global extinction in the wild due to the limited distribution of many species' specialized habitat requirements and the intensive collection of plants for horticulture.

Factors Threatening Species

Species are threatened with extinction primarily because of habitat destruction. Species are also driven to extinction when their habitat is degraded to the point where they can no longer exist. This might happen when a grassland is heavily grazed by domestic animals, a forest is repeatedly logged, or uncontrolled fires burn shrub land. Fully 81 percent of the endangered species of the United States are threatened by habitat degradation and loss. Species are also lost from habitats fragmented by human activity, when habitats are broken up into smaller pieces by roads, fences, power lines, residential areas, and ranches. The remaining fragments may be so altered in micro-climate, and so much more vulnerable to other human activities, that many plant species are no longer able to survive.

The second most significant threat to species diversity is competition and **predation** from exotic invasive species, which is a threat for 57 percent of the endangered plant species of the United States. In many cases, exotic species of animals such as cattle, sheep, goats, rabbits, and pigs selectively remove certain native plant species. For example, pigs introduced in Hawaii have removed all wild individuals of numerous plant species. Invasive exotic plants have often overwhelmed natural communities and outcompeted the native species. For example, in bottomland communities of the southern United States, Japanese honeysuckle plants have replaced the rich wildflower

predation the act of preying upon; consuming for food

communities, and in the rangeland of the western United States European grasses outcompete native grasses and wildflowers. As a result, native species decline at the expense of the introduced species.

Overharvesting of plants, often for food, medicinal purposes, or by horticulturists, threatens 10 percent of the endangered plant species of the United States. A notable example is ginseng, an herb used in Asian medicine, which has been so overharvested throughout its range that only a small number of plants remain. Many rare wildflowers, such as orchids, have been so severely overcollected by gardeners that they are in danger of extinction in the wild. Information on the location of the last remaining plants is often kept secret to prevent the theft of these individuals.

compound a substance formed from two or more elements

Pollution threatens 7 percent of the plant species of the United States. Water pollution can alter the water chemistry so severely that aquatic plants cannot grow. Increased inputs of nitrogen and phosphorus **compounds** into the water from sewage and agricultural fertilizers can result in algal blooms that shade out and kill native plants. In the land environment air pollution in the form of smog, acid rain, and nitrogen deposition can cause plants to slow down in growth or die. In some cases, this death may be related to the decline and death of the sensitive soil fungi (mycorrhizae) that have **mutualistic** relations with plants, providing water and mineral nutrients and receiving carbohydrates in return. And lastly, about 1 percent of plant species is threatened by disease and parasites. While this number may not seem very great, some of the most important woody plants in the forests of North America, such as chestnuts, elms, and dogwoods, are in severe decline due to introduced diseases.

mutualism a symbiosis between two organisms in which both benefit

What Can Be Done?

The most important way to protect plant biological diversity is to establish protected areas that include high concentrations of species, particularly those species in danger of extinction or in decline. These protected areas may be established by governments, conservation organizations, or private individuals. Management plans must be developed and implemented, and these protected areas must be monitored to ensure they are meeting their goals. Many management plans for protected areas include some forms of public education, because public support is often crucial for the success of a park.

Where it is not possible to maintain plant species in the wild due to ongoing threats, plants can often be grown in botanical gardens or kept as stored seed samples in seed banks. Networks of botanical gardens and seed banks are making a concerted effort to increase their holdings of endangered species and species of potential agricultural and economic importance. The goal of many botanical gardens is to increase knowledge of plants, to educate the public concerning plants, and to return plants eventually to their natural habitats.

The diversity of plant species provides us with the agriculture crops that are our food, many of the medicines that keep us healthy, wood that is needed in construction, fodder that feeds our domestic animals, ornamental plants that enrich our gardens and homes, and even the oxygen that we breathe. People could not live without the diversity of plants, and many plant species will live in the wild only if we take care of them. SEE ALSO

ASTERACEAE; BOTANICAL GARDENS AND ARBORETA; ENDANGERED SPECIES; GINGKO; HUMAN IMPACTS; INVASIVE SPECIES; RAIN FORESTS; SEED PRESERVATION; WETLANDS.

Richard B. Primack

Bibliography

Falk, D. A, C. I. Millar, and M. Olwell, eds. *Restoring Diversity; Strategies for the Reintroduction of Endangered Plants.* Washington, DC: Island Press, 1996.

Mittermeier, R. A., N. Myers, P. R. Gil, and C. G. Mittermeier. *Hotspots: Earth's Richest and Most Endangered Terrestrial Ecoregions.* Mexico City: Agrupacion Sierra Madre, SC, 1999.

Primack, R. *A Primer of Conservation Biology.* Sunderland, MA: Sinauer Associates, 2000.

Quammen, D. *The Song of the Dodo: Island Biogeography in an Age of Extinctions.* New York: Scribner, 1996.

Schneider, S. *Laboratory Earth: The Planetary Gamble We Can't Afford to Lose.* New York: Basic Books, 1998.

Stein, B. A., and S. R. Flack. *Species Report Card: The State of U.S. Plants and Animals.* Arlington, VA: The Nature Conservancy, 1997.

Biogeochemical Cycles

Nutrients are elements that plants require for growth. In most terrestrial **ecosystems**, a lack of essential nutrients may limit plant primary productivity. Net primary productivity (NPP), other ecosystem processes, and ecosystem structure and function may be best understood by examining and studying the cycles of these nutrients. To trace the movement of a nutrient—such as nitrogen (N), phosphorus (P), sulfur (S), or carbon (C)—as it travels between the living (biotic) and nonliving (abiotic) components of an ecosystem is to trace its biogeochemical cycle.

ecosystem an ecological community together with its environment

The Phosphorus Cycle

A generalized biogeochemical cycle of phosphorus, for example, starts with its release from apatite (phosphorus-containing rock). Inorganic, plant-available forms of phosphorus in most soils derive from apatite. Mechanical and chemical weathering reactions release phosphorus from apatite into the soil solution. Plants take up available forms of phosphorus, such as orthophosphate ($H_2PO_4^{3-}$), from the soil solution into their roots. After uptake from the soil, phosphorus travels as the phosphate anion HPO_4^{2-} through the plant before accumulating in leaves and other living tissues. Phosphate is present in plant cells and circulating fluids at a concentration of about 10^{-3} m. Plants also incorporate inorganic phosphate into organic forms that may be used for various metabolic processes. Because there are no gaseous forms of phosphorus and soil reserves are small, phosphorus is difficult for plants to acquire. As a result, plants hoard phosphorus. Rather than releasing it back into the environment, plants send the phosphorus to the roots for storage before dropping their leaves. This process, called **translocation**, ensures that the plant will have a sufficient supply of phosphorus for the next growing season. Any phosphorus remaining in the dead leaves falls to the ground in leaf litter. This phosphorus gradually returns to the soil organic matter after microorganisms, such as fungi and bacteria, break down the litter through decomposition, and the cycle commences again.

translocate to move, especially to move sugars from the leaf to other parts of the plant

The time that it takes for the phosphorus to move from apatite into the soil solution is called the flux rate. This represents the amount of time it takes a given amount of a certain element to move between the pools, or reservoirs. Flux rates can be very slow or very rapid. It may take hundreds of years for the phosphorus in the apatite to move into the soil solution. In contrast, once plant-available phosphorus is in the soil solution it is rapidly taken up by the plant roots. The mean residence time (MRT) is the length of time that elements remain in a pool. The MRT for phosphorus in apatite may be thousands of years, but within a plant, the MRT may be only one year. Nutrients move between pools through meteorological, geological, hydrological, biological, or **anthropogenic** mechanisms.

anthropogenic human-derived

Transport Mechanisms

Meteorological mechanisms of nutrient transport are generally related to precipitation in the form of rain, fog, snow, or ice. For example, nitrogen has various gaseous phases including ammonia (NH_3) and nitrous oxides (NO_x). The nitrogen-containing gas may dissolve in precipitation, whereupon the nitrogen is subsequently deposited on plant and soil surfaces. In contrast, phosphorus, which has no gaseous phase, is not incorporated in rain but may be transported as dust by wind currents through the atmosphere. Nutrients also move slowly over the long term (hundreds of thousands of years) and over long distances via geological mechanisms, such as **sedimentation**, **uplift**, and volcanism. For example, carbon (C) may be stored in combination with calcium (Ca) as calcium carbonate ($CaCO_3$) in seashells. The shells fall to the ocean floor and through sedimentation processes become calcite, or calcium carbonate rock. Over thousands or millions of years, this carbon may be released slowly to the atmosphere from near-shore sedimentary rocks. Eventually, the nitrogen deposited on the land by precipitation and the carbon released from the calcite become incorporated into organic matter, the biological component of ecosystems.

sedimentation deposit of mud, sand, shell, or other material

uplift raising up of rock layers, a geologic process caused by plate tectonics

Biological mechanisms generally refer to the microbial transformations of elements that are stored in organic matter into inorganic forms of nutrients that may be used by plants. For example, soil bacteria and fungi release acids that break down leaf litter and release the phosphorus and nitrogen that are bound in it. The phosphorus and nitrogen then combine with oxygen or hydrogen to form plant-available **compounds**.

compound a substance formed from two or more elements

Biological mechanisms of nutrient distribution can also include movement of nitrogen or phosphorus from one area to another via mammals or birds. Studies of bison movement in Oklahoma's tallgrass prairie ecosystem show that, when nitrogen-containing bison fecal pats decompose due to fire or chemical breakdown, they create a spatially patchy distribution of soil nitrogen; this patchiness of nitrogen may influence plant distributions. Likewise, a trip to the Caribbean island chain Los Roques, off the coast of Venezuela, provides a striking example of phosphorus distribution by seabirds. Guano, the white bird droppings that coat the island's rock outcrops, contains some of the highest phosphorus concentrations in the world.

vectors carriers, usually carriers who are not affected by the thing carried

Humans are probably the most important biological **vectors** for nutrient transport on Earth, particularly for carbon, nitrogen, sulfur, and phosphorus. Anthropogenic combustion of fossil fuels releases carbon dioxide

(CO_2) to the atmosphere in quantities that exceed the combined releases of CO_2 from plant, animal, and microbial respiration, natural forest and grassland fires, and volcanic emissions. This has contributed to the build-up of CO_2 in Earth's atmosphere and may alter the biogeochemical cycles of other elements. Fossil fuel combustion also releases nitrogen and sulfur, which ultimately contributes to the formation and deposition of acid rain. Mining of phosphorus, such as in Los Roques, has altered the long-term storage of phosphorus, increased the flux rate of the global phosphorus cycle, and contributed to the phosphorus pollution of freshwater ecosystems worldwide. These and other human activities are altering the biogeochemical cycles of nitrogen, phosphorus, sulfur, and carbon at the global scale, with largely unknown consequences for Earth's inhabitants and ecosystems. SEE ALSO BIOGEOGRAPHY; CARBON CYCLE; NITROGEN FIXATION; NUTRIENTS.

Anne Fernald Cross

Bibliography

Berner, E. K., and R. A. Berner. *Global Environment: Water, Air, and Geochemical Cycles.* Upper Saddle River, NJ: Prentice-Hall, 1996.

Mackenzie, F. T., and Judith A. Mackenzie. *Our Changing Planet: An Introduction to Earth System Science and Global Environmental Change.* Upper Saddle River, NJ: Prentice-Hall, 1995.

Schlesinger, W. H. *Biogeochemistry: An Analysis of Global Change.* San Diego, CA: Academic Press, 1997.

Biogeography

Biogeography is the study of the patterns of distribution of the world's living organisms. It tries to determine where plants and animals occur, why they occur where they do, and when and how the patterns developed. Biogeographic patterns are largely determined by climate, geology, soil conditions, and historical events. Individual plant species are generally restricted to particular habitats, but many plants have widely overlapping ecological requirements so that many different kinds grow together in communities.

Impact of Climate

Rainfall has a significant impact on the distribution of plant types. Savannas, steppes, and prairies occur where rainfall patterns result in long, dry periods at certain times of the year. During the dry season, fires often sweep through these areas. Woody plants, with buds for future vegetative growth borne above ground, are killed by the flames. Grasses and other herbaceous plants, whose reproductive buds are produced on underground shoots, and, therefore, protected from fires survive and thrive. Where annual rainfall is greater and more uniform throughout the year, fires are less frequent and woodlands develop. In contrast, deserts develop where rainfall is severely limited.

Vegetation is also influenced by temperature and length of growing season. In the Arctic, where the ground is frozen for several months of the year and the growing season is measured in weeks, only a relatively few, specialized species of dwarf plants are able to grow. Diversity under such conditions is considerably less than in the tropics, where annual temperatures

A Montana tallgrass prairie in summer.

epiphytes plants that grow on other plants

physiology the biochemical processes carried out by an organism

vernal related to the spring season

and rainfall often remain favorable, and the growing season extends throughout the year. Trees in the tropics can grow to a large size and provide further habitats for **epiphytic** plants and animals among their branches in the forest canopy.

Other Factors

While climate is a major force in determining the patterns of biogeography, other factors are also important, including the **physiological** requirements and tolerances of individual species. Although many plants overlap in their ecological tolerances, they all vary from each other. Individual species of plants rarely occur continuously in the landscape to the exclusion of all others. For instance, the red maple (*Acer rubrum*) in eastern North America is a plant of acid soils and commonly grows with other wetland species in lowlands from eastern Canada to Florida and from the Atlantic to the Mississippi, but it can also grow on dry ridges and hilltops with a different association of plants within the same geographic region. When we examine the distribution of red maple carefully, we also see that the individual plants are not continuous, but occur only where growing conditions are favorable. Some individuals may occur next to each other, but others live some distance away. The individuals within a reasonably close distance to each other, and which are capable of interbreeding, are called populations. Populations, just like individuals, may occur next to each other or be widely separated. Populations occurring far from the main range of distribution of a species are generally referred to as disjunct populations, or simply as disjuncts.

Highly specialized habitats such as bogs, barrens, rock outcrops, and **vernal** pools, which themselves occur in a scattered fashion across the landscape, are frequently home to disjunct species that are especially adapted to those particular ecological conditions. These habitats can be further divided by soil types. Barrens may occur over serpentine, limestone, sandstone, granite, and other less common types of rocks, and each supports a different group of plants particularly adapted to that specific habitat. One particular plant that has a wide distribution in North America from the southeastern United States to eastern and central Canada is the pitcher plant (*Sarracenia purpurea*). When the populations are plotted on a map the species appears to have a continuous distribution throughout its range, but in reality, individual populations occur only in scattered, highly acidic, boggy situations.

Intercontinental Disjunctions

Looking at the distribution of plants today, we see it only as a single slice of time. Studying historical data, we find a very different picture of the position of continents and the distribution of plants and animals. One of the most challenging problems faced by biogeographers is to explain intercontinental disjunctions, in which closely related plants are found on opposite sides of the world from each other and separated by major oceans. One intercontinental disjunction that has attracted particular attention is the one between eastern Asia and eastern North America. About seventy-five **genera** of plants are restricted to these two areas and occur nowhere else in the world. These plants have no or few close relatives in their respective regions, and there is no confusion over their close relationship to their disjunct sister **taxa**. Swedish botanist Carl Linnaeus first noticed that closely related plants grew in these two areas in 1750, but it was not until Asa Gray published a series of papers between 1840 and 1860 that this disjunction was brought into prominence. In fact, Gray's series of papers, which were written in response to requests by Charles Darwin for statistics on the North American flora, are often considered to be the seminal papers in the field of biogeography.

The genera belonging to this pattern often occur in what are considered to be ancient **lineages**, and include Magnoliaceae, Berberidaceae, Schisandraceae, Illiciaceae, Hamamelidaceae, and Saururaceae, but some more modern groups such as Rubiaceae and Asteraceae also contain a few genera with close relatives on opposite sides of the world and nowhere else. Gray tried to explain this pattern by proposing migrations across a Bering land bridge connecting the Asian and American continents during periods when sea levels were lower and corridors for migration were available in the center of North America. This was a simple and plausible explanation, but in reality the origin of this pattern of distribution has proven to be much more complex.

Later, the German botanist Adolf Engler (1844–1930), in writing about the vegetational history of Earth, made use of rapidly accumulating fossil evidence, particularly from the Arctic, to show that the forests in which these disjunct plants now occurred had once been more widespread and continuous at higher latitudes in the northern hemisphere: they essentially circled the globe in a zone where boreal forests now exist. Engler believed that deteriorating climates and the uplifting of mountains worldwide, and increasing aridity in the western part of North America, led to the extinction of this vegetation type in large portions of the world during the latter portion of the **Tertiary period.** (This group of plants is still frequently referred to as the **Arcto-Tertiary geoflora.**) It was also believed that the Pleistocene glaciations of the last two million years further contributed to the extinction of many of the plants in North America and Europe. It has been postulated that the major east-west mountain ranges in Europe—the Pyrenees, Alps, Carpathians, and Balkans—would have blocked the migration of plants in front of the southwardly moving ice sheet, thereby resulting in extinc-

genera plural of genus

taxa a type of organism, or a level of classification of organisms

lineage ancestry; the line of evolutionary descent of an organism

Tertiary period geologic period from sixty-five to five million years ago

Arcto-Tertiary geoflora the fossil flora discovered in arctic areas dating back to the Tertiary period; this group contains magnolias (*Magnolia*), tulip trees (*Liriodendron*), maples (*Acer*), beech (*Fagus*), black gum (*Nyssa*), sweet gum (*Liquidambar*), dawn redwood (*Metasequoia*), cypress (*Taxodium*), and many other species

tion. In contrast, north-south ranges, such as the Appalachians, allowed southerly migration and survival.

Many of the plants and animals restricted to eastern Asia and eastern North America today are known from fossils in Europe and western Asia, and geological evidence indicates that the Bering land bridge was not the only route available for migration between Eurasia and America. Until about forty-nine million years ago and perhaps as recently as about thirty-seven million years ago, North America, Greenland, Iceland, and Europe existed close enough to each other to allow direct migration of plants and animals across the North Atlantic. At that same time, the connection across the Bering Straight was also at a higher latitude than it is today, and climate may have been a controlling factor in plant and animal migrations. It is interesting to note that many genera of plants—*Magnolia, Liriodendron, Juglans, Sassafras, Acer*, and so forth—that now occur primarily or have their greatest diversity in eastern and southeast Asia and eastern North America are known from the Miocene of Iceland. According to Malcolm McKenna in the *Annals of the Missouri Botanical Garden* (1983), the closest relatives of Iceland's plants at that time were in North America. Since the end of the Pleistocene glaciations, the composition of Iceland's flora has become more European in character.

Island Biogeography

Islands require special examination. In a sense, islands are like isolated laboratories where long-term experiments in adaptation and evolution are taking place. Many factors have to be considered to understand the origin and development of an island's **biota**. Such factors include size and elevation of the island, latitude, distance from nearest landmass, age of the island and how long it has remained above sea level, past connections to mainlands, source of migrants, frequency of arrival of new colonists, wind direction, and rainfall patterns. Extinctions and recolonizations, too, have to be analyzed to understand the biological patterns present on islands.

Hawaii and the Galapagos Islands are classic examples where processes of island biogeography have been studied. Hawaii has never been connected to another landmass but instead sits over one of Earth's geological hot spots. As the Pacific plate moves to the west-northwest in conveyor belt fashion, new islands are created as magma flows up through Earth's crust to form volcanoes that eventually reach far above sea level. Activity of the hot spot is apparently intermittent, since the volcanoes are separated by gaps of varying sizes. As the islands move away from the hot spot, they are gradually eroded by the elements and eventually consumed as the Pacific plate dives under the Asian continent. This process has been going for at least seventy million years. Since the islands were barren at their creation, the plants and animals on the Hawaiian islands must have originally come from elsewhere. The nearest major landmasses to Hawaii, and the most likely sources of plant and animal colonists, are more than 4,000 kilometers away.

The first colonists to reach Hawaii would have encountered a rich diversity of wide-open ecological niches ranging from sea level to the tops of mountains (some of which exceed 4,000 meters). The diversity of unoccupied habitats is thought to have promoted rapid **speciation**. Because of the great distance from the major sources of colonists, the number of successful colonizations is estimated to be only 270 to 280 species of plants. These

biota the sum total of living organisms in a region of a given size

speciation creation of new species

have evolved to about 1,000 native species today, although some botanists who place greater emphasis on minor variations consider the number to be much higher. The Hawaiian flora is also considered to be disharmonious, meaning its species distribution differs from that of similar mainland regions. For example, only three native orchids are found on Hawaii, although one would expect many more because of the archipelago's tropical location and wide range of habitats. Conversely, the Campanulaceae (bluebell family) is the most **speciose** family in the islands, with 110 species of native plants. In other regions of the tropics, the family is an insignificant portion of the flora. SEE ALSO BIODIVERSITY; EVOLUTION OF PLANTS; GRAY, ASA; ORCHIDACEAE.

David E. Boufford

speciose marked by many species

Bibliography

Carlquist, S. *Island Biology.* New York: Columbia University Press, 1974.

Cox, C. B., and P. D. Moore. *Biogeography: An Ecological and Evolutionary Approach.* New York: John Wiley & Sons, 1973.

Daubenmire, R. *Plant Geography: With Special Reference to North America.* New York: Academic Press, 1978.

De Laubenfels, D. J. "Botany of Japan and Its Relations to That of Central and Northern Asia, Europe, and North America." *Proceedings of the American Academy of Arts and Sciences* 4 (1860): 130–35.

———. *A Geography of Plants and Animals.* Dubuque, IA: William C. Brown Co., 1972.

McKenna, M. C. "Holarctic Landmass Rearrangement, Cosmic Events, and Cenozoic Terrestrial Organisms." *Annals of the Missouri Botanical Garden* 70 (1983): 459–89.

Pears, N. *Basic Biogeography.* Whitstable, KY: Whitstable Litho Ltd., 1977.

Pielou, E. C. *Biogeography.* New York: John Wiley & Sons, 1979.

Stott, P. *Historical Plant Geography.* London: George Allen & Unwin, 1981.

Wagner, W. L., D. R. Herbst, and S. H. Sohmer. *Manual of the Flowering Plants of Hawaii,* rev. ed. Honolulu, HI: University of Hawaii Press, Bishop Museum Press, 1999.

Biomass Fuels

Biomass fuel is fuel produced from organic material of recent biological origin. Biomass suitable for the production of fuels is classified as either biomass waste or energy crops.

biomass the total dry weight of an organism or group of organisms

Biomass waste is any material of recent biological origin that has been discarded because it has no apparent value. Examples of biomass waste include residues from agricultural crops, municipal solid waste, and even sewage. Because this waste originates from biomass that recycles to the environment on a nearly annual basis, it is a sustainable energy resource; that is, the resource will be available for future generations.

Energy crops are defined as plants grown specifically as an energy resource. An energy crop is planted and harvested periodically. The cycle of planting and harvesting over a relatively short period assures that the resource is used in a sustainable fashion. Energy crops include woody crops harvested on a rotation of five to seven years and herbaceous energy crops harvested on an annual basis. Examples of woody crops include **hybrid**

hybrid a mix of two species

poplars and willows. Examples of herbaceous crops include switchgrass and sweet sorghum. Peat moss is also harvested and used as a fuel.

Solid fuels such as biomass are at an enormous disadvantage when compared to petroleum and natural gas because they are more difficult to transport and handle. The goal of many biomass conversion processes is to convert solid fuel into more useful gaseous or liquid forms. Gaseous fuels can substitute for natural gas in machinery to produce heat and power. Liquid fuels can substitute for gasoline or diesel fuel in automobiles and trucks. Both gaseous and liquid fuels can also be used to produce chemicals and materials currently made from petroleum resources.

anaerobic without oxygen

Either **anaerobic** digestion or thermal gasification can produce gaseous biomass fuels. Anaerobic digestion is the decomposition of organic solids to gaseous fuel by bacteria in an oxygen-free environment. The product is a mixture of methane, carbon dioxide, and some trace gases. Thermal gasification is the conversion of solid fuels into flammable gas mixtures consisting of carbon monoxide, hydrogen, methane, nitrogen, carbon dioxide, and smaller quantities of higher hydrocarbons.

Liquid biomass fuels can be produced from solid biomass by three processes: fermentation to ethanol, processing of vegetable oils to biodiesel, or thermal processing to pyrolysis oils. Pyrolysis is the high-temperature decomposition of organic compounds in the absence of oxygen to produce liquids. The mixture of oxygenated hydrocarbons is similar to that found in fuel oil.

compound a substance formed from two or more elements

Fermentation is the decomposition of complex organic molecules into simpler **compounds** by the action of microorganisms. A variety of carbohydrates (such as sugars, starches, hemicellulose, and cellulose) can serve as feedstock in ethanol fermentation as long as they can be broken down to sugars that are susceptible to microbial biological action. Cellulose and hemicellulose found in the plant cell walls of woody and herbaceous energy crops can also be converted to fermentable sugars, but the process is relatively difficult.

Vegetable oils from soybeans, peanuts, and other grains and seeds can be used as fuel in diesel engines after chemical modification to improve their combustion properties. SEE ALSO AGRICULTURE, MODERN; FORESTRY; OILS, PLANT-DERIVED; PEAT BOGS.

Robert C. Brown

Bibliography

Brown, Robert C. "Capturing Solar Energy Through Biomass." In *Principles of Solar Engineering*, 2nd ed. D. Y. Goswami, F. Kreider, and F. Kreith, eds. Washington, DC: Taylor & Francis, 1999.

Needham, Cynthia, Mahlon Hoagland, Kenneth McPherson, and Bert Dodson. *Intimate Strangers: Unseen Life on Earth.* Washington, DC: ASM Press, 2000.

Wayman, Morris, and Sarad R. Parekh. *Biotechnology of Biomass Conversion.* Milton Keynes, England: Open University Press, 1990.

Biome

biogeography the study of the reasons for the geographic distribution of organisms

A biome is a particularly useful **biogeographic** unit that results from large-scale climatic patterns. A portion of a biome, such as the tropical rain forest found in the Amazon basin, may cover thousands of hectares. It will have

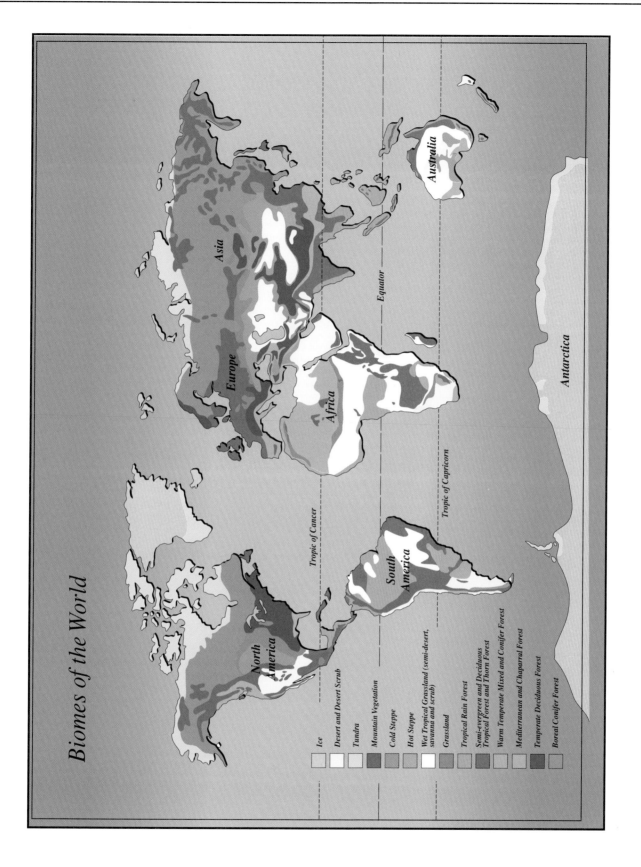

Biomes of the World

North America

South America

Europe

Asia

Africa

Australia

Antarctica

Tropic of Cancer

Equator

Tropic of Capricorn

Ice

Desert and Desert Scrub

Tundra

Mountain Vegetation

Cold Steppe

Hot Steppe

Wet Tropical Grassland (semi-desert, savanna and scrub)

Grassland

Tropical Rain Forest

Semi-evergreen and Deciduous Tropical Forest and Thorn Forest

Warm Temperate Mixed and Conifer Forest

Mediterranean and Chaparral Forest

Temperate Deciduous Forest

Boreal Conifer Forest

Mean annual precipitation and temperature of biomes. *Source:* Reprinted from Aber and Melillo, 1991, p. 16.

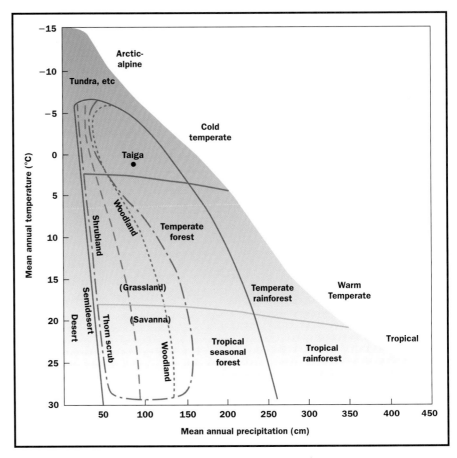

recognizable vegetation features that impart a sameness that defines the unit. The fact that this region differs from others, such as the desert biome, is evident to even the most untrained observer. Frederic Clements (1874–1945) and Victor Shelford (1877–1968) observed in 1939 that not only was the vegetation characteristic, but that these were plant–animal formations with associated fauna. In the 1960s an ecological research effort, the International Biological Program, sought to characterize the structure and function of major biomes through intense study. American botanist and ecologist Robert Whittaker (1920–1980) summarized some characteristics of the biomes in his book *Communities and Ecosystems*, in which he arranged them graphically according to interacting gradients of mean annual temperature and moisture availability (see accompanying figure).

The Influence of Rainfall

You can bring this model to life though observation as you travel within the continental United States. The Interstate Highway System allows easy movement across the country along latitudes, parallel to the equator, or the longitudes, perpendicular at the equator. Travel on Interstate 80 from New York City to San Francisco during the summer growing season reveals an obvious gradient of change in vegetation. The deciduous forests of central New York State are lush green in most years, with trees predominating where human development has not occurred. In the Midwest, traveling from Illinois into Iowa and Nebraska, the trees are absent except along rivers, and grasses and broad-leaved nonwoody **forbs** cover the landscape like a carpet.

forbs broad-leaved, herbaceous plants

Much of this region is now dominated by fields of grain such as corn and wheat, **domesticated** replacements of the native vegetation that once was predominant in the grasslands. (Remnants of the native prairie are rare.) In August, the green prairies begin to show some signs of the golden color of mature fields as the various annual grasses produce seeds that will ultimately produce plants for the following year. Meanwhile the perennials will die back to ground level by late fall, and then start growth again the following year.

The farther west one travels, the sparser the vegetation and the less luxuriant the crops, until dry short-grass prairies merge into deserts and badlands with more widely spaced plants and soil that is frequently bare. The predominant color throughout the year in the deserts tends toward earth tones of beige and brown with small green leaves being less evident. Two major north-south mountain barriers, the Rocky Mountains and the Sierra Nevada range in California, interrupt the gradual transition. In these areas, elevation-dependent differences produce a complex mosaic of vegetation that does not fit the overall pattern. Finally, on the West Coast, moisture-laden air deposits rain on the windward sides of the coastal mountains and abruptly changes the pattern. Lush temperate rain forest vegetation forms a margin along the western edges of California north of San Francisco, just as in coastal Oregon and Washington. Southward, the forests are replaced by coastal shrub lands because rainfall is not sufficient to support extensive forests in most places, and the inland deserts are even closer to the ocean shores. This east-west gradient across the country parallels a decline in moisture availability, the first of two major climatic factors that determine the character of biomes.

The Influence of Temperature

A similar trip along Interstate 75 in January from the Canadian border at Sault Ste. Marie, Michigan, to Florida provides evidence of the second major climatic factor gradient. In northern Michigan, it is likely that the ground will be snow covered most of the month. Ohio and Kentucky can present occasional periods with persistent snow cover; by the time you reach Georgia, however, snow generally disappears shortly after it falls, and Florida has only rain. This gradient is not so much a result of differences in volume of precipitation (the amount of rain or snowfall), but the prevailing temperatures. When the north to south temperature gradient overlays the east to west moisture gradient, the type of biological community that will be supported is determined. Similar interactions of temperature and moisture availability determine the presence of other biomes globally as indicated in the map of their distribution. Toward the poles, Canadian boreal forests change over to tundra and illustrate the results of extending the temperature gradient.

Tropical rain forests occur where the temperature is greater near the equator and daily tropical rains maintain high moisture levels. This tropical region along the equator forms a boundary with the temperature gradients in the Southern and Northern Hemispheres being mirror images of each other. In the tropical forest biomes, there is little seasonal change; the prevailing conditions are wet and warm. Seasonal temperature variation is minimal in regions adjacent to tropical forests, but ultimately at increasing distance from the equator, alternating wet and dry periods produce fluctuations in growth rates in subtropical seasonal forests. This moisture-dependent al-

domesticate to tame an organism to live with and to be of use to humans

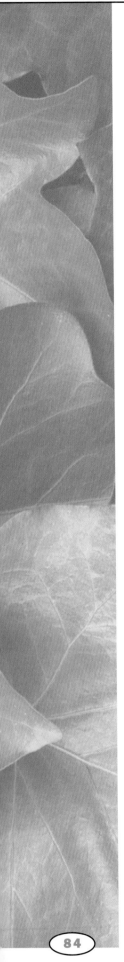

ternation is different from the temperate biomes covering the United States and Canada where the seasons are produced by the alternation of a cold winter and relatively warmer summer.

The classification of biogeographic areas into biomes is only one of several different methods of organizing terrestrial environments. Michael Barbour, in *Terrestrial Ecosystems*, gives a brief historical review of other classification systems, and Robert Bailey, in *Ecosystem Geography*, updates various ways of classifying the Earth's surface. Barbour uses the term *vegetation types* to classify landscape patterns and points out significant differences between the various subdivisions that can be identified, while Bailey prefers the term *ecoregion* as the unit of subdivision at the level of assemblages of landscapes.

Since the distribution of biomes is dependent on global climate patterns, one may question what impact global climatic change could have on these biogeographic units. A continuation of global warming would change the boundaries by moving warmer conditions closer to the poles.

In addition, the climatic changes do not just involve changes in temperature; they also involve changes in air movement patterns, alteration of temperatures (known as El Niño and La Niña) within the oceans, and storm distributions that change the annual growth of both plants and animals. This is not a new phenomenon on Earth. Cold periods have existed in the past, and biome boundaries have shifted in response. This is known from the pollen record left in lakes and bogs over many thousands of years. The challenge to plants and animals is not so much the extent or duration of expected temperature changes, but the rate of those changes. Vegetation can respond to changes that take hundreds or thousands of years to occur by gradually dispersing into new areas or evolving. It cannot move or reproduce fast enough to adapt to the same changes if they occur over tens or hundreds of years. The total ecologic impact of these potential rapid changes is not currently known. SEE ALSO AQUATIC ECOSYSTEMS; BIODIVERSITY; CHAPARRAL; CLINES AND ECOTYPES; COASTAL ECOSYSTEMS; CONIFEROUS FORESTS; DECIDUOUS FORESTS; DEFORESTATION; DESERTIFICATION; DESERTS; ECOLOGY; ECOSYSTEM; GLOBAL WARMING; GRASSLANDS; PLANT COMMUNITY PROCESSES; RAIN FORESTS; SAVANNA; TUNDRA.

W. Dean Cocking

Bibliography

Aber, John, and Jerry Melillo. *Terrestrial Ecosystems.* Philadelphia, PA: Saunders College Publishing, 1991.

Bailey, Robert G. *Ecosystem Geography.* New York: Springer-Verlag, 1996.

Barbour, Michael G., ed. *Terrestrial Plant Ecology,* 3rd ed. New York: Addison-Wesley, 1998.

Clements, Frederic E., and Victor Shelford. *Bio-ecology.* New York: John Wiley & Sons, 1939.

Whittaker, Robert. *Communities and Ecosystems,* 2nd ed. New York: Macmillan, 1975.

Bioremediation

The word "bioremediation" was coined by scientists in the early 1980s as a term to describe the use of microorganisms to clean polluted soils and waters. The prefix *bio* defined the process as biological, that is, carried out by living organisms. The noun remediation defined the process as one that re-

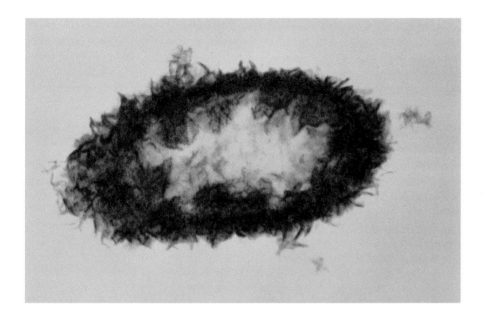

Desulphovibrio sp., a sulphur-eating bacterium used in toxic waste treatment. In anaerobic conditions such as those found in waste effluents, the bacterium obtains oxygen from sulphate ions. This liberates sulphide ions, which may bond with iron in the waste water to form a precipitate, seen here as the hairlike coating, which attracts toxic metals. The bacterium and its toxic coat may then be isolated by magnetic separation.

sulted in the cleaning, or remediation, of the environment, via complete degradation, sequestration, or removal of the toxic pollutants as the result of microbial activity. Degradation means that the microorganisms decompose the pollutants to harmless natural products such as carbon dioxide (CO_2), water (H_2O), or other nontoxic naturally occurring **compounds**. Sequestration means that the pollutant is trapped or changed in a way that makes it nontoxic or unavailable to biological systems. Removal means that while the pollutant is not necessarily degraded, the microbes physically remove it from the soil or water so that it can be collected and disposed of safely.

The principal goal of bioremediation is to return polluted environments to their natural state. Examples of the many contaminants that are amenable to bioremediation via degradation include organic chemicals such as pesticides, insecticides, herbicides, and pollutants derived from petroleum as the result of oil or fuel spills, or oil refining activities. Research in the 1990s has shown that even synthetic chemicals previously thought to be totally resistant to degradation, such as the insecticide DDT or the explosive TNT, are, in fact, degradable by microorganisms when they are supplied the right growth conditions. Examples of pollutants that can be **sequestered** or removed by microorganisms include toxic heavy metals such as lead (Pb), cadmium (Cd), and arsenic (As), and radioactive metals such as uranium (U). Toxic levels of metals are found in soils or waters previously contaminated as the result of military, industrial, or mining activities. Metals are found in various chemical forms, but unlike organic compounds, metals cannot be degraded. They can be changed only to some other chemical form. Therefore, the goal of metal bioremediation is to use microbes to change the metals into a form that is either sequestered in the soil in an insoluble form, or changed into a soluble form that can be removed from the soil with water, and then recovered later.

Various processes are used to carry out bioremediation. They include ex situ techniques, where contaminated soil is excavated, bioremediated in a vessel or pile, and then returned to the environment. Alternatively, with

compound a substance formed from two or more elements

sequester remove from circulation; lock up

PHYTOREMEDIATION

Phytoremediation uses plants to remove both soilborne and waterborne pollutants. It is proving especially useful for treating heavy metal contamination, an exceptionally difficult type of cleanup job. Plants need soil nutrients and are efficient absorbers of all kinds of minerals. Some species, called hyperaccumulators, can concentrate metals thousand of times above normal levels. Indian mustard (*Brassica juncea*) will hyperaccumulate lead, chromium, cadmium, nickel, selenium, zinc, copper, cesium, and strontium. Detoxifying the soil is as simple as harvesting the plants.

in situ techniques, the contamination is treated where it occurred. This approach is particularly suited to treating contaminated groundwater in deep aquifers. Bioremediation can involve the inoculation of a contaminated environment with the specific microorganisms needed to carry out the bioremediation, or supplementation of the environment with nutrients that will promote the activity of microbes already naturally present. When supplementation is done in situ, it is sometimes called naturally accelerated bioremediation. The microorganisms naturally present in some contaminated environments may sometimes slowly bioremediate that environment without any human intervention. This type of bioremediation is called natural attenuation, a process that usually occurs very slowly over many years. Because it is effective and affordable, bioremediation is often the method of choice for cleaning polluted soils, groundwaters, aquatic areas, wetlands, and other environments. SEE ALSO HUMAN IMPACTS; SOIL, CHEMISTRY OF.

Don L. Crawford

Bibliography

Chaudhry, G. Rasul, ed. *Biological Degradation and Bioremediation of Toxic Chemicals.* Portland, OR: Dioscorides Press, 1994.

Crawford, Ronald L., and Don L. Crawford, eds. *Bioremediation: Principles and Applications.* New York: Cambridge University Press, 1996.

Quensen, J. F., S. A. Mueller, M. K. Jain, and J. M. Tiedje. "Reductive Dechlorination of DDE to DDMU in Marine Sediment Microcosms." *Science* 280 (1998): 722–24.

Bonsai

Bonsai is a Japanese word formed by two ideogram characters, the first meaning "pot" or "container" and the second "to cultivate." It is a term that can be applied to any plant grown in a pot. Today it is applied to a tree or shrub grown usually in a ceramic pot, trained or styled by clipping or wiring or both. But it is so much more.

Bonsai is an ancient art form with its origins in China at least as far back as the fourth century. Soon the art spread to Korea and was found in Japan by the sixth and seventh centuries. During the last hundred years the art of bonsai spread and now enjoys worldwide popularity.

Even today, bonsai continues to touch one's soul and intellect with its beauty, tranquility, and natural character of age, just as one would react to viewing a masterpiece of art. Despite its small size, one can sense a large old tree sometimes shaped by wind, often with branches weighed down by imaginary heavy snows, and a sense of balance and perfection in this small plant in a ceramic pot. Bonsai is that ideal tree in nature.

There are two general methods used to transform a plant into a bonsai. A young tree may be grown from seed or from nursery stock. In this case the intent is to concentrate on the development of the trunk by keeping many lower branches. Alternatively, a mature tree may be collected from the field or mountains and then styled.

Care includes almost daily watering and monthly fertilizer applications. Bonsai may be trained into one of many styles. Among them are formal upright (straight trunk), informal upright (curvy trunk), slanted, windswept,

A man shapes and prunes a pine tree bonsai to the desired form.

cascade, multiple trunk, clump, raft, rock planting, broom, raised roots, forest planting, and literati (a variation on the others with sparse branches). Usually, the growth and structural characteristics of the tree determine the style chosen.

Once the plant is selected, the training of bonsai begins with the selection of which side will be the front of the tree, based on the width of the trunk and the sense of stability imparted by the tree. Branches on the left, right, and backside of the plant are then selected and trained. The profile of the tree as seen from all directions, especially the front, is triangular, the corners of which are formed by the apex and the ends of the major left and right branches. Copper or aluminum wire of various sizes is used over a period of several months to bend and hold branches until they retain their position. Highly specialized hand tools are used during this training process. A suitable pot is selected based on how the styled tree harmonizes with the color, shape, width, and depth of the pot. The tree is potted in a coarse or medium well-draining soil mixture.

Several species are more frequently used for bonsai. These include most junipers, pines, and many deciduous or flowering/fruiting shrubs or trees such as the *Prunus* family and azaleas.

It is highly recommended that beginning bonsai enthusiasts receive instruction in styling bonsai since this is more difficult than it sounds.

John Yoshio Naka of the United States is arguably the world's foremost expert in bonsai. He began his bonsai career in Los Angeles, California, in the 1940s. For his accomplishments in bonsai, Naka was recognized with Japan's highest honor for a noncitizen and a national Heritage Fellowship from the U.S. National Endowment for the Arts. At the turn of the twenty-first century he still continued to teach and work on his bonsai daily.

Bonsai can be formally displayed indoors for up to a week. The potted trees are placed on display stands or slabs of finished wood and accompanied with an accent plant that suggests grasses and other plants that typically grow under a tree. Almost all bonsai must be kept outdoors on large tables or individual stands, except during harsh, freezing weather.

Bonsai may be seen in several collections open to the general public. The National Bonsai Foundation has several collections at the National Arboretum in Washington, D.C. Other public bonsai displays are the Pacific Rim collection in Tacoma, Washington, and the Bonsai Pavilion and Garden at the Wild Animal Park in Escondido, California. The Golden State Bonsai Federation has two collections, one at Lakeside Park in Oakland, California, and another at the Huntington Garden in San Marino, California.

Bonsai is an art that will continue to fascinate and amaze people of all races, cultures, and age with its universal appeal. SEE ALSO HORTICULTURE; TREE ARCHITECTURE; TREES.

Sherwin Toshio Amimoto

Bibliography

American Bonsai Society. [Online] Available at http://www.absbonsai.org.

Bonsai Clubs International. [Online] Available at http://www.bonsai-bci.com.

Golden State Bonsai Federation. [Online] Available at http://www.gsbf-bonsai.org.

Naka, John Y. *Bonsai Techniques I*. Whittier, CA: Bonsai Institute, 1984.

———. *Bonsai Techniques II*. Whittier, CA: Bonsai Institute, 1985.

———, Richard K. Ota, and Kenko Rokkaku. *Bonsai Techniques for Satsuki*. Los Angeles: Ota Bonsai Nursery, 1979.

National Bonsai Foundation. [Online] Available at http://www.bonsai-nbf.org.

Nippon Bonsai Association. *Classic Bonsai of Japan*. John Bester, tr. New York: Kodansha International, 1989.

Borlaug, Norman E.

American Microbiologist and Agronomist
1914–

Norman E. Borlaug, perhaps the world's best-known plant breeder, was born on a small farm near Cresco, Iowa, in 1914. He studied plant pathology at the University of Minnesota.

In October 1944 Borlaug began work with the Rockefeller Foundation in Mexico. The foundation had begun a new program in Mexico in 1943 aimed at increasing the agricultural yields of the country. Borlaug's primary scientific achievements were as an applied wheat geneticist with the foundation. He oversaw a highly successful use of Mendelian genetics to create new varieties of wheat.

His work involved the identification of parent varieties with useful traits, such as disease resistance and high yield. He then dusted pollen (male reproductive cells) from the flowers of one variety onto flowers from another variety, from which the stamen had been removed. The transferred pollen cells fertilized the ovules (female reproductive cells) of the recipient flowers. The wheat seeds produced by the female parent were harvested and grown into new plants. Borlaug and his team then identified offspring with desired, novel combinations of traits and used them for further crosses. They released offspring offering high promise and reliability to farmers for commercial **cultivation**.

Norman Borlaug.

cultivation growth of crop plants

88

Borlaug used a practice considered controversial at the time: shuttle breeding. This involved shuttling breeding stock between two different geographic regions in order to achieve two crossings per year rather than just one. With this technique, he successfully shortened the time needed to obtain new varieties from about ten years to about five years. His shuttle breeding also enabled him to create new wheat varieties that were widely adaptable. In wheat, this wide adaptability was due in part to eliminating day-length sensitivity (photoperiodism) in flowering.

Borlaug's work was of profound significance. Within ten years, he and his team were able to create varieties of wheat well suited to different regions of Mexico, which enabled Mexican wheat farmers to more than triple production, from 365 thousand tons (750 kilograms per hectare) in 1945 to 1.2 million tons (1,370 kilograms per hectare) in 1956. As a result, Mexico stopped importing wheat and began exporting it.

In 1953 wheat varieties bearing **semidwarfing** genes came to Borlaug from Orville Vogel in Washington State. Vogel had successfully incorporated these genes, obtained from Japanese varieties, into wheats suited to Washington. These varieties responded well to fertilizer and gave substantially higher yields. Borlaug incorporated the semidwarfing genes into his already successful new varieties, which enabled Mexican wheat growers by the early 1960s to obtain over 6,000 kilograms per hectare. In 1963 Borlaug subsequently recommended that India import the new semidwarf varieties, and these plants were equally successful there.

Borlaug's scientific work led to his receipt of the Nobel Peace Prize in 1970. His successes, plus those of his other colleagues in wheat and rice breeding, are often referred to as the Green Revolution. High-yielding varieties of wheat and rice are now grown in all parts of the world. They are very significant in the production of food supplies adequate for the growing human population. SEE ALSO BREEDER; BREEDING; GRAINS; GREEN REVOLUTION; PHOTOPERIODISM.

John H. Perkins

semidwarfing a variety that is intermediate in size between dwarf and full-size varieties

Bibliography

Easterbrook, Gregg. "Forgotten Benefactor of Humanity." *Atlantic Monthly* 279 (January 1997): 75–82.

Perkins, John H. *Geopolitics and the Green Revolution: Wheat, Genes, and the Cold War.* New York: Oxford University Press, 1997.

Boreal Forest   *See Coniferous Forest.*

Botanical and Scientific Illustrator

The botanical or scientific illustrator creates accurate artworks under the close supervision of the scientist or author. Most works are made for publication in books or journals, but some may be for transparencies, charts, maps, diagrams, models, or murals. Curiosity, patience, and precision are required, as well as artistic creativity. This career could be ideal for people who enjoy spending hours looking for minute details on pressed **specimens** in a museum, or relish the idea of sketching live ones in the wild. Much sat-

specimen object or organism under consideration

Durchschnitt eines Schlauchblattes.

1. Dischidia Rafflesiana.

3. Dischidia imbricata.

8. Tillandsia usneoides.

2. Polypodium quercifolium.

4. Oncidium Limminghii.

5. Ficus religiosa.

6. Tillandsia bulbosa.

7. Platycerium grande.

An undated lithograph of Irish moss (right), creeping vine (center), ferns, figs, and other plants found in the American South.

isfaction can come from seeing publication of a drawing that is both beautiful and scientifically accurate.

The work of the botanical or scientific illustrator may be found in publications (particularly those dealing with plant taxonomy) and exhibitions of natural history museums, nature centers, and parks; and also in periodicals devoted to gardening, cooking, and health. Good artists accurately and artistically convey the author's ideas. Illustrators may have to decide how to show sections, magnifications, and various processes such as pollination or seed dispersal. A preliminary drawing could involve hours of comparing specimens and measurements under a microscope.

For persons interested in pursuing a career as a botanical or scientific illustrator, recommended courses at the high school level include basic design and drawing and science. Knowledge of Latin may be useful with scientific names; Spanish or Portuguese would be invaluable for work in the New World tropics. Computer graphics are opening additional career opportunities. The illustrator should also learn about printing techniques and will have to address issues of copyright and contracts.

Numerous universities and other institutions offer education in this field. Undergraduate degrees and master's degrees in botanical and scientific illustration are available. Various certificate programs, diplomas, courses, and internships are also offered at many institutions. The names of excellent private teachers, particularly in Great Britain, may be obtained from the Guild of Natural Science Illustrators (GNSI), American Society of Botanical Artists (ASBA), and Hunt Institute for Botanical Documentation.

A position might involve duties other than illustration, such as teaching, program and exhibition planning, collection curation, and writing. Many scientific illustrators work freelance, especially at first. The beginner may have to negotiate with a publisher before settling on a fee (a few hundred dollars in 1999) for a drawing. SEE ALSO HERBARIA; TAXONOMY.

James J. White

Bibliography

American Society of Botanical Artists. [Online] Available at http://huntbot.andrew. cmu.edu/ASBA/ASBotArtists.html.

Blunt, Wilfrid, and William T. Stearn. *The Art of Botanical Illustration.* Woodbridge, Suffolk, UK: Antique Collectors' Club, 1994.

Guild of Natural Science Illustrators. [Online] Available at http://www.gnsi.org/.

Hodges, Elaine R. S., ed. *The Guild Handbook of Scientific Illustration.* New York: Van Nostrand Reinhold, 1989.

Hunt Institute for Botanical Documentation. [Online] Available at http://huntbot. andrew.cmu.edu/HIBD/HuntInstitute.html.

West, Keith. *How to Draw Plants: The Techniques of Botanical Illustration.* London: Herbert Press in association with the British Museum (Natural History), 1983.

Botanical Gardens and Arboreta

Botanical gardens and arboreta are living museums. Their collections are plants, and like any museum **specimens**, they are carefully identified, **accessioned**, labeled, and displayed for public enjoyment and education. They provide a rich opportunity for both the professional and interested public to learn more about the diverse world of plants, how to grow them, and the benefits they offer to society.

People have been collecting and displaying plants for hundreds of years. During the sixteenth century the study and use of herbs for medicinal purposes motivated the founding of botanical gardens. The first were in Italy, at Pisa in 1543, and Padua and Florence in 1545. These gardens were initially associated with the medical schools of universities. Physic gardens, developed by professors of medicine who were the botanists of this period, served as both a teaching resource and a source of plants to make medicines. Interestingly, these original gardens are still in existence today. During the eighteenth and nineteenth centuries, the focus shifted towards taxonomy and the collection of specimens from around the world. Herbaria and libraries joined living collections as components of botanical gardens. Today, botanical gardens and arboreta are devoted mainly to plant culture and the display of ornamental plants and plant groups of special interest. Botanical exploration, taxonomy, and research can also be part of an individual garden's

specimen object or organism under consideration

accessioned made a detailed record of an acquistion

A trellis with a cupola stands among the many flower beds on the 88-acre site of the Niagara Parks Botanical Garden in Ontario, Canada.

efforts. The latest estimates, derived from research for the International Union for Conservation of Nature and Natural Resources/World Wildlife Fund for Nature Botanic Gardens Conservation Strategy, indicate that there are approximately fourteen hundred botanical gardens and arboreta in the world. These may range in size from one or two acres to thousands of acres.

Botanical gardens and arboreta may be based on a design that gathers the trees, shrubs, and herbaceous plants in their respective taxonomic groups. Or, they may be grouped according to the region of the world where the plant grows in its native environment. Often, plants are used to create small, landscaped display gardens such as a rhododendron, wildflower, medicinal, or Japanese style garden, or examples of gardens for the home landscape.

In addition to their gardens and outdoor plant collections, botanical gardens and arboreta may include herbaria for the collection and preservation of dried plant specimens, libraries, research laboratories, production and display greenhouses, conservatories for the indoor display of tropical plants, educational classrooms, areas for interpretive exhibits, and public amenities such as a gift shop or restaurant.

Such diverse resources and facilities require a skilled staff of workers. The most important consideration in maintaining botanical gardens and arboreta is good plant-care practices. Horticulturists, trained in these practices, spend time on everything from lawn maintenance to systematic pruning of tree and shrub collections. Horticulturists are also responsible for collecting new plants, **propagating** seeds and cuttings, and maintaining accurate records of growth and health characteristics.

Other types of professional staff depend upon the objectives of the individual garden. They might include a plant pathologist or specialist in plant diseases, a landscape architect, research scientists, educators, librarian, and a membership and fund-raising specialist. A director is responsible for coordinating the entire botanic garden program.

Botanic gardens and arboreta may be independently established, part of a government agency, or connected to a college and university. Funding to support their activities may be derived through memberships, fees, tax support, or endowment funds, or a combination of these methods. SEE ALSO CURATOR OF A BOTANICAL GARDEN; TAXONOMY.

Paul C. Spector

Botany

Botany is the study of plants. Plants make up a large fraction of all living organisms, and the study of botany is equally broad, including the **physiology**, genetics, anatomy, and **morphology** of plants, as well as their taxonomy, evolution, ecological relationships, and the many ways in which plants are used by people.

Like other scientific endeavors, the field of botany has grown immensely during the last decades of the twentieth century. It might also be said to have shrunk, however, as botanists have more carefully defined what a plant is. Fungi, algae, and photosynthetic bacteria, which were once classified as plants, are now placed in other kingdoms. Nonetheless, many who study these organisms still consider themselves botanists, and many university botany departments continue to include these organisms as topics of study within their departments.

Plants have an enormous influence on our lives through their use as foods, fibers, and fuels, as well as their critical role in recycling the gases of the atmosphere. More complete knowledge of botany improves our understanding of these influences, allowing us to use them more effectively, and more wisely. SEE ALSO ECOLOGY, HISTORY OF; EVOLUTION OF PLANTS, HISTORY OF; PHYSIOLOGY, HISTORY OF.

Richard Robinson

Bibliography

Raven, Peter H., Ray F. Evert, and Susan E. Eichhorn. *Biology of Plants*, 6th ed. New York: W. H. Freeman and Company, 1999.

Breeder

Plant breeding is the art and science of improving plant characteristics through the process of sexual reproduction. The goal of a plant breeder is to transfer genes from one plant to another and to select offspring that

propagate to create more of through sexual or asexual reproduction

physiology the biochemical processes carried out by an organism

morphology shape and form

A plant breeder performing research at the Volcani Institute in Israel.

population a group of organisms of a single species that exist in the same region and interbreed

physiology the biochemical processes carried out by an organism

have superior growth, yield, pest and disease resistance, or some other desirable trait.

To achieve this goal the breeder often begins the breeding process using primitive or wild forms of a particular plant species. Through a process of repeated sexual crossing and selection of improved forms, the breeder gradually reaches the goal. Often the hybridization process is lengthy, requiring time for the seed to grow into a mature flowering plant, which can then be compared to a **population** of seedlings from previous crosses. The newly selected plant is again sexually crossed with other improved plant types and gradually the desired trait or traits are incorporated into the new hybrid selection.

Plant breeders are trained in the science of genetics. Some receive a bachelor's degree in science, while others go on to earn a doctoral degree. This training is usually combined with a specialization in one or more types of crops such as grains, oilseeds, fruits, vegetable forage crops, or ornamental plants. A successful plant breeder must thoroughly understand the **physiology** and reproductive patterns and characteristics of the breeding materials.

Selecting for improved traits requires both the application of genetic principles as well as the ability to recognize sometimes small but very important changes in the plants when they are selected from one generation to the next during the breeding process. A well-trained plant breeder will also have knowledge of the "new genetics" of molecular biology and molecular genetics. Modern plant breeding combines the classical approach of sexual breeding with an understanding of gene structure. This knowledge allows the breeder to more rapidly combine desirable traits in the breeding population by establishing molecular genetic markers that can be associated with those traits.

Creativity is an important part of plant breeding. And developing a new plant that will increase the food supply or contribute to the beauty of the environment is quite rewarding. There are many career choices available to a plant breeder with training in molecular biology and classical breeding principles. One career path involves the application of genetic principles to plant improvement in a field or greenhouse. This is the role of the traditional breeder in the development of new plant varieties. There is a great need for individuals who possess these skills. Combining this role with training in molecular genetics increases the effectiveness of the breeder. Molecular genetics training also enables the breeder to work in a laboratory environment. Information developed in the laboratory can be transferred to breeders who use the information in a classical breeding program.

Typically, a plant breeder may teach and conduct research in a university or government laboratory. Many seed companies and biotechnology organizations employ plant breeders as well. Entry-level salaries in the 1990s ranged from $40,000 in an academic or government job to $60,000 to $80,000 in private industry. SEE ALSO BREEDING; GENETIC ENGINEER.

Roger H. Lawson

Breeding

The vast majority of the human population and most civilizations have depended on the productivity of plant-based agriculture for sustenance, vitality, and quality of life during the preceding five to fifteen millenia. During this time, and especially since the rediscovery of Gregor Mendel's principles of heredity in the late nineteenth century, the genetic content (genome) of crop plants has become a more important resource for crop management and production. The dynamic genomes of crop plants contain tens of thousands of genes that interact with themselves and the environment to determine the many traits affecting crop productivity. Gradually, humans have learned that the genomes of crop species and their relatives contain a range of genetic variation for many traits; how the genomes are transmitted from parent to progeny; a few of the myriad relationships among genomes, genes, the environment, and traits; some methods and mechanisms for maintaining or modifying the genomes; and how to select, capture, **propagate** and deliver the desirable genetic variation in forms suited to the agricultural systems and their societies. Much remains to be learned and understood.

propagate to create more of through sexual or asexual reproduction

Daniel Sarria, a
Colombian corn breeder,
inspects corn kernels on
a light table.

holistic including all the
parts or factors that
relate to an object or
idea

Plant breeding is the science ultimately concerned with the **holistic** and systematic creation of cultivars, cultivated varieties of plant species better suited to the needs and pleasures of human societies. In many ways, plant breeding is analogous to a large river system such as the Mississippi: it has a primary source (the gene pool of the plant species), a main river (the elite gene pool of plant breeding methods), tributaries (new technology and scientific disciplines), the ability to adapt to the prevailing conditions and forces of nature, and it is replenished by recycled water (germplasm, all genotypes of a species). Plant breeders devise and deploy methods that, in accordance with their resources, the nature of the plant and production environment, and the prevailing goals of society, integrate information and material from the tributaries to produce better cultivars. The scientific tributaries have included the biological (e.g., genetics, botany, biochemistry, plant pathology, entomology), physical (e.g., mathematics, chemistry, computer), and analytical (e.g., experimental design and statistics) sciences. Some important technological tributaries include methods for storing seed or other propagules, the computer for data analysis and management, and tools or machines for conducting the many experiments and evaluating the progeny needed to create a superior cultivar. New tributaries include genomics, molecular biology, and genetic engineering. While the tributaries have varied with the nature of the crop species and the resources and goals of the societies they support, the primary roles of the plant breeder—integration, evaluation, and selection—have been constant.

Components and Challenges of Plant Breeding Programs

Plant breeding programs consist of several steps that are usually conducted as reiterative procedures:

1. hire talented and cooperative scientists (e.g., plant breeder, scientists in other disciplines, and technical staff)

2. understand the ecology of the plant, the target environment, the system of crop production, and the consumers

3. define the target environment for crop production (e.g., Where and how are the crops grown? What is the prevailing ecology therein?)

4. assemble and maintain the necessary physical resources

5. identify clear goals for selection regarding the type of cultivar, the traits, and their expression

6. select or create testing environments representative of the target environment

7. survey and choose germplasm to serve as parents and sources of genes (the crop and other species, cultivars, accessions [individual samples of seed] from germplasm reserves, and genes)

8. identify and create genetic variation among the parents and their progeny by evaluating the parents, mating the parents, and evaluating their progeny and occasionally by modifying the parents' genome or introducing genes through genetic engineering and transformation

9. evaluate and select the progeny that optimize production in the target environment.

When practiced on a continuous basis, these steps have achieved impressive results for several species and target environments.

Plant breeding programs negotiate numerous challenges along the path of improvement. The reproductive biology and growth habit of the plant are primary factors that dictate breeding methods, their implementation, progress from selection, and the type of cultivar (e.g., **hybrid**, pure line, clonal, **population**, or other). Some important considerations include the mode of reproduction (sexual, vegetative, or both), flower structure (perfect or imperfect), prevailing type of pollination (e.g., autogamous [self] or allogamous [other], wind, or insect), and methods to induce flowering, make controlled matings between the selected parents, and produce an adequate supply of progeny for evaluation and distribution. Considerations of the growth habit would include the length of the juvenile period (especially with trees) and if the species has an annual or perennial habit in the target environment.

The organization of the plant's genome also affects breeding strategy and the rate of progress. The plant genome is partitioned into the nucleus, mitochondrion (mt), and plastid (pt; e.g., chloroplast). The mt and pt genomes contain relatively few genes (hundreds) and in most **angiosperm** species are transmitted to the progeny exclusively through the cytoplasm of the female gametes (the egg cell in the embryo sac). The maternal inheritance of those genomes may dictate which parents are used as males and females. Plant nuclear genomes contain tens of thousands of genes as parts of several independent chromosomes, are inherited biparentally through the male (sperm nuclei in the generative cell of the pollen grain) and female gametes, and often contain more than two complete sets of chromosomes (polypoidy). For example, maize (*Zea mays* L.) and rice (*Oryza sativa* L.) are **diploid** because the nuclei of their somatic cells contain two complete sets of chromosomes, one each from the maternal and paternal parents. In contrast, cultivated alflalfa (*Medicago sativa* L.) and bread wheat (*Triticum aestivum* L.) are autotetraploid and allohexaploid because their somatic cells

hybrid a mix of two species

population a group of organisms of a single species that exist in the same region and interbreed

angiosperm a flowering plant

diploid having two sets of chromosomes, versus having one (haploid)

progenitor parent or ancestor

polyploidy having multiple sets of chromosomes

contain four (from the same species) and six (from three different **progenitor** species) complete sets of chromosomes, respectively. **Polyploidy** challenges breeders because it leads to more complex inheritance patterns and may hinder identification of desirable progeny in segregating populations.

The ecology of the target environment and the plant affect the evaluation and selection of parents and progeny in myriad ways (e.g., climate, soil, organic diversity, and the subsequent stress on crop production). The relative merit of the germplasm (e.g., parent, progeny, or cultivar) may vary greatly and depend upon certain elements of the environment (i.e., genotype and environment interaction, GxE). For example, a disease-resistant cultivar may have superior productivity when evaluated in a disease-laden environment but the same cultivar may be inferior when tested in a disease-free environment. GxE is a major challenge for every plant-breeding program because so many factors could influence the plant's growth and productivity during its life cycle. GxE is managed by testing germplasm in samples of relatively few environments and treatments intended to resemble the prevailing conditions of the target environment. Inadequate testing may result in a poor choice of genotypes, less genetic progress, and, sometimes, truly inferior cultivars.

Accomplishments of Plant Breeding Programs: Some Examples

Plant breeders have achieved some significant genetic modifications of plant species. Crop **domestication**, although unrecorded for most plants, provided the critical foundation for subsequent cycles of distribution, adaptation, mating, and selection. Some products of those cycles include rice and wheat of short stature and increased yield, beets (*Beta vulgaris* L.) with increased sucrose concentration, *Brassica napus* L.with edible oil, the forms of *Brassica oleracea* L. (e.g., cauliflower, cabbage, kale, broccoli, kohlrabi, and brussels sprouts), and high-yielding maize (corn). The achievements with rice and wheat (the Green Revolution) significantly enhanced food production for billions of persons and were partially recognized in 1970 when Norman Borlaug received a Nobel Prize for his role in developing and promoting new cultivars of wheat.

domesticate to tame an organism to live with and to be of use to humans

In the United States maize is an example of a crop that has been quickly and significantly modified through plant breeding. Maize is a tropical grass domesticated by central American natives, possibly from the wild relative teosinte (*Zea mexicana*). It was cultivated throughout the Americas before the colonization by Europeans, who adopted and expanded maize production. In the 1920s breeding methods changed dramatically: inbred lines (parents) were developed through generations of self-pollination and selection; the inbred lines were mated in specific combinations; many combinations were tested; a few combinations exhibited exceptional vigor and productivity; and the seed produced from selected matings was grown as the crop (i.e., the F1 or hybrid generation of the mating between the inbred lines). Previously, breeding methods in the United States emphasized selection of seed and individual plants produced through random, uncontrolled matings within locally adapted varieties and such open-pollinated seed was grown as the crop. In the 1930s farmers quickly substituted hybrid cultivars for the open-pollinated cultivars because the hybrids had higher and more consistent yield. Concomitantly, management practices changed. The average grain yield of maize increased from 30 to 120 bushels per acre from the 1930s to the 1990s. About 50 percent of the increase is due to genetic changes mediated by breeding for higher yield of grain, resistance to **biotic** and **abiotic** stress, and the ability to respond to more intensive management (e.g., increased application of fertilizer and seeding rates).

biotic involving or related to life

abiotic nonliving

Plant Breeding Programs and Germplasm Reserves. The target environment and societies' goals sometimes change in dynamic and unpredictable ways that render existing cultivars obsolete. Cultivars with improved adaptation may be bred if genetic variation (i.e., genes and combinations thereof) exists for the traits of interest. To manage this uncertainty, germplasm reserves or gene banks have been established worldwide with the primary goals of collecting and maintaining the broadest possible array of genetic variation for economically important plant species. In the United States a network of Plant Introduction Stations are financed by the federal and state governments to provide this service. The reserves are important because:

- the gene pool of existing cultivars represents only a subsample of the genetic variation for a given species

- favorable genes are certainly contained in other gene pools

- human activity has reduced the native gene pools of most crop species and their wild relatives in agricultural and natural settings

- the reserves have provided useful genes

- methods for investigating gene pools have been crude but there are good prospects for improvement

- our ability to engineer genes and complete organisms to meet the demands of crop production is woefully inadequate and will need all the help provided by nature. SEE ALSO BREEDER; CULTIVAR; GENETIC ENGINEERING; GREEN REVOLUTION; HYBRIDS AND HYBRIDIZATION; POLYPLOIDY; PROPAGATION; REPRODUCTION, SEXUAL; SEEDS.

Michael Lee

Bibliography

Crabb, Richard. *The Hybrid Corn-Makers.* Chicago, IL: West Chicago Publishing Company, 1993.

Fehr, Walter R. *Principles of Cultivar Development*, Vol. 1: *Theory and Technique.* New York: Macmillan, 1991.

Sauer, Jonathan D. *Historical Geography of Crop Plants: A Select Roster.* Boca Raton, FL: CRC Press, 1993.

Smartt, J. and N. W. Simmonds. *Evolution of Crop Plants.* Essex, England: Longman Scientific & Technical, 1995.

Wallace, Henry Agard, and William L. Brown. *Corn and Its Early Fathers.* Ames, IA: Iowa State University Press, 1988.

Breeding Systems

Breeding systems in plants refer to the variety of ways plants answer the general question of "Who mates with whom" by answering specific questions such as whether flowers mature at the same time, whether a plant has more than one kind of flower or differs from other plants in types of flow-

Wind blows pollen off the male cone of a pine tree.

ers, and whether there are chemicals that keep certain plants from mating with each other.

Outcrossing and Inbreeding

Most vertebrate species consist of separate male and female individuals. In contrast, the majority of flowering plants are hermaphroditic, with both pollen and ovules produced by the same plant. As a consequence, many flowering plants are capable of self-fertilization (selfing), with seeds resulting from pollen and eggs produced by the same plant. The self pollen that fertilizes the egg may be produced by the same flower (called autogamy) or by different flowers on the same plant (geitonogamy). Selfing or mating among close relatives (inbreeding) often results in offspring that have reduced vigor and produce fewer offspring compared to offspring from matings between unrelated plants (outcrossing). This reduction in fitness of selfed offspring relative to outcrossed offspring is referred to as inbreeding depression. If both selfing levels and levels of inbreeding depression are high, natural selection may favor mechanisms that promote outcrossing. High levels of inbreeding depression are likely to be found in populations that have been outcrossing for a long time. In contrast, in populations that have been inbreeding (high selfing rates) for many generations, inbreeding depression levels may now be low because harmful genes have already been eliminated from the population by natural selection.

Selfing may also have direct advantages. Selfing plants may have an *automatic selection advantage* and contribute more genes to the next generation because they contribute both maternal genes (through the egg) and paternal genes (through pollen) to selfed seeds, and they also contribute pollen (and thus paternal genes) to other plants, spreading their genes further. In contrast, outcrossing plants contribute pollen to other plants, but only maternal genes to their own seeds. This automatic selection advantage will lead to selection for selfing if selfing does not decrease outcrossing (thereby limiting the spread of genes), and if inbreeding depression is not too severe. In addition, selfing tends to produce offspring more similar to the parent plant than outcrossing. If seeds are dispersed locally into habitat similar to that of the parent, these selfed offspring may do better than outcrossed offspring. In habitats where pollen is limited because of low population density or because there are few pollinators, selfing may also provide *reproductive assurance* with a guaranteed source of pollen. Some plants, such as touch-me-not (*Impatiens*) and some violet species (*Viola*) have evolved flowers that are pollinated autogamously and never open (called cleistogamy), as well as the more showy open flowers (chasmogamy).

Heterostyly

Several factors may promote outcrossing, including separation of male and female function in time or space. In **heterostylous** plants such as the primrose (*Primula*) described by English naturalist Charles Darwin (1809–1882), there are two floral forms (distyly). In one form, pin flowers have long styles and short stamens. Thrum flowers have short styles and long stamens. This positioning favors outcrossing with transfer of pollen between the pin and thrum plants by pollinators.

heterostylous having styles (female flower parts) of different lengths, to aid cross-pollination

Dichogamy

In dichogamy, pollen is released and the stigma is receptive (ready to receive pollen) at different times. There are two types: in protandry ("early male"), the pollen is shed before the stigmas are receptive, while in protogyny ("early female"), the stigmas are receptive before the pollen is shed. Even greater outcrossing is promoted by synchronizing all of the flowers on the plant for the same sex, so that all stigmas are receptive together, either before or after all pollen is shed.

Dioecy

Spatial separation of the sexes onto different flowers or different plants may also promote outcrossing. An individual flower may have only stamens (male) or only **pistils** (female), or both (hermaphroditic) in the same flower, and plants and populations may have various combinations of flowers. Monoecious ("one house") populations have both sexes of unisexual flowers on each plant (e.g., corn has tassels of male flowers and an ear of female flowers on the same plant). Gynodioecious populations, consisting of female and hermaphroditic plants, are also possible. Dioecious ("two-house") populations consist of male-only and female-only plants (e.g., marijuana, or *Cannabis*). Dioecy has arisen independently in the flowering plants many times. About 6 percent of flowering plant species are dioecious, and the incidence of dioecy is particularly high in the Hawaiian Islands (14.7 percent) and in New Zealand (12 to 13 percent). Flowering plants also have more complicated patterns of sex expression, and some plants are even capable of switching sex through time.

pistil the female reproduction organ

Two major theories have been proposed to explain the evolution of dioecy. One theory suggests that dioecy has evolved as a mechanism to avoid inbreeding depression and enforce outcrossing between unisexual plants. The other theory suggests that patterns of resource allocation between male and female function (sex allocation) are critical. According to this theory, dioecy should evolve from hermaphroditism when greater investment of resources in flowers of one sex yields a disproportionate gain in reproductive

success. In such cases, it would be advantageous to separate the sexes to allow more efficient resource allocation.

Self-incompatibility

Even without spatial or temporal (time-related) separation, chemical incompatibility between the stigma or style and pollen of the same plant can also promote outcrossing. Molecular data suggest that self-compatibility is the ancestral condition in flowering plants and that self-incompatibility has evolved independently many times. In plants such as tobacco (*Nicotiana*) that have **gametophytic** self-incompatibility (GSI), pollen tubes germinate but fail to grow through the style if they are chemically incompatible. In GSI, the incompatibility reaction is determined by the combination of the self-incompatibility (SI) genes of the maternal plant and the SI genes of the pollen grain. GSI is found in several species, including tobacco and some grasses.

In sporophytic self-incompatibility (SSI), the incompatibility reaction is controlled by the combination of maternal plant SI genes in the stigma and the SI genes of the plant that produced the pollen, rather than those of the pollen grain itself. Incompatible reactions cause the pollen tube to stop growing on or near the stigma. Multi-allelic SSI systems have many incompatibility types, and proteins that cause the incompatibility reaction are produced by the anthers and are present in the outer layer of the pollen grain. Broccoli and many other members of the mustard family (Brassicaceae) have multi-allelic SSI.

In contrast, many plants with SSI have only two or three incompatibility types, but are heterostylous (e.g., shamrock [*Oxalis*], and water hyacinth [*Eichhornia*], a noxious, invasive aquatic weed). SEE ALSO FLOWERS; POLLINATION BIOLOGY; REPRODUCTION, ASEXUAL; REPRODUCTION, FERTILIZATION AND; REPRODUCTION, SEXUAL; SEED DISPERSAL.

Ann K. Sakai

gametophyte the haploid organism in the life cycle

Bibliography

Bertin, Robert I. "Pollination Biology." In *Plant-Animal Interactions.* Warren G. Abrahamson, ed. New York: McGraw-Hill, 1989.

Briggs, D., and S. M. Walters. *Plant Variation and Evolution,* 3rd ed. Cambridge, UK: Cambridge University Press, 1997.

Sakai, Ann K., and Stephen G. Weller. "Gender and Sexual Dimorphism in Flowering Plants: A Review of Terminology, Biogeographic Patterns, Ecological Correlates, and Phylogenetic Approaches." In *Sexual and Gender Dimorphism in Flowering Plants,* eds. Monica A. Geber, Todd E. Dawson, and Lynda F. Delph. Heidelberg: Springer-Verlag, 1999.

Britton, Nathaniel

American Botanist
1859–1934

Nathaniel Lord Britton was an American botanist who helped found the New York Botanical Garden and build it into a premier research institution. Britton was born in 1859 in Staten Island, New York, and received both his undergraduate and graduate degrees in geology and mining engineering from Columbia University. His professional interest in botany began while he was working for the New Jersey Geologic Survey, during which time he prepared a list of plants found in the state. He became a professor at Columbia, first in geology and later in botany. In 1885 he married Elizabeth Knight, one of the foremost **bryologists** in the country.

Britton and his wife were inspired by a visit to the Royal Botanic Gardens at Kew, England, and returned in 1891 to the United States to begin planning for what would become the New York Botanical Garden. Britton was its first director, a post he held until his retirement in 1929. Through his administrative skill, scholarship, energy, and force of personality, Britton built the garden into a world-class center for research in plant taxonomy, and the finest botanical garden in the country.

Britton was a prolific author, writing hundreds of scientific papers and several important books. He was the principal author of the *Illustrated Flora* of the northeastern United States, a text that was at one time the major guide to the plants of this region. He published many papers on the flora of the West Indies, and was coauthor of *The Cactaceae of the World*. A large number of **genera** of flowering plants bear his name, as does *Brittonia*, a major journal of American plant taxonomy published by the New York Botanical Garden.

Britton undertook a major revision of the nomenclature of the plants of North America, creating the American Code of Botanical Nomenclature in 1892. Britton meant this system to replace the International Code used widely at that time. Although most major research institutions did not adopt his system, the U.S. Department of Agriculture did, assuring it a prolonged life, if not widespread use. The American Code, however, fell further and further out of favor after Britton's death in 1934, and is no longer used today. SEE ALSO BOTANICAL GARDENS AND ARBORETA; CURATOR OF A BOTANICAL GARDEN; TAXONOMIST; TAXONOMY; TAXONOMY, HISTORY OF.

Richard Robinson

Bibliography

Isely, Duane. *One Hundred and One Botanists*. Ames, IA: Iowa State Univeristy Press, 1994.

bryologist someone who studies bryophytes, a division of nonflowering plants

genera plural of genus

Brongniart, Adolphe

French Paleobotanist
1801–1876

Adolphe Brongniart is considered to be the founder of French paleobotany (the study of fossil plants), but his influence and that of his family extends far beyond the borders of France. Born 1801 in Sèvres, France, where his father ran a porcelain factory, Adolphe came from a very well-known family. His grandfather, Alexandre-Théodore Brongniart, was a respected architect who designed the Bourse (the Paris Stock Exchange); his father, Alexandre Brongniart (1770–1847), and Georges Cuvier (1769–1832) are considered the fathers of **stratigraphic geology**. They developed geologic mapping on a scale that could be both interpretive and predictive, and were pioneers in using fossils to determine the age of rocks.

stratigraphic geology the study of rock layers

Adolphe greatly benefited from his father's wide-ranging interests. Before he was twenty, they had traveled together to many areas of the continent, including western France, the Jura Mountains, Switzerland, and Italy. In 1824 and 1825 they visited Scandinavia and the British Isles. These trips focused on botany, geology, or both, so that Adolphe was exposed to fossil plants from a variety of places while still relatively young, giving him a more global view of fossil floras than many scientists of his day.

In 1822 Adolphe Brongniart published his initial classification of all fossil plants then known, a system that was also adopted for the living plants in the Museum of Natural History in Paris. In 1828 he published the first of two volumes of a more complete description of the fossil plants of the world, *Histoire des Végétaux Fossiles.* At the age of twenty-five, he received a doctor of medicine degree with a thesis on the living plant family Rhamnaceae (the buckthorn family). He was already known for his research on fossil plants at this time. In 1831 he was appointed as a naturalist aide at the museum and two years later became a professor of botany there. More than any other interest, paleobotany occupied him until he died.

silicified composed of silicate minerals

Although Brongniart published numerous works on compression fossils (thin, carbonaceous films on the rock surface), he is equally well known for his studies of internal anatomy in ancient plants. One of his first papers on this subject was on Carboniferous ferns and was published in 1837. Brongniart used comparative anatomy of fossil and living plants to better understand the classification of the fossils and was clearly a pioneer in the area of using thin sections to study the internal structure of fossil plants. His study of the structure of **silicified** Carboniferous seeds, *Recherches sur les Graines silicifiées du Terrain houiller de St.-Etienne* (1881), has been called a model of comparative anatomy of fossil plants. Unfinished at his death in 1876, the book was published posthumously.

Adolphe Brongniart was the first to publish a classification of all known fossil plants and pioneered the use of comparative anatomy in the study of plant fossils. Because of his broad knowledge of fossil plants from many regions, he was able to recognize a distinct succession of floras through time and regularly correlated fossils with particular rocks (biostratigraphy). Finally, Brongniart was probably the first to spend his life working in paleobotany as a primary pursuit and not just as a sideline to medicine or business, making him the first professional paleobotanist in history. SEE ALSO EVOLUTION OF PLANTS; EVOLUTION OF PLANTS, HISTORY OF; TAXONOMY.

Edith L. Taylor and Thomas N. Taylor

Bibliography

Andrews, H. N. *The Fossil Hunters: In Search of Ancient Plants.* Ithaca, NY: Cornell University Press, 1980.

Bryophytes

vascular related to transport of nutrients

epiphytes plants that grow on other plants

Plant scientists recognize two kinds of land plants: bryophytes (nonvascular land plants) and tracheophytes (**vascular** land plants). Bryophytes are small, herbaceous plants that grow closely packed together in mats or cushions on rocks or soil or as **epiphytes** on the trunks and leaves of forest trees.

Bryophytes are distinguished from tracheophytes by two important characteristics. First, in all bryophytes the ecologically persistent, photosynthetic phase of the life cycle is the **haploid, gametophyte** generation rather than the **diploid sporophyte**; bryophyte sporophytes are very short-lived, are attached to and nutritionally dependent on their gametophytes, and consist of only an unbranched stalk, or seta, and a single, terminal sporangium. Second, bryophytes never form xylem tissue, the special lignin-containing, water-conducting tissue that is found in the sporophytes of all vascular plants. At one time, all bryophytes were placed in a single phylum, intermediate in position between algae and vascular plants. Modern studies of cell **ultrastructure** and molecular biology, however, confirm that bryophytes comprise three separate evolutionary **lineages**, today recognized as mosses (phylum Bryophyta), liverworts (phylum Marchantiophyta), and hornworts (phylum Anthocerotophyta). Following a detailed analysis of land plant relationships, Paul Kenrick and Peter R. Crane proposed that the three groups of bryophytes represent a structural level in plant evolution, identified by their monosporangiate life cycle. Within the bryophytes, liverworts are the geologically oldest group, sharing a fossil record with the oldest vascular plants (Rhyniophytes) in the Devonian era.

Mosses

Of the three phyla of bryophytes, greatest species diversity is found in the mosses, with up to fifteen thousand species recognized. A moss begins its life cycle when haploid spores, which are produced in the sporophyte capsule, land on a moist **substrate** and begin to germinate. From the one-celled spore a highly branched system of **filaments**, called the protonema, develops. Cell specialization occurs within the protonema to form a horizontal system of reddish-brown anchoring filaments and upright green filaments. Each protonema, which superficially resembles a **filamentous** alga, can spread over several centimeters to form a fuzzy green film over its substrate. As the protonema grows, some cells of the specialized green filaments form leafy buds that will ultimately form the adult gametophyte shoots. Numerous shoots typically develop from each protonema so that, in fact, a single spore can give rise to a whole clump of moss plants. Each leafy shoot continues to grow **apically**, producing leaves in spiral arrangement on an elongating stem. In many mosses the stem is differentiated into a central strand of thin-walled water-conducting cells, called hydroids, surrounded by a **parenchymatous** cortex and a thick-walled epidermis. The leaves taper from a broad base to a pointed apex and have lamina that are only one-cell-layer thick. A hydroid-containing midvein often extends from the stem into the leaf. Near the base of the shoot, reddish-brown multicellular rhizoids emerge from the stem to anchor the moss to its substrate. Water and mineral nutrients required for the moss to grow are absorbed, not by the rhizoids, but rather by the thin leaves of the plant as rain water washes through the moss cushion.

As is typical of bryophytes, mosses produce large, multicellular sex organs for reproduction. Many bryophytes are unisexual, or sexually **dioicous**. In mosses male sex organs, called antheridia, are produced in clusters at the tips of shoots or branches on the male plants; female sex organs, the archegonia, are produced in similar fashion on female plants. Numerous motile sperm are produced by **mitosis** inside the brightly colored, club-shaped an-

haploid having one set of chromosomes, versus having two (diploid)

gametophyte the haploid organism in the life cycle

diploid having two sets of chromosomes, versus having one (haploid)

sporophyte the diploid, spore-producing individual in the plant life cycle

ultrastructural the level of structure visible with the electron microscope; very small details of structure

lineage ancestry; the line of evolutionary descent of an organism

substrate the physical structure to which an organism attaches

filament a threadlike extension

filamentous thin and long

apically at the tip

parenchyma thin-walled cells of various sizes

dioicous having male and female sexual parts on different plants

mitosis the part of the cell cycle in which chromosomes are separated to give each daughter cell an identical chromosome set

DISTINGUISHING CHARACTERISTICS OF MOSSES, LIVERWORTS, AND HORNWORTS

Characteristics	Mosses (Bryophyta)	Liverworts (Marchantiophyta)	Hornworts (Anthocerotophyta)
Protonema	Filamentous, forming many buds	Globose, forming one bud	Globose, forming one bud
Gametophyte form	Leafy shoot	Leafy shoot or thallus; thallus simple or with air chambers	Simple thallus
Leaf arrangement	Leaves in spirals	Leaves in three rows	Not Applicable
Leaf form	Leaves undivided, midvein present	Leaves divided into two-plus lobes, no midvein	Not Applicable
Special organelles	None	Oil bodies	Single plastids with pyrenoids
Water-conducting cells	Present in both gametophyte and sporophyte	Present only in a few simple thalloid forms	Absent
Rhizoids	Brown, multicellular	Hyaline, one-celled	Hyaline, one-celled
Gametangial position	Apical clusters (leafy forms)	Apical clusters (leafy forms) or on upper surface of thallus	Sunken in thallus, scattered
Stomates	Present on sporophyte capsule	Absent in both generations	Present in both sporophyte and gametophyte
Seta	Photosynthetic, emergent from gametophyte early in development	Hyaline, elongating just prior to spore release	Absent
Capsule	Complex with operculum, theca, and neck; of fixed size	Undifferentiated, spherical, or elongate; of fixed size	Undifferentiated, horn-shaped; growing continuously from a basal meristem
Sterile cells in capsule	Columella	Spirally thickened elaters	Columella and pseudoelaters
Capsule dehiscence	At operculum and peristome teeth	Into four valves	Into two valves

flagellae threadlike extensions of the cell membrane, used for movement

ephemeral short-lived

theridia while a single egg develops in the base of each vase-shaped archegonium. As the sperm mature, the antheridium swells and bursts open. Drops of rainwater falling into the cluster of open antheridia splash the sperm to nearby females. Beating their two whiplash **flagellae**, the sperm are able to move short distances in the water film that covers the plants to the open necks of the archegonia. Slimy mucilage secretions in the archegonial neck help pull the sperm downward to the egg. The closely packed arrangement of the individual moss plants greatly facilitates fertilization. Rain forest bryophytes that hang in long festoons from the trees rely on torrential winds with the rain to transport their sperm from tree to tree, while the small pygmy mosses of exposed, **ephemeral** habitats depend on the drops of morning dew to move their sperm. Regardless of where they grow, all bryophytes require water for sperm dispersal and subsequent fertilization.

Embryonic growth of the sporophyte begins within the archegonium soon after fertilization. At its base, or foot, the growing embryo forms a nutrient transfer zone, or placenta, with the gametophyte. Both organic nutrients and water move from the gametophyte into the sporophyte as it continues to grow. In mosses the sporophyte stalk, or seta, tears the archegonial enclosure early in development, leaving only the foot and the very base of the seta embedded in the gametophyte. The upper part of the archegonium remains over the tip of the sporophyte as a caplike calyptra. Sporophyte growth ends with the formation of a sporangium (the capsule) at the tip of the seta. Within the capsule, water-resistant haploid spores are formed by meiosis. As the mature capsule swells, the calyptra falls away. This allows the capsule to dry and break open at its tip when the spores are mature. Special membranous structures, called peristome teeth, that are folded down into the spore mass now bend outward, flinging the spores into the drying

The bryophyte common liverwort (*Marchantia polymorpha*).

winds. Moss spores can travel great distances on the winds, even moving between continents on the jet streams. Their walls are highly protective, allowing some spores to remain **viable** for up to forty years. Of course, if the spore lands in a suitable, moist habitat, germination will begin the cycle all over again.

viable able to live or to function

Liverworts and Hornworts

Liverworts and hornworts are like mosses in the fundamental features of their life cycle, but differ greatly in organization of their mature gametophytes and sporophytes. Liverwort gametophytes can be either leafy shoots or flattened **thalli**. In the leafy forms the leaves are arranged on the stem in one ventral and two **lateral** rows or ranks, rather than in spirals like the mosses. The leaves are one cell-layer thick throughout, never have a midvein, and are usually divided into two or more parts called lobes. The ventral leaves, which actually lie against the substrate (soil or other support), are usually much smaller than the lateral leaves and are hidden by the stem. Anchoring rhizoids, which arise near the ventral leaves, are colorless and unicellular. The flattened ribbonlike to leaflike thallus of the thallose liverworts can be either simple or structurally differentiated into a system of dorsal air chambers and ventral storage tissues. In the latter type the dorsal epidermis of the thallus is punctuated with scattered pores that open into the air chambers. Liverworts synthesize a vast array of volatile oils, which they store in unique **organelles** called oil bodies. These **compounds** impart an often spicy aroma to the plants and seem to discourage animals from feeding on them. Many of these compounds have potential as antimicrobial or anticancer pharmaceuticals.

thallus simple, flattened, nonleafy plant body

lateral away from the center

organelle a membrane-bound structure within a cell

compound a substance formed from two or more elements

Liverworts. Liverwort sporophytes develop completely enclosed within gametophyte tissues until their capsules are ready to open. The seta, which is initially very short, consists of small, thin-walled hyaline cells. Just prior to capsule opening, the seta cells lengthen, thereby increasing the length of the seta up to twenty times its original dimensions. This rapid elongation

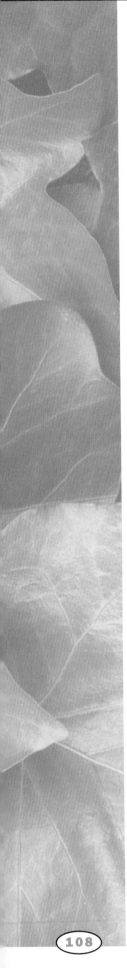

sterile not capable or involved in reproduction

symbiosis a relationship between two organisms from which each derives benefit

cyanobacteria photosynthetic prokaryotic bacteria formerly known as blue-green algae

chloroplast the photosynthetic organelle of plants and algae

meristem the growing tip of a plant

montane growing in a mountainous region

community a group of organisms of different species living in a region

pushes the darkly pigmented capsule and upper part of the whitish seta out of the gametophytic tissues. With drying, the capsule opens by splitting into four segments, or valves. The spores are dispersed into the winds by the twisting motions of numerous intermixed **sterile** cells called elaters. In contrast to mosses, which disperse their spores over several days, liverworts disperse the entire spore mass of a single capsule in just a few minutes.

Hornworts. Hornworts resemble some liverworts in having simple, unspecialized thalloid gametophytes, but they differ in many other characters. For example, colonies of the **symbiotic cyanobacterium** *Nostoc* fill small cavities that are scattered throughout the ventral part of the hornwort thallus. When the thallus is viewed from above, these colonies appear as scattered blue-green dots. The cyanobacterium converts nitrogen gas from the air into ammonium, which the hornwort requires in its metabolism, and the hornwort secretes carbohydrate-containing mucilage, which supports the growth of the cyanobacterium. Hornworts also differ from all other land plants in having only one large, algal-like **chloroplast** in each thallus cell. Hornworts get their name from their long, horn-shaped sporophytes. As in other bryophytes, the sporophyte is anchored in the gametophyte by a foot through which nutrient transfer from gametophyte to sporophyte occurs. The rest of the sporophyte, however, is actually an elongate sporangium in which meiosis and spore development take place. At the base of the sporangium, just above the foot, is a mitotically active **meristem**, which adds new cells to the spore-producing zone throughout the life span of the sporophyte. In fact, the sporangium can be releasing spores at its apex at the same time that new spores are being produced by meiosis at its base. Spore release in hornworts takes place gradually over a long period of time, and the spores are mostly dispersed by water movements rather than by wind.

Mosses, liverworts, and hornworts are found throughout the world in a variety of habitats. They flourish particularly well in moist, humid forests like the fog forests of the Pacific Northwest or the **montane** rain forests of the Southern Hemisphere. Their ecological roles are many. They provide seed beds for the larger plants of the **community**, they capture and recycle nutrients that are washed with rainwater from the canopy, and they bind the soil to keep it from eroding. In the Northern Hemisphere peatlands, wetlands often dominated by the moss *Sphagnum*, are particularly important bryophyte communities. This moss has exceptional water-holding capacity, and when dried and compressed forms a coal-like fuel. Throughout northern Europe, Asia, and North America, peat has been harvested for centuries for both fuel consumption and horticultural uses, and today peat lands are managed as a sustainable resource. SEE ALSO EVOLUTION OF PLANTS; GAMETOPHYTE; NITROGEN FIXATION; PEAT BOGS; REPRODUCTION, ALTERNATION OF GENERATIONS AND; SPOROPHYTE.

Barbara Crandall-Stotler

Bibliography

Crandall-Stotler, Barbara. "Morphogenetic Designs and a Theory of Bryophyte Origins and Divergence." *BioScience* 30 (1980): 580–85.

Hébant, Charles. *The Conducting Tissues of Bryophytes.* Vaduz: J. Cramer, 1977.

Kenrick, Paul, and Peter R. Crane. *The Origin and Early Diversification of Land Plants: A Cladistic Study.* Washington, DC: Smithsonian Institution Press, 1997.

Miller, Norton G. "Bogs, Bales and BTUs: A Primer on Peat." *Horticulture* 59 (1981): 38–45.

Schofield, W. B. *Introduction to Bryology*. New York: Macmillan, 1985.

Shaw, Jonathon A., and Bernard Goffinet, eds. *The Biology of Bryophytes*. Cambridge, England: Cambridge University Press, 2000.

Burbank, Luther

American Horticulturist
1849–1926

Luther Burbank was the most well-known plant breeder of the Age of Agriculture. He was born March 7, 1849, in Lancaster, Massachusetts. He had little formal science training, but his efforts to better the human condition by improving useful plants made him a folk hero throughout the world. Burbank's work is said to have advanced the science of horticulture by several decades.

Burbank's first, and foremost, contribution is evidenced with every baked potato and french fry eaten today. At the age of twenty-four, Burbank discovered a seed ball on the normally **sterile** Early Rose potato. Inspired by English naturalist Charles Darwin's *The Variation of Animals and Plants Under Domestication*, Burbank cultivated these seeds and used them to "build" the first white potato, the basis for the modern Burbank Russet Idaho potatoes.

In 1875, with $150 in proceeds from the sale of most of his potato stock, Burbank journeyed by train to California in search of a suitable climate for year-round **cultivation**. Burbank saw greater potential in the soil and climate of the state than in its famed gold mines. After a few rough years, Burbank was able to establish himself in Santa Rosa as a **nurseryman** who tried, and usually delivered, the impossible. After fulfilling an order for twenty thousand bearing prune trees from seed in nine months, Burbank earned a reputation as one who could succeed where others feared to try.

In 1893 Burbank's "New Creations in Fruits and Flowers" catalog created an international sensation, causing some to object that Burbank claimed powers of creation reserved only for God. Burbank believed that his plants were inventions that were developed in concert with God's agent: nature.

At his nursery, greenhouses, and experimental gardens, Burbank specialized in horticultural novelties, working on an at-demand basis for nurserymen. At any one time, Burbank might have tens of thousands of plants in cultivation and hundreds (perhaps thousands) of experiments in progress.

Burbank worked with flowers, fruits, trees, cacti, grasses, grains, and vegetables. His long-running experiments and his keen awareness of the correlation of nascent plant features with desirable traits in mature plants, helped him introduce or develop more than eight hundred varieties throughout his fifty-year career—that's a new plant every twenty-three days.

Among the many varieties he developed several are still widely used today: the Paradox Walnut (*Juglans Regina x J. Californica var.*), developed as a fast-growing hardwood tree for the furniture industry, today the most com-

Luther Burbank.

sterile not capable or involved in reproduction

cultivation growth of crop plants, or turning the soil for this purpose

nurseryman a worker in a plant nursery

complex hybrid
hybridized plant with more than two parent plants

quadruple hybrid
hybridized plant with four parents

mon rootstock for walnuts; the 1906, Santa Rosa plum, a **complex hybrid,** still among the most cultivated varieties in the United States; and the **quadruple hybrid** Shasta daisy (*Chrysanthemum leucanthemum hybridum*), introduced in 1901, one of the most popular flowers in cutting gardens today.

Some of Burbank's more unusual novelties include: more than thirty-five varieties of spineless cacti for improved fruit and better forage for livestock; the plumcot, the first creation of an entirely new stone fruit; and the white blackberry, a flavorful berry without pigment to stain hands and clothing.

Burbank's methods were not unique, but he applied them on a greater scale than previously known. A wider range of experimental varieties, a longer period of study, and a greater number of experiments underway at a given time gave Burbank an unmatched breadth of experience and genetic variability from which to work. Using space- and time-saving methods such as grafting (sometimes hundreds of varieties on one nurse tree) and budding allowed him to grow several million plants during his career.

Burbank imposed environmental changes and numerous cross-fertilizations on imported plants from across the globe to induce as many perturbations or variants as possible. From the most promising plants Burbank continued to select, hybridize, reselect, and rehybridize for several generations until he developed a marketable plant.

He employed all of his senses to judge the worthiness of his creations. His criteria for success included both attractiveness and utility. "The urge to beauty," according to Burbank, "is as important as the urge to bread." (Explanation: Beauty is as fundamental as bread.)

Although Burbank had little formal scientific training in his early years, he enjoyed the friendship and support of many leading scientists. Favorable impressions of his work led to a prestigious and lucrative five-year Carnegie Foundation grant. His brand of applied scientific practice and the increasingly astounding accounts of his new creations, however, provoked scientists' ire as well as imagination.

Burbank believed heredity and environmental circumstances governed a plant's "life force." He asserted, as did French naturalist Jean-Baptiste Lamarck (1744–1829), that acquired characteristics (accrued forces) were inheritable, a position that became increasingly unacceptable in the scientific world. He felt that many of the mutations heralded by ever more popular Mendalians were simply hybrids.

As his career progressed, Burbank became as well known for his unorthodox social and religious beliefs as for his plant developments. In 1907 he wrote a book entitled *The Training of the Human Plant* that advocated that children should learn from natural surroundings until the age of ten, foregoing formal schooling. Burbank stated publicly that he felt himself to have supernatural powers.

Just before his death in 1926, Burbank was quoted in an article as proclaiming himself an "infidel," like Christ, a man who did not believe in traditional religion. This caused a firestorm of debate across the country. Burbank later clarified his meaning on national radio, "I am a lover of man and of Christ as a man and his work, and all things that help humanity. . . . I prefer and claim the right to worship the infinite, everlasting, almighty God of this vast universe as revealed to us gradually, step by step, by the demonstrable truths of our savior, science."

Burbank groomed no successors to his work. Although Burbank kept copious notes, he did not have the protection of plant patent laws, and he was protective of his practices. His efforts to institute such laws eventually encouraged their passage, but not until after his death. For years, despite his secretiveness, Burbank allowed visitors who paid admission to see his experiments. In 1905 a one-hour visit to the Sebastopol, California, experiment farm cost $10.

Burbank was twice married but had no children. He was laid to rest under a cedar of Lebanon tree he had planted from seed in front of his original home place. In death, he said, he should like to feel that his strength was flowing into the strength of the tree.

Burbank's birthday continues to be celebrated as Arbor Day in California. His legacy lives on in the form of hundreds of useful plants that benefit the world today and in his example of a man who lived a life true to his beliefs. SEE ALSO AGRICULTURE, HISTORY OF; BREEDER; BREEDING; HYBRIDS AND HYBRIDIZATION.

Rebecca Baker

Bibliography

Dreyer, Peter. *A Gardener Touched with Genius: The Life of Luther Burbank*. Santa Rosa, CA: Luther Burbank Home and Gardens, City of Santa Rosa, 1985.

Jordan, David Starr, and Vernon L. Kellogg. *The Scientific Aspects of Luther Burbank's Work*. San Francisco: American Robertson, 1909.

Williams, Henry Smith, et al., eds. *Luther Burbank: His Methods and Discoveries and Their Practical Application*. Santa Rosa, CA: Luther Burbank Press, 1915.

Cacao

As currency, beverage, and divine plant, cacao (*Theobroma cacao*, family Sterculiaceae) has played an important role in ancient Central American cultures. To the Mayans, the plant was a gift from their gods—implied in the name *Theobroma*, Latin for "food of the gods." The dried seeds were important in Aztec society as a unit of currency (used in the Yucatan Peninsula until the 1850s), and as part of a drink reserved for the nobility. Today, cacao is probably best known for the sweet, rich food produced from the seeds called chocolate.

Cacao is typically a small- to medium-sized deciduous tree of the New World tropical forests. The small, cream-colored flowers are produced directly from the woody trunks and branches of the tree, not in the leaf axils, where most other flowering plants produce flowers. Following pollination, pods are produced, ranging in color from green through yellow to red-brown. Each pod contains between twenty and sixty seeds that are surrounded by a thick, whitish pulp. Seed dispersal in the wild is usually by monkeys.

Although presently distributed throughout Central America due to migration and dispersal by the Mayans, cacao is thought to have its origin in the eastern Andes. **Cultivation** has led to the production of two

cultivation growth of crop plants

111

A harvester in Ecuador selects the seeds from cacao pods to use in making chocolate.

forms of cacao: *Criollo*, from Central America, and *Forastero*, from South America. *Trinitario* is a form produced by breeding criollo and forastero types. At the turn of the twenty-first century, cacao is grown commercially in parts of West Africa, Malaysia, Brazil, Central America, and parts of Mexico.

Processing Cacao

The process of producing chocolate from cacao seeds is complex. Following harvesting, ripe pods are opened, the seeds removed, and the pulp scraped away from the seeds. At this point, the light-brown seeds have no discernible chocolate taste. Piles of cleaned seeds are allowed to ferment for up to one week, during which time the chocolate flavor begins to develop as polyphenols start to break down. During the fermentation process, the embryos of the seeds are killed and any remaining pulp is broken down. The color of the seeds also changes to purple. Following fermentation, the seeds are dried, sorted, and shipped to processing factories.

At the processing factory, roasting the seeds removes any remaining water and acids and allows the chocolate flavor to develop. Roasting is done at 121°C for seeds used to produce chocolate, higher for cocoa powder. The roasted seeds are then cracked and the seed coats removed, leaving the cotyledons (known as chocolate nibs), which are then ground using rollers.

During the grinding process, sufficient heat is generated to melt fats in the chocolate nibs, producing a fine paste called chocolate liquor. Baking chocolate is molded, set chocolate liquor. Subjecting the nibs to high pressure prior to grinding removes up to 30 percent of the fats and yields a dry cocoa powder. The fats are called cocoa butter, and they may be used later in the production procedure. Most chocolate is treated with alkalis to neutralize organic acids that are still present in the chocolate. This process, called dutching, produces a mild, dark chocolate.

Milk chocolate is produced by adding condensed milk to chocolate liquor. Stirring the chocolate results in very finely ground cacao particles, which yields a very smooth chocolate. Finally, the addition of extra cocoa butter produces some of the smoothest and creamiest of chocolates.

Chocolate acts as a mild stimulant due to the presence of the alkaloids theobromine, caffeine, and theophylline. The caffeine can be extracted from the discarded seed coats and used in drinks and medicines; extracted theobromine can also be chemically converted into caffeine. SEE ALSO ALKALOIDS; ECONOMIC IMPORTANCE OF PLANTS.

Charles A. Butterworth

Cacti

The members of family Cactaceae are a group of dicotyledonous flowering plants that are primarily native to various dry or seasonally dry habitats in North and South America. Due to the presence of specialized fleshy stems, they are classified as stem succulents. Leaves are not produced in most species, although there are some leafy species in a few genera. There are more than sixteen hundred species of cacti, which are contained in approximately one hundred genera. All cacti share the unique **morphological** features of having most, if not all, of their secondary stems condensed into structures called areoles. These are the places on the stems from which the spines develop. Spines are modified leaves that have become hardened and sharp, thereby providing protection for the plants from **herbivores** in addition to providing some shade to the stems.

morphological related to shape

herbivore an organism that feeds on plant parts

Morphological Adaptations

The plant body of a typical cactus is composed of one or more stem segments that are succulent—that is, having water storage tissue (parenchyma) in their central portions—and a photosynthetic outer skin that is covered by a thickened epidermis and a thick layer of waxy **cuticle**. At various places upon these stem segments are areoles from which both spines and flowers arise. In some columnar and barrel cacti, the stems have developed ribs that assist the plant by providing more surface area to encour-

cuticle the waxy outer coating of a leaf or other structure, providing protection against predators, infection, and water loss

113

Saguaro cacti in the Sonoran Desert of Arizona.

xerophytes plants adapted for growth in dry areas

crassulacean acid metabolism a water-conserving strategy used by several types of plants

biomass the total dry weight of an organism or group of organisms

age heat loss, to accommodate rapid stem diameter increases following uptake of large amounts of water during rare rain events, and to provide shade in some species. Almost all cacti are **xerophytes** and have evolved adaptations to conserve water that is typically scarce in the habitats they occupy. These anatomical adaptations, in addition to the evolution of **crassulacean acid metabolism** for carbon fixation, have enabled the cacti to flourish in otherwise inhospitable habitats. Some cacti have even become geophytic, with the largest portions of their **biomass** below ground, where they store water in enlarged roots; the aboveground photosynthetic stems are small by comparison.

Geographic Distribution and Ecological Role

Cacti are widely distributed throughout both North and South America, having maximal centers of diversity in the Sonoran and Chihuahuan Deserts of North America, the central Andean region (including Chile, Argentina, Bolivia, and Peru), and the dry scrub forests of eastern Brazil (the Caatinga) in South America. In many habitats, cacti play an important role in the ecology of the region and are often a major component of the arid zone flora in New World deserts. Nearly all forms of animal-mediated pollination syndromes are found in the cacti, with insect (bee and beetle), hummingbird, hawkmoth, and bat pollination types found in species from both North and South America. This accounts for the wide range of variation in floral morphologies seen in various groups of cacti throughout their range.

Diversity

Classification of the cactus family is considered to be highly problematic and difficult due to the effects of convergent or parallel evolution. Systematic studies have shown that there are four major **lineages** of cacti that are recognized at the subfamily rank. Of these, the two primitive groups (*Maihuenia* [two species] and *Pereskia* [sixteen species]) are found mainly in South America and have persistent true leaves, a limited degree of succulence, and are not as well adapted to heat and water stress as are members of the two remaining groups, the subfamilies Opuntioideae and Cactoideae.

The *Opuntia* group has approximately three hundred species of cacti or more, and typical members of subfamily Opuntioideae have well-defined stem segments, an unusual kind of specialized seed structure, and a unique type of reverse-hooked small spines (glochids), which penetrate the skin and are easily dislodged from their attachment points in the areoles. These cacti include the prickly pears and chollas (pronounced CHOY-yas), which produce showy flowers that are often pollinated by bees, and develop fleshy (occasionally dry) edible berries called tunas. This group is the most widespread of any in the Cactaceae, ranging from southern Canada southwards almost continuously to the cold habitats of Patagonia in southernmost Argentina. They are found from sea level to high elevation (4,000 meters and higher) and have adapted to a wide variety of habitat types. Species of *Opuntia* introduced into suitable habitats in Africa and Australia have become noxious invasive pests, and removing these escaped cacti has become an significant ecological concern.

The largest subfamily of the cacti (subfamily Cactoideae) contains approximately thirteen hundred species and provides examples of extreme morphological variation in the family. There is a tremendous range of variation in spine form and color, flowering types, formation of ribs and tubercles, and other morphological characters in members of this subfamily. Plants in this group range from plants with narrow upright stems that sometimes branch (a columnar habit) to plants with globular or ball-shaped forms (the barrel cactus types) to **epiphytic** plants that either hang from trees in a pendant fashion (such as in *Schumbergera* or *Rhipsalis*) or are lianas and climb up the surfaces of trees with a vining habit. The most easily recognizable cactus species, the saguaro (*Carnegiea gigantea*), is the state flower of Arizona and the symbol of the American desert. It is also among the tallest of all cacti, with individual plants recorded over 15 meters (50 feet) in height. Some cacti produce special alkaloid **compounds**, notably the peyote cactus (*Lophophora williamsii*), which is known for its **hallucinogenic** properties.

Horticultural Interest

Due to their extreme morphological diversity and their ability to tolerate a wide range of growing conditions, the cacti have received much interest by horticulturists since they were first brought to Europe by Christopher Columbus in the 1490s. The Indian fig, or *Opuntia ficus-indica*, is now widely cultivated throughout the Mediterranean region and in other places for its tasty and sweet multiseeded berries. Other species of cacti are grown for food for humans: nopales/nopalitos are young *Opuntia* stems, while the dragon fruit favored by southeast Asians is the berry of an epiphytic cactus, *Hylocereus undatus*, originally from Central America. Perhaps the most widely grown cactus is also an epiphyte, originating from mountainous regions in south cen-

lineage ancestry; the line of evolutionary descent of an organism

epiphytes plants that grow on other plants

compound a substance formed from two or more elements

hallucinogenic capable of inducing hallucinations

115

tral Brazil. The Christmas cactus (*Schlumbergera*, or *Zygocactus truncata*), often sold during holiday times in winter, is a freely flowering epiphytic cactus that was selected for its showy flowers and ease of cultivation. Tens of thousands of cactus horticulturists around the world collect a wide variety of cacti as a hobby, and a number of international and national societies have been established to promote the understanding, cultivation, and conservation of cactus species. SEE ALSO DESERTS; DICOTS; PHOTOSYNTHESIS, CARBON FIXATION AND; DEFENSES, PHYSICAL; RECORD-HOLDING PLANTS; SUCCULENTS.

Robert S. Wallace

Bibliography

Benson, L. *The Cacti of the United States and Canada.* Stanford, CA: Stanford University Press, 1982.

Cullmann, W., E. Götz, and G. Gröner. *The Encyclopedia of Cacti.* Sherborne, England: Alphabooks, 1986.

Gibson, A. C., and P. S. Nobel. *The Cactus Primer.* Cambridge, MA: Harvard University Press, 1986.

Calvin, Melvin

American Biochemist
1911–1997

Melvin Calvin was a biochemist whose prolific career included fundamental work on the biochemistry of photosynthesis. His work led to a Nobel Prize and had *Time* magazine calling him "Mr. Photosynthesis."

Calvin was born in St. Paul, Minnesota, on April 8, 1911, of immigrant parents. The family moved to Detroit, Michigan, where Calvin graduated from high school in 1927. He graduated from the Michigan College of Mining and Technology (now Michigan Technological University) as its first chemistry major in 1931. He received his Ph.D. from the University of Minnesota in 1935. He worked two years at Manchester University with British chemist and philosopher Michael Polanyi (1875–1946), who introduced him to the multidisciplinary approach that later characterized his own scientific career.

In 1937 Calvin became an instructor at the University of California at Berkeley and remained there for the rest of his career. He eventually became a professor (1947), director of the Laboratory of Chemical Biodynamics (1963), and associate director of the Lawrence Radiation Laboratory (1967; now the Lawrence Berkeley Laboratory).

Together with American physical chemist Gilbert Newton Lewis (1875–1946), Calvin studied the color of organic **compounds**, which introduced him to the importance of the electronic structure of organic molecules. He collaborated with chemist G. E. K. Branch and cowrote *The Theory of Organic Chemistry* (1941), the first American book on the subject to use quantum mechanics.

In 1942 Calvin married Genevieve Jemtegaard, a juvenile probation officer who spent a great deal of time in her husband's laboratory, both assisting and collaborating with him. After their first child died of Rh incompatibility they sought to determine the chemical factors causing the

Melvin Calvin.

compound a substance formed from two or more elements

illness. After the 1973 oil embargo they sought new fuel sources from plants (e.g., the genus *Euphorbia*) to convert solar energy into hydrocarbons, an economically unsuccessful project.

During World War II (1939–41) Calvin devised a method for obtaining pure oxygen from the atmosphere onboard destroyers or submarines. He purified and decontaminated the irradiated uranium in fission products and isolated and purified plutonium by his solvent extraction process.

After the radioisotope carbon-14 (because of its long-lived radioactivity, it could be used to follow otherwise untraceable chemical reactions) became available, Calvin began his work on the chemical pathways of photosynthesis. This occupied him from 1946 to 1961 and won him the 1961 Nobel Prize in chemistry. He introduced carbon dioxide (CO_2) labeled with carbon-14 as a tracer into a thin, round flask filled with the single-cell green alga *Chlorella pyrenoidosa* in suspension. The apparatus was illuminated, allowing the alga to incorporate the labeled CO_2 into compounds involved in photosynthesis. Calvin isolated and identified the radioactively labeled constituents, thus determining the steps by which CO_2 is converted into carbohydrates. This set of steps is now known as the Calvin-Benson cycle. Using isotopes, he also traced the path of oxygen in photosynthesis.

The Calvin-Benson cycle is named in honor of Melvin Calvin and Andrew Benson.

Calvin worked on chemical evolution and organic geochemistry, and he examined the organic constituents of Moon rocks for the National Aeronautics and Space Administration. His varied research interests also included photochemistry, free radicals, artificial photosynthesis, radiation chemistry, brain chemistry, the molecular basis of learning, and the philosophy of science.

In 1987 Genevieve died of cancer. Because Calvin's personal and professional life had been built around her presence, her loss was a blow from which he never recovered. Calvin died in Berkeley, California, on January 8, 1997, after several years of declining health. SEE ALSO PHOTOSYNTHESIS, CARBON FIXATION AND; PHYSIOLOGIST; PHYSIOLOGY; PHYSIOLOGY, HISTORY OF.

George B. Kauffman

Bibliography

Bassham, James A., and Melvin Calvin. *The Path of Carbon in Photosynthesis.* Upper Saddle River, NJ: Prentice-Hall, 1957.

———. *The Photosynthesis of Carbon Compounds.* New York: W. A. Benjamin, 1962.

Calvin, Melvin. *Following the Trail of Light: A Scientific Odyssey.* Washington, DC: American Chemical Society, 1992.

Kauffman, George B., and Isaac Mayo. "Melvin Calvin's Trail of Light." *World & I* 9, no. 5 (1994): 206–13.

———. "Multidisciplinary Scientist—Melvin Calvin: His Life and Work." *Journal of Chemical Education* 73, no. 5 (1996): 412–16.

———. "Melvin Calvin (1911–1997)." *Chemical Intelligencer* 74, no. 1 (1998): 54–56.

Candolle, Augustin de

Swiss Botanist
1778–1841

Augustin de Candolle was a Swiss botanist who advanced significant ideas concerning the classification of plants and developed a taxonomic scheme that provided the foundation for much work in taxonomy up to the present.

As did most learned men of science in his day, Candolle trained in medicine, earning a medical degree from the University of Paris in 1804. During this time, he became friends with several other scientific luminaries working in Paris, including the evolutionary theorist Jean-Baptiste Lamarck (1744–1829) and the paleontologist Georges Cuvier (1769–1832). Candolle became an assistant to Cuvier for a time and helped to revise Lamarck's treatise on French flora.

By this time, Candolle had become professionally interested in botany, and in 1806 obtained a commission to conduct a botanical and agricultural survey of France, an endeavor conducted over the next six years. In 1808 he was appointed professor of botany at the University of Montpellier, where he began work on his *Théorie Élémentaire de la Botanique* (Elementary Theory of Botany), published in 1813.

In this work, Candolle laid out his most significant intellectual contribution to plant taxonomy (and in fact coined the word "taxonomy" as well). Candolle believed that a natural classification scheme should be based on the anatomic characteristics of plants, and in particular the positional relations among parts. Candolle argued, for instance, that in the flower, the position of the stamens in relation to the petals provides important information about whether two species are closely or more distantly related: the more similar the arrangement of parts, the more likely the two species are closely related. While strong adaptational pressures might cause two close relatives to diverge in shape, color, or size, the relation of parts—what Candolle called "symmetry"—would not be as likely to change, since these relations reflected a developmental program that would be much more resistant to large evolutionary changes in a short time. While modern taxonomists use other criteria besides those Candolle proposed, his essential insight into the significance of positional relationships remains an important part of the taxonomist's toolbox.

Candolle became professor of natural history at the University of Geneva in 1817, where he remained until his death. He was the first director of the botanical gardens there, and established what is now one of the world's largest herbarium. He expanded on his theories of classification in *Regni vegetabilis systema naturale* (Natural Classification for the Plant Kingdom), published in 1818, and began the most ambitious task of his life, the *Prodromus systematis naturalis regni vegetabilis*, intended to be a descriptive classification of all known seed plants. Candolle's goal was not only to classify every known species, but also to include ecology, evolution, and the **biogeography** of each (Candolle was, in fact, a pioneer in the field of biogeography). Candolle died in 1841 having completed only seven volumes, but the work was carried on by his son, Alphonse de Candolle (1806–1893), and eventually reached seventeen volumes.

biogeography the study of the reasons for the geographic distribution of organisms

Hundreds of individual plant species were first described and named by Augustin de Candolle, including purple coneflower (*Echinacea angustifolia*), the source of the popular herbal remedy echinacea. Genetic studies of *Arabidopsis* have borne out Candolle's belief that positional relationships are deeply embedded in the genetic program. His son Alphonse, in addition to completing the *Prodromus*, was a leading botanist in his own right. Candolle the younger made major contributions to the theory of the origin of cultivated plants, laying out ideas taken up and expanded upon by Russian geneticist N. I. Vavilov (1887–1943), and published an important early work on plant biogeography. SEE ALSO ARABIDOPSIS; BIO-GEOGRAPHY; HERBARIA; TAXONOMIST; TAXONOMY; TAXONOMY, HISTORY OF; VAVILOV, N. I.

Richard Robinson

Bibliography

Isely, Duane. *One Hundred and One Botanists.* Ames, IA: Iowa State University, 1994.

Cannabis

Cannabis sativa (of the family Cannabaceae) is the Latin name for marijuana and hemp. The cannabis plant has been cultivated and used for many centuries by a variety of cultures, primarily for two distinct purposes. The long, tough fibers of the stem have been (and still are) used for making rope and cloth (hemp). The leaves and flowers produce a resin (marijuana) that has been (and still is) smoked to attain an altered state of consciousness. In the United States and many other countries, possession and use of marijuana is against the law under most circumstances, although a number of changes in these laws have recently been made to allow it to be used for medical treatment in some states.

Cannabis grows as a woody annual plant. It favors deep, well-drained, loamy soils, but can, and does, grow in almost any soil. The fibers of the stem are formed from tough sclerenchyma cells, joined together to make long strands. The leaves are compound, with five to seven serrated leaflets arranged palmately in a fan shape. The flowers, which form at the end of the summer, are separated by sex onto different plants. Full-grown plants can attain a height of ten feet or more, and a breadth of several feet, but when planted for fiber, seeds are sown so thickly that little branching occurs and stems remain very thin.

A budding cannabis plant.

psychoactive causing an effect on the brain

To harvest the fibers, the plants are cut before flowering and left to cure for days to weeks in the field. This allows retting, or rotting of the stem to loosen the fibers. The fiber is extracted by macerating the plant in water and removing the pulp. Hemp fibers, each from three to six feet long, can be corded into a strong and durable rope. Historically, hemp rope pulled the water bucket from the village well, hanged the criminal on the gallows, and outfitted the great sailing ships of the voyages of discovery. Cannabis varieties grown for hemp contain extremely low levels of **psychoactive** substances. Despite this, hemp went largely out of use as a fiber source in the United States during the mid-twentieth century, due mainly to the political difficulties of keeping it in production while marijuana as a drug was being outlawed.

Leaves and flowers are harvested and dried before the plant reaches full maturity, and most commonly before the seeds have set. Female flowers contain more of the active ingredient THC (delta-tetrahydrocannabinol) than either the male flowers or the leaves, and the THC content decreases after fertilization. Because of this, male plants are often removed from stands being grown for their THC. This simultaneously increases the soil nutrients available to the female plants and prevents fertilization of the flowers.

spasticity abnormal muscle activity caused by damage to the nerve pathways controlling movement

Late in the twentieth century in the United States, the legal use of marijuana has been promoted because of its potential for treating several medical conditions, including glaucoma (high fluid pressure within the eye), **spasticity**, and nausea during chemotherapy. Several states, most notably California, have passed "compassionate use" laws that allow patients to legally obtain marijuana for smoking. At the same time, several states are moving forward with legislation to allow fiber hemp to be grown legally, though these efforts will require the cooperation of the U.S. Drug Enforcement Administration. Currently, hemp fiber for use in the United States is imported from Canada, China, and several other countries where it is grown legally. SEE ALSO CULTIVAR; DEFENSES, CHEMICAL; FIBER AND FIBER PRODUCTS; PSYCHOACTIVE PLANTS.

Richard Robinson

Bibliography

Clarke, Robert C. *Marijuana Botany*, 2nd ed. Berkeley, CA: Ronin Publishing, 1992.

Carbohydrates

compound a substance formed from two or more elements

empirical formula the simplest whole number ratio of atoms in a compound

Carbohydrates are a diverse group of **compounds** composed of the elements carbon (C), hydrogen (H), and oxygen (O) with the **empirical formula** $[CH_2O]_n$, where n represents the number of CH_2O units in the compound. The ultimate source of all carbohydrates is photosynthesis, in which the energy of sunlight is used to chemically fix atmospheric CO_2 into carbohydrate. Carbohydrates constitute as much as 80 percent of the dry weight of a plant. This is largely due to the presence of cell walls made of complex carbohydrates surrounding each plant cell.

Sugars, also called saccharides, are carbohydrates. Common sugars occurring in nature have from three (glyceraldehyde) to seven (sedoheptulose) carbon atoms bonded together to form the molecule's backbone. Sugars can be classified chemically as either aldehydes or ketones, and contain OH (**hydroxyl**) groups attached to their carbon backbones. Glucose (an aldehyde sugar) and fructose (a ketose sugar) are two examples of common six-carbon sugars that occur widely in plants. These molecules form ring structures, with glucose forming a six-member ring, and fructose a five-member ring.

hydroxyl the chemical group -OH

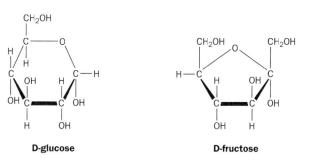

D-glucose

D-fructose

Individual sugars are called monosaccharides. Two sugars linked together chemically are called disaccharides; three are trisaccharides; four are tetrasaccharides, and so on. A generic term for several sugars linked together is oligosaccharide. Molecules with many sugars linked together to form a **polymer** are called polysaccharides. Sucrose (table sugar) is the most abundant disaccharide and is comprised of glucose and fructose. A large amount of sucrose is formed in plant leaves from photosynthetic products. Sucrose is **translocated** over long distances in plants in specialized conductive tissue known as phloem. Sucrose can be broken down, and its components (glucose and fructose) metabolized for energy and as the initial raw material for building cellular components in plant cells distant from photosynthetic leaves. Sucrose also can be stored. High concentrations are found in storage organs such as fruits, sugarcane stems, and enlarged roots of sugar beets. The latter two are commercial sources from which sucrose is refined.

polymer a large molecule made from many similar parts

translocate to move, especially to move sugars from the leaf to other parts of the plant

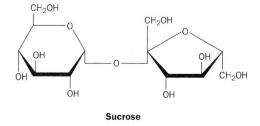

Sucrose

Two important plant polysaccharides, cellulose and starch, are composed exclusively of glucose units bonded together. Cellulose is the most abundant polysaccharide in plant cell walls, and thus, the most abundant polysaccharide on Earth. In cell walls, cellulose occurs along with other complex polysaccharides, each of which is composed of more than one type of sugar. Because of the way glucose is linked in cellulose, individual chains, hundreds of glucose molecules long, are able to bond together by hydrogen bonding in a crystalline arrangement to form a cable-like structure known as a microfibril. These microfibrils are interwoven and give cellulose its strength in plant cell walls and in cotton fabric and paper.

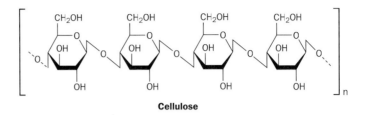

Cellulose

Starch and cellulose differ in the way the glucose molecules are bonded together. Starch is a storage compound in plants, and is broken down as needed into glucose for metabolic use.

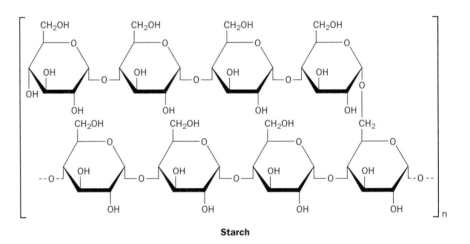

Starch

Carbohydrates are important in human nutrition, often constituting the major source of calories in the diet. Glucose, fructose, sucrose, and starch are readily digested by humans. Cellulose and the other complex carbohydrates of the plant cell wall are not readily digested, but constitute useful dietary fiber.

Cellulase, an **enzyme** that can degrade cellulose, is made by many different fungi and some microorganisms. This enzyme allows these organisms to decompose plant material, an important step in the recycling of materials in food webs. SEE ALSO PHOTOSYNTHESIS, CARBON FIXATION AND; SUGAR.

D. Mason Pharr and John D. Williamson

Bibliography

Taiz, Lincoln, and Eduardo Zeiger, eds. *Plant Physiology*, 2nd ed. Sunderland, MA: Sinauer Associates, 1998.

Carbon Cycle

All life on Earth is based on carbon, the sixth element of the periodic table. The term carbon cycle refers to the movement of carbon in various forms between Earth's biogeochemical reservoirs: the oceans, the atmosphere, plants, animals and soils on land (the land biosphere), and the geosphere (rocks). Carbon dioxide (CO_2) in the air traps heat, contributing to warm-

> Treatment of denim with cellulase has largely replaced pumice stone in the production of "stone-washed" jeans.

enzyme a protein that controls a reaction in a cell

ing of Earth's surface (called the greenhouse effect) and thereby influencing the climate. Human activities such as burning fossil fuels and clearing forests are causing the amount of CO_2 in the atmosphere to increase rapidly. Concern that global climate change may result has led to a pressing need for scientific research to better understand the global carbon cycle.

The Path of Carbon

To illustrate some of the important processes of the carbon cycle one can follow a carbon atom as it moves through the biogeochemical reservoirs of the cycle. Begin with a carbon atom that is in the atmosphere in the form of CO_2. In the atmosphere CO_2 is the fifth most abundant gas, behind nitrogen (N_2), oxygen (O_2), argon (Ar), and water vapor (H_2O). Nevertheless, of every million molecules of air, fewer than four hundred are CO_2.

The CO_2 molecule contacts the leaf of an apple tree. It is removed from the air by the process of photosynthesis, also called carbon fixation, whereby plants use light energy from the Sun and water from the soil to convert CO_2 to carbohydrate (sugar) and O_2 gas. The carbohydrate may be converted to other **compounds** that the plant needs to grow and reproduce. The carbon atom may be used by the plant to grow an apple, which may be picked and eaten. The body uses the carbohydrate in the apple for fuel, converting the carbon back into CO_2, which is breathed out to the air. Or, perhaps the apple falls to the ground and gradually rots, meaning that the carbon is converted to CO_2 by decomposers in the soil, including insects, worms, fungi, and bacteria. Either way, this process of converting the carbon in the apple to CO_2 consumes O_2 from the air and is called respiration. About one-tenth of all the CO_2 in the atmosphere is taken up by photosynthesis on land each year, and very nearly the same amount is converted back to CO_2 by respiration. Most of the carbon fixed each year on land is used by plants to make new leaves, which eventually die and fall to the ground where they are decomposed, just like the apple. The rich, dark brown material in the top several centimeters of most soil is mainly decomposing plant material.

compound a substance formed from two or more elements

The CO_2 molecule rides on the wind out over the ocean. It crashes into the ocean surface and dissolves, like sugar dissolving in a glass of water. Since CO_2 is very soluble in water the oceans contain about fifty times as much carbon as the atmosphere. About one-eighth of all the CO_2 in the atmosphere dissolves into the ocean waters each year, but nearly the same amount returns to the atmosphere because the total amount of CO_2 in the ocean is approximately in equilibrium with the amount in the air, and CO_2 is constantly moving into and out of the seawater. The CO_2 molecule, dissolved in the water, is taken up by a single-celled marine plant called a coccolithophore. The carbon is used by the coccolithophore to add to its hard protective coating, which is made of calcium carbonate ($CaCO_3$). When the coccolithophore dies its coating sinks to the bottom of the ocean and becomes part of the marine sediment. Most of the carbon in the sediment is recycled rapidly by respiration or dissolution, but a small amount remains in the sediment and eventually (over millions of years) becomes sedimentary rock.

Being trapped in a sedimentary rock is not the end of the cycle for the carbon atom. If that were the case eventually all of the carbon in the atmosphere, the plants and soils, and the oceans would have ended up in rocks, and the carbon cycle would have stopped long ago. Fortunately, a

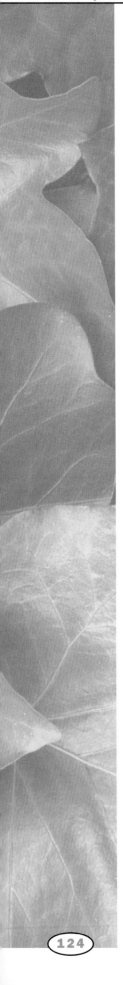

The carbon cycle. Note that the geosphere (sedimentary rock) is by far the largest pool of carbon on Earth, but it exchanges only very slowly with the more active pools in the atmosphere, land biosphere, and oceans. Burning fossil fuels represents a huge increase in the transfer of carbon from the geosphere to the atmosphere, causing an increase in the amount of CO_2 in the air (on average 3.1 billion tons of carbon accumulated in the atmosphere each year during the 1990s). More CO_2 in the air drives large net uptake of carbon by the land biosphere and oceans. In pre-industrial times the atmosphere, oceans, and land biosphere were roughly in balance, and net exchanges between these pools were about zero.

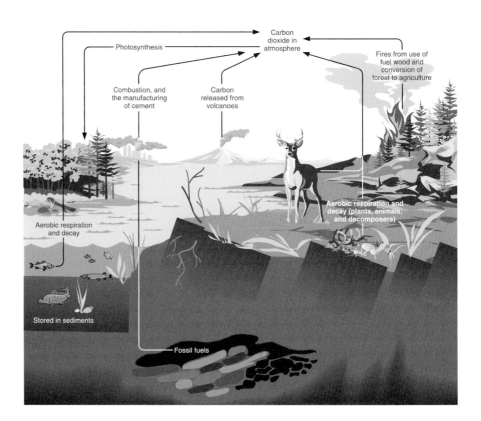

little of this carbon is returned to the atmosphere each year, mainly by volcanism. The amount of CO_2 that is emitted by volcanoes and geothermal vents is small, but it is enough to have kept the carbon cycle turning for billions of years.

Following a carbon atom through some pathways of the carbon cycle touches on many important processes. The balance between photosynthesis and respiration on land, the transfer of CO_2 into and out of the oceans, and the incorporation of carbon into sedimentary rocks and return to the atmosphere via volcanic activity all represent recycling of carbon atoms. It is important to understand that the carbon cycle is a dynamic process, it is constantly changing and an adjustment or change in one carbon cycle process will cause changes in many other parts of the cycle. For example, if the amount of CO_2 in the atmosphere increases for some reason, more CO_2 will dissolve into the oceans. Also, since plants require CO_2 as a nutrient, a larger amount of CO_2 in the air will increase plant growth, a process called CO_2 fertilization.

Carbon and Climate

A very important part of the carbon cycle is the influence of CO_2 on Earth's climate. Carbon dioxide is one of several gases in the air (water vapor is the most important one) that trap heat near the surface, causing the surface to be warmed. This process is known as the greenhouse effect. If there were no greenhouse gases in the atmosphere the surface temperature would be about 35°C colder on average than it is, and life on Earth would be very different. More CO_2 means more warming, that is, higher average surface temperature. That means that the amount of CO_2 and other greenhouse gases in the air has a strong influence on the climate of Earth. Furthermore, since many parts of the carbon cycle, such as the plants and soils on land, and the chemistry of the oceans, are sensitive to climate, a change in climate can cause a change in the carbon cycle. For example, in the temperate zone during a warm spring, leaves will come out on the trees earlier than in a cool spring. With a longer growing season the plants can remove more CO_2 from the air, and will grow faster.

Human Influences on the Carbon Cycle

Humans are causing large changes in the carbon cycle. First, humans have altered the land biosphere by cutting forests to clear land for agriculture; for lumber, pulp, and fuel wood; and to make room for cities. Natural grasslands have also been plowed for agriculture. In the early 1990s about 38 percent of Earth's land surface was used for agriculture including croplands and pastures, according to United Nations statistics. When land is cleared, most of the carbon stored in the plants and much of that stored in the soils is converted to CO_2 and lost to the atmosphere. Second, since the mid-1800s humans have learned to harness the energy stored in fossil fuels, mainly coal, oil, and natural gas. The term fossil fuels refers to the fact that these materials are composed of the fossil remains of ancient plants. When fossil fuels are burned, energy that can be used to light and heat our homes, drive our cars, and manufacture all the goods that we use from day to day is released. Burning fossil fuels also consumes O_2 and releases CO_2 to the air. In 1996, 6.5 billion metric tons of carbon were released to the atmosphere from fossil fuels. That's a little more than 1 ton of carbon per person per year worldwide. The use of fossil fuel, however, is not evenly distributed. The United States, with less than 5 percent of Earth's population, used 22 percent of the fossil fuels in 1996, and on a per-person basis residents of the United States used about nineteen times as much fossil fuel as the residents of Africa. The use of fossil fuels is growing rapidly, particularly in developing countries such as China.

Carbon dioxide from fossil fuels and land clearing caused a 25 percent increase in CO_2 in the atmosphere between the eighteenth century and the 1990s. Only about one-half of the CO_2 that has been emitted into the atmosphere has remained there, the rest has been taken up by the oceans and the land biosphere. Scientists do not know exactly how much of the added CO_2 has gone into the oceans and how much has gone into the land biosphere, nor do they understand precisely why the land biosphere is taking up a lot of CO_2. One reason that the land biosphere may be taking up carbon is the CO_2 fertilization effect mentioned above. Another explanation is that forests that were cleared for agriculture and lumber in the 1800s and early 1900s may be regrowing. These are important questions for future research. The answers will affect our ability to regulate the amount of CO_2 in the atmosphere in order to lessen climate change.

Burning fossil fuels represents a huge increase in the transfer of carbon into the atmosphere from sedimentary rocks in Earth's crust. Unless an alternative source of energy is found, it is likely that in a few hundred years humans could burn all of the coal, oil, and gas that is believed to exist on Earth, and that took many millions of years to form. If this occurs the amount of CO_2 in the atmosphere will be several times the preindustrial amount,

saturate containing as much dissolved substance as possible

dissipate to reduce by spreading out or scattering

and the oceans will become completely **saturated** with CO_2, which would drastically alter their chemical composition. Also, the increased greenhouse effect would cause very substantial but currently unpredictable changes in climate. Because the leak of carbon out of the oceans and atmosphere into the sediments and eventually into the sedimentary rocks is very slow, the added carbon would take thousands of years to **dissipate** from the oceans and atmosphere. SEE ALSO BIOGEOCHEMICAL CYCLES; DECOMPOSERS; GLOBAL WARMING; HUMAN IMPACTS; PHOTOSYNTHESIS, CARBON FIXATION AND.

Peter S. Bakwin

Bibliography

Tans, P. P. "Why Carbon Dioxide from Fossil Fuel Burning Won't Go Away." In *Perspectives in Environmental Chemistry*. Ed. D. Macalady. New York: Oxford University Press, 1998.

Vitousek, P. M., H. A. Mooney, J. Lubchenco, and J. M. Melillo. "Human Domination of Earth's Ecosystems." *Science* 277 (1997): 494–99.

Carnivorous Plants

Plants that trap and digest tiny animals have fascinated people for centuries. It was known by 1790 that sundews, pitcher plants, and the Venus's-flytrap could catch insects. This interest led Thomas Jefferson to collect Venus's-flytraps near Charleston, South Carolina, for study. A century later, Charles Darwin referred to the Venus's-flytrap as one of the most wonderful plants in the world. More recently, certain adventurous, twentieth-century Hollywood movies depicted man-eating plants as inhabiting mysterious tropical jungles. Carnivorous plants, in fact, are relatively small and do not live in dark swamps and jungles, and the largest animal ever found trapped in one of the plants was a small rat. Carnivorous plants catch mostly insects, and hence are often referred to as insectivorous plants.

Carnivorous plants are defined as plants that attract, catch, digest, and absorb the body juices of animal prey (referred to as the carnivorous syndrome). The major types of carnivorous plants are sundews, pitcher plants, butterworts, bladderworts, and the unique Venus's-flytrap. More than 150 different types of insects have been identified as victims, but also arachnids (spiders and mites), mollusks (snails and slugs), earthworms, and small vertebrates (small fish, amphibians, reptiles, rodents, and birds) are known to have been caught.

Many different kinds of plants have insect-attracting structures such as colorful leaves and flower parts and produce sweet sugar secretions (like nectar). Others may ensnare and kill small animals using sticky hairs, thorns, cupped leaves, poisonous liquids, or a combination of these tactics. In some cases it is known that the juices of dead animals can be absorbed through the surfaces of plant leaves. However, only true carnivorous plants have the ability to obtain nutrients from animal prey.

It is known that carnivorous plants can survive without catching prey. However, botanists believe that the added nutrition derived from carnivory helps the plants grow faster and produce more seeds, thus allowing the plants to survive better and spread into new areas. In general, carnivorous plants grow in poor soils where nitrogen, phosphorus, and potassium are lacking.

MAJOR CARNIVOROUS PLANT GROUPS

Genus	Common Name	Number of Species (approximate)	Geographical Distribution
Sarracenia	Trumpet pitcher plant	10	Southeastern United States, with one species extending across Canada
Darlingtonia	California pitcher plant	1	Northern California and adjacent Oregon
Heliamphora	South American pitcher plant	5	Venezuela, Guyana, Brazil
Nepenthes	Tropical pitcher plant	75	Southeast Asian tropics, from Australia, Malaysia, and India to Madagascar
Cephalotus	Australian pitcher plant	1	Western Australia
Drosera	Sundew	110	Worldwide, especially South Africa and Australia
Dionaea	Venus's-flytrap	1	Southeastern North Carolina and adjacent South Carolina
Pinguicula	Butterwort	60	Mostly Northern Hemisphere
Utricularia	Bladderwort	200	Worldwide

They obtain these nutrients, especially nitrogen and phosphorus, from their prey, and they are quickly absorbed through the leaf surface and transported throughout the plant. Although carnivorous plants do absorb nutrients from a weak fertilizer, for instance, high concentrations of fertilizer, as are suitable for garden crops and houseplants, normally kill carnivorous plants.

Habitats

There are more than 450 different species of carnivorous plants found in the world. At least some occur on every continent except Antarctica. They are especially numerous in North America, southeastern Asia, and Australia. Carnivorous plants typically live in wet habitats that are open and sunny, with nutrient-poor soils having an acidic **pH**. They do not like competition from other plants, and thus seem to thrive in the nutrient-poor habitats where other types of plants do not grow very well. These plants may be found in wet meadows in the southeastern United States or in peat-moss bogs in northern North America and Eurasia. Some are true aquatics, growing in the quiet waters of ponds and ditches around the world. Still others grow on wet, seeping, rocky cliffs or moist sand. In many cases they grow in places that have periodic fires that act to cut down on competition, keep their habitats open, and release nutrients into the soil.

pH a measure of acidity or alkalinity; the pH scale ranges from 0 to 14, with 7 being neutral; low pH numbers indicate high acidity; high numbers indicate alkalinity

Types of Traps

The traps of carnivorous plants are always modified leaves. They may be active or passive in their mechanism. Active traps have sensitive trigger hairs and moving parts, such as the sticky, glue-tipped hairs that cover the leaves of sundews. The paired leaf blades of the Venus's-flytrap snap shut like jaws when trigger hairs are touched inside. The aquatic bladderworts have little inflated pouches that suck in microscopic animals and mosquito larvae. The passive traps of terrestrial butterworts consist of flat leaves covered with a greasy, sticky surface that are effective at catching crawling insects much like flypaper traps flies. The elegant pitcher plants have passive pitfall traps that are hollow, tubular leaves. Insects fall in, die, and sink to the bottom to be digested. The hoods on most pitcher plants keep out rainwater and prevent prey from flying out. In many cases, especially in pitcher plants that hold water, bacteria may aid in digesting prey. It is also known that several species of mites and fly larvae live inside the trumpet leaves of

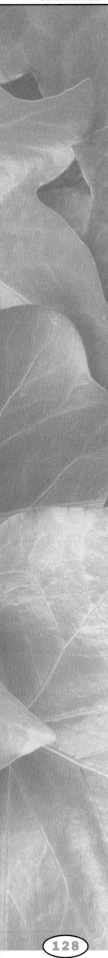

An oblong-leaved sundew flower (*Drosera intermedia*) traps a white-legged damselfly.

chitin a cellulose-like molecule found in the cell wall of many fungi and arthropods

pitcher plants, without themselves being harmed, and help break down prey for digestion. Pitcher plants may be terrestrial, growing in clumps of erect pitcher leaves (such as the *Sarracenia* pitcher plants) in the North American temperate zone, or they may grow as sprawling vines in the Malaysian tropics, with pitchers hanging from the tips of their flat leaf blades (such as the *Nepenthes* pitcher plants).

Microscopic glands are present on each type of trap. They are specialized cells that perform various jobs. They may act as receptors to detect the presence of prey, or they may secrete digestive fluids to dissolve the animal bodies with only the outer shell of **chitin** of arthropods (insects, spiders, and their relatives) remaining undigested. The glands also absorb the products of digestion, taking them into the leaves of the plant. For example, the sticky hairs of the sundew trap the insect and slowly curve over to press the victim onto the leaf surface where digestive juices are secreted and nutrients absorbed.

While a variety of carnivorous plants are scattered around the world, the area with the most numerous types is the Green Swamp Nature Preserve in southeastern North Carolina (Brunswick County). Occurring in this area are four species of *Sarracenia*, four species of *Drosera*, ten species of *Utricularia*, three species of *Pinguicula*, and the single species of *Dionaea*. SEE ALSO EVOLUTION OF PLANTS; INTERACTIONS, PLANT-INSECT; PEAT BOGS; WETLANDS.

T. Lawrence Mellichamp

Bibliography

Cheers, Gordon. *A Guide to Carnivorous Plants of the World.* New York: Collins Publishers, 1992.

D'Amato, Peter. *The Savage Garden: Cultivating Carnivorous Plants.* Berkeley, CA: Ten Speed Press, 1998.

Lloyd, Francis E. *The Carnivorous Plants.* First printed in 1942. New York: Dover Publications, 1976.

Schnell, Donald E. *Carnivorous Plants of the United States and Canada.* Winston-Salem, NC: John F. Blair Publisher, 1976.

Carotenoids

The carotenoids are red, orange, and yellow pigments synthesized by all green plants and some microbes. They have an essential function in photosynthesis and in attracting the attention of animals. Several of these pigments also have an important nutritional function for animals and some of the familiar colors of animals are derived from plant or microbial carotenoids they consume.

Structure and Occurrence

Carotenoids are synthesized in the plastids of a plant cell and typically contain forty carbon atoms derived from eight subunits of the five-carbon compound, isoprene. Larger and smaller carotenoids do occur. Two categories of carotenoids occur in nature. These are the carotenes that contain only carbon and hydrogen, and the xanthophylls (also termed oxycarotenoids) that contain carbon, hydrogen, and oxygen atoms. Each carotenoid has its own distinctive color. Their chemical structure makes carotenoids very insoluble in water, but they are fat-soluble. Therefore they are usually associated with cell membranes and lipids, the primary water-insoluble component of cells. Some plant carotenoids occur as crystals in a protein matrix, and in some animals carotenoids occur with proteins. These animal carotenoproteins can be a very different color than their component carotenoids. For example, the carotenoprotein responsible for the distinctive blue color of some live lobsters breaks into a bright red carotenoid and colorless protein upon heating. Over six hundred carotenoids occur in plants, animals, and microbes. Since only plants and some microbes can synthesize carotenoids, those carotenoids in animals all come from their dietary sources. Typically several different carotenoids occur in plant tissue containing this class of pigments. For example, orange carrots contain at least six different carotenes that account for their color. All green leaves contain beta-carotene and three xanthophylls, lutein, neoxanthin, and violaxanthin. Most leaves also contain alpha-carotene and several other xanthophylls as well.

Both chlorophylls and carotenoids occur in all green leaves, but chlorophylls mask the carotenoids to the human eye. When the chlorophylls break down as leaves senesce (mature), the yellow and orange carotenoids persist and the leaves turn yellow.

Role in Plants

In the process of photosynthesis, potentially harmful oxidizing **compounds** are generated. The carotenoids occur in photosynthetic tissues along with chlorophyll to protect them from **photooxidative** damage. In fact, this protection is essential for photosynthesis. The photoprotective role of carotenoids is demonstrated in plant mutants that cannot synthesize essential leaf carotenoids. These mutants are lethal in nature since without carotenoids, chlorophylls degrade, their leaves are white in color, and photosynthesis cannot occur. Carotenoids also assist chlorophylls in harvesting light. Carotenoids absorb wavelengths of blue light that chlorophylls do not. The energy that carotenoids harvest in the blue range of the spectrum and transfer to chlorophyll contributes significantly to photosynthesis. The growth and development of plants is often stimulated by light, and

compound a substance formed from two or more elements

photooxidize to react with oxygen under the influence of sunlight

129

A carrot harvest. Carrots contain at least six different carotenes that account for their color.

carotenoids have sometimes been implicated as the photoreceptors of light to trigger these responses.

Outside of photosynthesis, plant carotenoids also serve as one of the pigments, along with anthocyanins and betalains, that provide color to flowers, ripening fruit, and other plant parts. Familiar examples of carotenoids having this role are found in sunflowers, marigolds, bananas, peaches, oranges, tomatoes, peppers, melons, and yellow corn. Two root crops, carrots and sweet potatoes, also acquire their color from carotenoids. These colors attract insects, birds, and bats for pollinating flowers, and they attract a wide range of animals to aid in the dispersal of seeds and fruits.

Role in Animals

Beyond their role in attracting animals, carotenoids are important nutrients and colorants for animals that consume them. Vitamin A is an essential nutrient for humans and animals, and all vitamin A ultimately comes from dietary carotenoids. A small subset of all carotenoids, including beta-carotene, can be converted to vitamin A by animal metabolic systems. Animals cannot synthesize these provitamin A carotenoids or vitamin A itself from scratch, and humans around the world obtain about two-thirds of their vitamin A in this provitamin form from plants they eat. The rest is consumed as vitamin A from meat, eggs, and dairy products that ultimately came from carotenoids in the diets of these animal sources.

Animal products and tissues containing vitamin A, which has no color, often contain carotenoids as well. This is the case in egg yolk, butterfat, and the pink or red flesh color of certain fish, such as salmon and trout. Dietary carotenoids are readily visible in the striking and familiar colors of flamingoes, canaries, lobsters, prawn, goldfish, and ladybugs. Some of the coloration in human skin is also due to the carotenoids consumed. Beyond their important role as a source of vitamin A for humans, dietary carotenoids, including those that are not provitamin A carotenoids, have been implicated as protecting against certain forms of cancer and cardiovascular disease. Two carotenoids that appear to impart health benefits are lycopene and lutein.

Genetic engineering of rice may allow high expression of carotenoids. However, the normally white rice becomes yellow-orange in the process, which may not be appealing to consumers.

Lycopene is the red carotene that accounts for the typical color of tomatoes and watermelon. Lutein is a yellow xanthophyll common in all green leaves and responsible for much of the color of milk, butter, and egg yolks. The **antioxidant** properties that make carotenoids essential for photosynthesis may provide a similar type of protection in preventing human disease.

antioxidant a substance that prevents damage from oxygen or other reactive substances

Commercial Importance

The color of food is an important variable contributing to its selection for consumption. Carotenoids in plant extracts such as red palm oil, saffron, annatto, and paprika have been used as food colors through much of history. More recently, industrially produced (synthetic) carotenoids have also been used as food color. Poultry, fish, and mammalian food animal diets also are frequently supplemented with natural or synthetic carotenoids to not only provide a dietary vitamin A source, but primarily to color meat and animal products and make them more appealing for consumers. Medicines and cosmetic products are often colored with carotenoids to enhance their appeal. SEE ALSO PIGMENTS; PLASTIDS.

Philipp W. Simon

Bibliography

Bauernfeind, J. Christopher, ed. *Carotenoids as Colorants and Vitamin A Precursors.* New York: Academic Press, 1981.

Britton, George, Synnove Liaaen-Jensen, and Hanspeter Pfander, eds. *Carotenoids*, Vol. 1. Basel: Birkhauser Verlag, 1995.

Packer, Lester, ed. *Carotenoids, Methods in Enzymology*, Vols. 213 and 214. New York: Academic Press, 1993.

Carver, George Washington

American Botanist
1865–1943

George Washington Carver was born in 1865, near the end of the Civil War (1861–65). His mother was a slave on the Moses and Susan Carver farm close to Diamond Grove, Missouri. Carver was orphaned while still in his infancy and was raised by the Carvers. He received a practical education working on the farm and in 1877 was sent to attend a school for African-American children in the nearby town of Neosho. From Neosho, Carver traveled through several states in pursuit of a basic education. He took odd jobs to support himself and lived with families he met along the way.

In 1890 Carver began a study of art at Simpson College in Indianola, Iowa. The following year he left Simpson to pursue studies in agriculture at the Iowa State College of Agriculture and Mechanic Arts in Ames. He enrolled in 1891 as the first African-American student at Iowa State. Carver maintained an excellent academic record and was noted for his skill in plant **hybridization** using techniques of cross-fertilization and grafting. An appointment as assistant botanist allowed him to continue with graduate studies while teaching and conducting greenhouse studies.

In 1896 American educator Booker T. Washington (1856–1915) extended an invitation to Carver to head the agriculture department at Al-

George Washington Carver.

hybridization formation of a new individual from parents of different species or varieties

abama's Tuskegee Institute. Carver accepted the invitation and remained at Tuskegee until his death forty-seven years later in 1943. During his tenure at Tuskegee he taught classes, directed the Agricultural Experiment Station, managed the school's farms, served on various councils and committees, and directed a research department.

Carver's work focused on projects that held potential for improving the lives of poor southern farmers. Years of repeated planting of a single crop, cotton, and uncontrolled erosion had depleted southern soils. He advocated the wise use of natural resources, sustainable methods of agriculture, soil enrichment, and crop diversification.

One of Carver's first efforts was to find methods within reach of the farmer with limited technical and financial means for enriching the soils. He conducted soil analysis to determine what was needed to make soils more productive. Then Carver proceeded to set up scientific experiments to determine organic methods for building up the soil. He also tried planting and cultivating various plants and plant varieties so he could identify ones that could be successfully grown. Sweet potatoes, peanuts, and cowpeas were considered the most promising. These plants were favored because they could help enrich the soil, they could offer good nutritional value to animals and humans, they were easily preserved and stored, and they could be used as raw material for the production of useful products. Carver developed hundreds of products from these resources. He recognized that processing raw materials was a means of adding value to and increasing the demand for the agricultural products of the South.

When the United States entered World War I in 1917, shortages of certain goods were felt. This caused Carver's substitutes and alternatives to gain attention. Sweet potato products and peanut milk were especially of interest. In 1921 Carver appeared before a congressional committee to testify on the importance of protecting the U.S. peanut industry by establishing a tariff on imported peanuts, and a tariff was established. This event brought Carver national and international recognition as a scientist. Carver spent the remainder of his life conducting agricultural research and sharing his knowledge with individuals in the South and throughout the world. SEE ALSO AGRICULTURE, ORGANIC; BREEDER; BREEDING; ECONOMIC IMPORTANCE OF PLANTS; FABACEAE.

Janet M. Pine

Bibliography

Kremer, Gary R. *George Washington Carver in His Own Words.* Columbia, MO: University of Missouri Press, 1987.

McMurry, Linda O. *George Washington Carver, Scientist and Symbol.* New York: Oxford University Press, 1981.

Cell Cycle

During the cell cycle, cells grow, double their nuclear deoxyribonucleic acid (DNA) content through chromosome replication, and prepare for the next mitosis (chromosome separation) and cytokinesis (cytoplasm separation). In effect, the cell cycle is the proliferating cell's life history. Cells spend most of their time in interphase, the period between divisions, acquiring competence for division. For example, in the higher plant *Arabidopsis thaliana* at

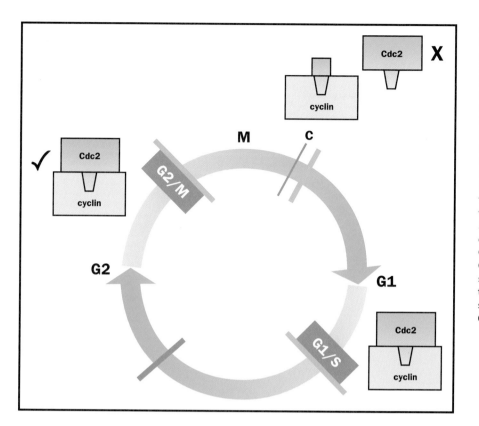

An idealized cell cycle, showing the order of mitosis (M), cytokinesis (C), postmitotic interphase (G1), DNA synthetic phase (S-phase), and postsynthetic interphase (G2). Major control points of the cell cycle at G1/S and G2/M are indicated as hatched rectangles. P34 (Cdc2 kinase) is shown bound to a cyclin at G2/M, where it exhibits catalytic activity (✓) while cyclin degrades at M/G1 and Cdc2 stops working (X). A Cdc2-cylin complex is also shown at G1/S, but note this is not necessarily the same cyclin as the one at G2/M.

23°C, **meristematic** cells are in interphase for eight hours but are in mitosis for only thirty minutes.

meristematic related to cell division at the tip

The Phases of the Cell Cycle

The cell cycle is commonly described as having four phases: M (mitosis), Gap 1 (postmitotic interphase), S-phase (period of DNA synthesis), and Gap 2 (postsynthetic interphase). Gaps 1 and 2 were initially thought to be resting stages between mitosis and S-phase. This description is a misnomer because numerous genes regulate cell growth in these phases. Appropriately, these terms became abbreviated to G1 and G2. Moreover, networks of cell cycle gene products constitute molecular checkpoints that in G1 determine whether a cell is competent to replicate its chromosomes during S-phase, and that in G2 sense whether the cell is ready to partition its chromatids during mitosis. Uniquely in plant cells, in late G2 an array of microtubules known as the preprophase band appears and chromosomes separate in a plane perpendicular to it.

Only in mitosis do chromosomes become visible by light microscopy; each one appears as two sister chromatids constricted at a specific point along their length, the centromere. At mitosis, a **diploid** parent cell passes through four phases: prophase, metaphase, anaphase, and telophase. During late prophase, the nuclear envelope disintegrates and spindles of microtubules span the cell. Unlike animal mitosis where the spindles attach to centrioles (and associated polar asters), there is no obvious anchoring structure for higher plant spindles. This led to the botanical term "anastral cell division." At metaphase, the chromosomes align at the cell's equator and attach to mitotic spindles via kinetochores, discs of structural protein that also

diploid having two sets of chromosomes, versus having one (haploid)

Arrows point to a developing cell plate, which divides the new daughter cells.

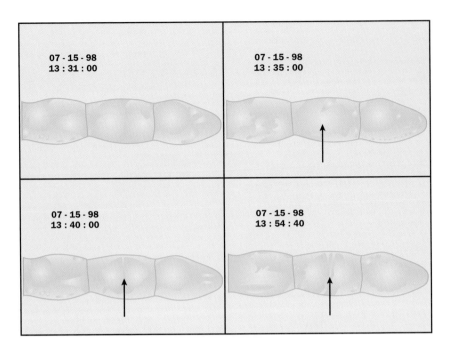

vesicle a membrane-bound cell structure with specialized contents

bind to the centromere of the chromosome. During anaphase, sister chromatids are pulled apart and move to opposite ends of the cell. In telophase, nuclear envelopes reform around each new diploid set of chromosomes followed by cytokinesis when a new wall forms between sibling cells. Cytokinesis requires the formation of a cell plate or phragmoplast that spans the cell center, and becomes dense with **vesicles** from the Golgi complex (also called the Golgi apparatus). The plasma membrane and the membrane surrounding the phragmoplast fuse, resulting in separation of the sibling cells. On the phragmoplast, cellulose forms the fibrillar component of the cell wall while hemicelluloses and pectins are added as a matrix. Trapped in the primary cell wall are cytoplasmic strands and microtubules that become plasmodesmata, the cytoplasmic connections between the new cells.

Regulation

ATP adenosine triphosphate, a small, water-soluble molecule that acts as an energy currency in cells

Most knowledge about regulatory cell cycle genes comes from studies of yeasts and vertebrate cells, but the molecular landscape of the plant cell cycle is being identified. In fact, an important discovery about the cell cycle stemmed from work on plant cells in the 1960s by Jack Van't Hof at the Brookhaven National Laboratory in New York. He discovered that when cultured pea root tips were deprived of carbohydrate, meristematic cells stopped dividing and arrested in either G1 or G2. If sucrose and inhibitors of protein synthesis or adenosine triphosphate (**ATP**) synthesis were then added to the medium, the cells continued to arrest in G1 or G2 despite nutrient availability. With confirmatory data from other species, in 1973 Van't Hof published his principal control point hypothesis: that there are two major control points of the cell cycle, one at G1/S and the other at G2/M, both of which are dependent on adequate nutrients, the generation of energy, and protein synthesis. Discovery of the proteins synthesized at these transitions and the genes that encode them occurred in the 1980s. Paul Nurse at the Imperial Cancer Research Fund (ICRF) in London discovered that a fission yeast cell division cycle (cdc) gene, cdc2, was absolutely required for the G2/M and G1/S transitions. Cdc2 encodes a protein kinase, an **enzyme** that catalyzes substrate phosphorylation. Although the kinase (also called p34 because its molecular weight is 34 kilodaltons), is not fully understood, it can phosphorylate lamin proteins that line the inside of the nuclear envelope. Notably, phosphorylated lamins become unstable, leading to nuclear envelope breakdown. Presumably, p34 drives a cell into mitosis at least partly because it phosphorylates lamins. Genes equivalent to cdc2 have been discovered in humans, frogs, insects, fish, and higher plants.

How does mitosis stop so abruptly when two siblings enter G1, even though p34 is still present? This puzzle was partly solved by Tim Hunt at the ICRF laboratories. A protein extract injected into immature frog oocytes caused them to undergo meiosis prematurely. Hunt noticed one protein in the extract that increased in concentration during the cell cycle but disappeared suddenly at the M to G1 phase transition. It was called cyclin. Data from the fission yeast and frog systems indicated that p34 depends on cyclin for its phosphorylating activity. In fact, p34 and cyclin bind together from late G2 until late mitosis and then, suddenly, cyclin is degraded, p34 stops working, and mitosis ends. Plant-like cyclins have also been identified in various higher plants including *Arabidopsis*, alfalfa, and rice, reflecting remarkable conservation of the key cell cycle genes among unrelated organisms. SEE ALSO CELLS; CELLS, SPECIALIZED TYPES; MERISTEMS.

Dennis Francis

Bibliography

Alberts, Bruce, D. Bray, J. Lewis, M. Raff, K. Roberts, and J. D. Watson. *The Molecular Biology of the Cell*, 3rd ed. New York: Garland, 1994.

Cells

Plants are multicellular organisms composed of millions of plant cells. Although individual cells may differ greatly from each other in mature structure, all plant cells share the same basic eukaryotic organization. That is, each plant cell possesses a nucleus and cytoplasm with subcellular **organelles.** In addition to these components, all plant cells possess a cell wall of cellulose. Although plant cells begin their life with a full complement of cellular components, some specialized cell types lose their nuclei and all or part of their cytoplasm as they mature.

Components of a Cell

Cell Wall. Plant cells, unlike animal cells, are surrounded by a relatively thin but mechanically strong cell wall. Plant cell walls consist of a complex mixture of **polysaccharides**, proteins, and phenolic **polymers** that are secreted by the **protoplast** and then assembled into an organized network linked together by **covalent** and hydrogen bonds. Cell walls function in the support of plant tissues and in mechanical protection from insects and **pathogens**. Plant cell walls are made up of cellulose microfibrils embedded in an amorphous matrix, an organization analogous to that of fiberglass or steel-reinforced concrete. Cellulose microfibrils consist of linear chains of glucose, with each chain composed of two thousand to twenty-five thousand glucose units. About fifty such chains are linked side by side through

enzyme a protein that controls a reaction in a cell

organelle a membrane-bound structure within a cell

polysaccharide a linked chain of many sugar molecules

polymer a large molecule made from many similar parts

protoplast the portion of the cell within the cell wall

covalent held together by electron-sharing bonds

pathogen disease-causing organism

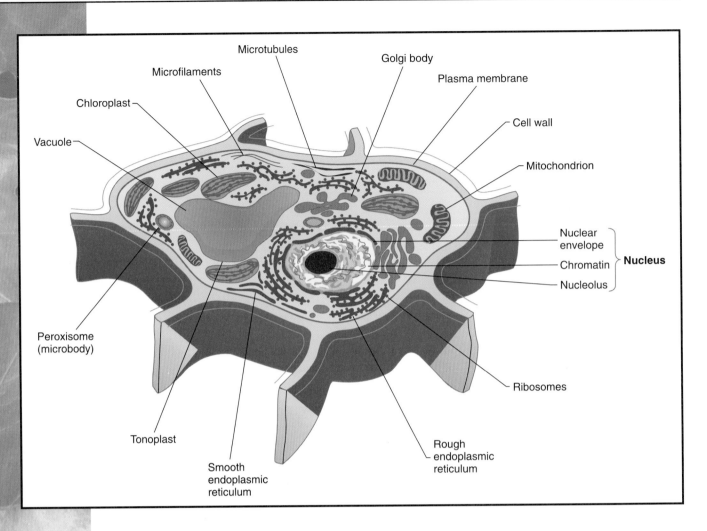

Microtubules

Microfilaments

Golgi body

Plasma membrane

Chloroplast

Cell wall

Vacuole

Mitochondrion

Nuclear envelope

Chromatin — **Nucleus**

Nucleolus

Peroxisome (microbody)

Ribosomes

Tonoplast

Rough endoplasmic reticulum

Smooth endoplasmic reticulum

Components of a plant cell.

compound a substance formed from two or more elements

hydrogen bonds to form one microfibril. Hydrogen bonding between adjacent glucose units forms highly crystalline regions within the cellulose microfibril, giving cellulose its stiffness and high tensile strength.

Cellulose microfibrils are embedded in a matrix composed of pectin, hemicelluloses, and proteins. Pectins and hemicelluloses are shorter chain polysaccharides that are either branched or unbranched and form cross-links between the cellulose microfibrils. In the presence of calcium ions, pectins form a highly hydrated gel (purified pectin is used in jam and jelly making). Cell wall carbohydrates are covalently linked to cell wall proteins that are rich in the rare amino acid hydroxyproline. Cell wall structural proteins vary greatly in their composition but are thought to provide strength, particularly in cells that are growing.

Specialized types of plant cells such as sclerenchyma fibers and xylem vessels require a hard, rigid cell wall in order to function. These cells synthesize a thick, inner wall layer called a secondary cell wall. The secondary cell wall is impregnated with a polymer of phenolic units called lignin. Lignins are much-branched, long chain phenolic **compounds** that form many cross-links with other wall components and give secondary cell walls great strength and rigidity.

Cell Membrane. The portion of the plant cell inside the cell wall is called the protoplast. The protoplast is bounded by a membrane known as the

COMPONENTS OF A PLANT CELL

Component	Number Per Cell (approximate)	Diameter/Thickness	Function
Cell wall	1	1 micrometer	Support, protection
Nucleus	1	10 micrometers	Site of most of cell's genetic information
Endoplasmic reticulum	1 interconnected network	30 nanometers (thickness of cisterna)	Protein synthesis, processing, and storage, lipid synthesis
Golgi apparatus	100	1 micrometer (thickness of cisterna)	Protein processing, secretion
Vacuole	1	100 micrometers	Osmotic regulation, storage
Mitochondrion	200	1 micrometer	Cellular respiration
Plastid	20	5 micrometers	Photosynthesis
Peroxisome	100	1 micrometer	Photorespiration
Microtubule	1000	25 nanometers	Cell shape, cell division
Microfilament	1000	7 nanometers	Chromosome movements, cytoplasmic streaming

cell membrane or the plasma membrane. Like all biological membranes, it consists of a double layer of phospholipids in which proteins are embedded. Phospholipids are a class of lipids in which glycerol is covalently linked to two fatty acids and to a phosphate group. The hydrocarbon chains of the fatty acids are **nonpolar** and form a region that is highly **hydrophobic**. The proteins associated with the lipid layer are of two types: integral and peripheral. Integral proteins span the entire thickness of the lipid layer. For example, the cellulose synthase **enzymes** that catalyze the synthesis of cellulose are integral proteins. They extend across the cell membrane, taking up glucose precursors on the inner side and extruding a cellulose microfibril on the outer side. Peripheral proteins are attached to one surface of the lipid layer. Peripheral proteins on the inner surface of the plasma membrane often function in interactions between the membrane and components of the cytoskeleton. Some peripheral proteins on the outer surface of the plasma membrane function in hormone perception and signaling.

All plant cell membranes share the same basic structure but differ in the makeup of specific components. All membranes also share the important property of semi-impermeability. Small molecules such as water move readily across the membrane, but larger molecules can move only if the appropriate integral proteins are present.

Nucleus. The nucleus is the most prominent structure within the protoplast and contains the genetic information responsible for regulating cell metabolism, growth, and differentiation. The nucleus contains the complex of deoxyribonucleic acid (DNA) and associated proteins, known as chromatin in the uncondensed state and as chromosomes in the condensed state. The chromatin is embedded in a clear matrix called the nucleoplasm. Nuclei also contain a densely granular region, called the nucleolus, that is the site of ribosome synthesis. The nucleus is bounded by a double membrane, the nuclear envelope. The two membranes of the nuclear envelope are joined at sites called nuclear pores. Each nuclear pore is an elaborate structure that allows macromolecules such as ribo-

nonpolar not marked by separation of charge (unlike water and other polar substances)

hydrophobic water repellent

enzyme a protein that controls a reaction in a cell

A micrograph of the nuclei of plant cells.

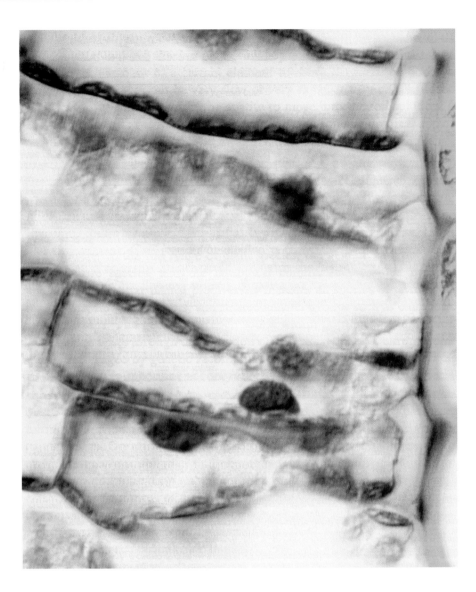

cisterna a fluid-containing sac or space

dictyosome any one of membranous or vesicular structures making up the Golgi apparatus

vesicle a membrane-bound cell structure with specialized contents

somal subunits and ribonucleic acid (RNA) to pass between the nucleus and the cytoplasm.

Endomembrane System. The cytoplasm of plant cells has a continuous network of internal membranes called the endomembrane system. The nuclear envelope forms part of this system and is continuous with another component, the endoplasmic reticulum (ER). The ER consists of flattened sacs or tubes known as **cisternae**. There are two types of ER, smooth and rough, that are interconnected but carry out different functions. Rough ER tends to be lamellar (formed into flattened sacs) and is covered with ribosomes. Rough ER functions in protein synthesis and in the processing and storage of proteins made on the outer surface. In contrast, smooth ER tends to be tubular and is a major site of the synthesis of lipids such as those making up membranes.

Another major component of the endomembrane system is the Golgi apparatus (or **dictyosome**). The Golgi apparatus consists of a stack of flattened membrane cisternae and associated **vesicles**. The two primary functions of the Golgi apparatus are the modification of proteins synthesized on the rough

COMPARISON OF PLANT AND ANIMAL CELLS

Component	Plant Cell	Animal Cell
Cell wall	Provides protection, support	Absent (some cells have extracellular matrix of protein)
Nucleus	Site of most of cell's genetic information	Site of most of cell's genetic information
Endoplasmic reticulum	Protein synthesis, processing, and storage, lipid synthesis	Protein synthesis, processing, and storage, lipid synthesis
Golgi apparatus	Protein processing, secretion	Protein processing, secretion
Vacuole	Provides turgor storage	Absent
Mitochondrion	Cellular respiration	Cellular respiration
Plastid	Photosynthesis, color, starch or lipid storage	Absent
Peroxisome	Oxidizes fatty acids, photorespiration in green tissues	Oxidizes fatty acids
Cytoskeleton	Regulates cell shape, moves chromosomes, cytoplasmic streaming	Regulates cell shape, moves chromosomes, cytoplasmic streaming
Centriole	Absent	Required for nuclear division

ER and packaging of processed proteins and carbohydrates to be secreted outside the plasma membrane. The Golgi apparatus is a very dynamic part of cell structure. Vesicles carrying newly synthesized proteins or other precursors fuse with a cisterna on the forming face of the Golgi apparatus. As its contents are processed, a cisterna moves through the stack until it reaches the maturing face of the stack. Here the cisterna breaks up into separate vesicles that release their contents at the plasma membrane. Golgi apparatus are very numerous in secretory cells such as those of nectaries or root caps, and they also play a role in the secretion of cell wall matrix polysaccharides.

Vacuole. The vacuole is a conspicuous component of the cytoplasm in most plant cells. It may occupy more than 90 percent of cell volume in unspecialized parenchyma cells. The vacuole is surrounded by a membrane called the tonoplast that, because of the high density of integral proteins that are ion channels, plays an important role in the osmotic relationships of the cell. The vacuole stores a wide range of inorganic and organic substances such as the compounds that give beets their color (the water soluble red pigment anthocyanin), apples their sweetness (sucrose), lemons their sourness (citric acid), and tea its bitterness (tannin). In some plants, the vacuoles function as part of the plants' defense systems: it may be filled with sharp crystals of calcium oxalate that help deter **herbivores**.

Chloroplast. Chloroplasts are organelles that function in photosynthesis and are another feature that distinguish plant from animal cells. Chloroplasts are bounded by a double membrane, the chloroplast envelope. The inner membrane of the envelope is invaginated (folded) to form flattened sacs within the chloroplast called thylakoids. Thylakoid membranes take two forms: stacks called grana, and sheets that connect the grana, called stroma thylakoids. Granal thylakoids contain photosynthetic pigments such as chlorophyll and carotenoids, as well as the proteins associated with the light reactions of photosynthesis. The carbon fixation reactions of photosynthesis take place within the amorphous portion of the chloroplast called the stroma. Chloroplast DNA is found in discrete regions within the stroma. The stroma also contains chloroplast ribosomes and other components required for protein synthesis. Therefore the chloroplast is semiautonomous, relying on the nuclear **genome** for only some of its proteins. Green chloro-

herbivore an organism that feeds on plant parts

genome the genetic material of an organism

plasts are just one of several types of plastids that share the same basic structure. Chromoplasts are red or orange plastids that contain large amounts of carotenoid pigments and give fruits such as tomatoes and oranges their color. The brilliant colors of autumn leaves results from both the conversion of chloroplasts to chromoplasts and the formation of anthocyanin in the vacuole. Amyloplasts, such as those found in a potato tuber, are plastids that store starch.

Other Organelles. Mitochondria are small organelles with a double membrane that function in cellular respiration. The inner membrane of the mitochondrial envelope is infolded to form cristae that are the sites of the electron transfer system. The inner membrane encloses the matrix region, the location of the Krebs cycle. Like plastids, mitochondria possess their own DNA, ribosomes, and protein-synthesizing machinery. Proteins encoded by the mitochondria genome include ribosomal proteins and components of the electron transfer system.

Peroxisomes are small, single-membrane-bound organelles that function in photorespiration, a process that consumes oxygen and releases carbon dioxide. These peroxisomes are often found in association with chloroplasts in green leaf tissue. Other peroxisomes, called glyoxysomes, function in the conversion of stored fats to sucrose and are common in the tissues of germinating seeds.

Cytoskeleton. All living plant cells possess a cytoskeleton, a complex network of protein **filaments** that extends throughout the cytosol. The cytoskeleton functions in **mitosis**, cytokinesis, cell growth, and cell differentiation. The plant cell cytoskeleton has two major components: hollow cylinders called microtubules that are composed of tubulin protein, and solid microfilaments composed of actin protein. Microtubules guide chromosome movements during mitosis and the orientation of cellulose microfibrils during cell wall synthesis. The **contractile** microfilaments play a role in chromosome movement and in cytoplasmic streaming. SEE ALSO CARBOHYDRATES; CELL CYCLE; CELLS, SPECIALIZED TYPES; CELLULOSE; CELL WALLS; CHLOROPLASTS; PLASTIDS.

Nancy G. Dengler

filament a threadlike extension

mitosis the part of the cell cycle in which chromosomes are separated to give each daughter cell an identical chromosome set

contractile capable of contracting

Bibliography

Purves, William K., Gordon H. Orians, H. Craig Heller, and David Sadavai. *Life: The Science of Biology*. Sunderland, MA: Sinauer Associates/W. H. Freeman, 1998.

Raven, Peter H., Ray F. Evert, and Susan E. Eichhorn. *Biology of Plants*, 6th ed. New York: W. H. Freeman and Company, 1999.

Taiz, Lincoln, and Eduardo Zeiger. *Plant Physiology*, 2nd ed. Sunderland, MA: Sinauer Associates, 1998.

Cells, Specialized Types

vascular related to the transport of nutrients

The specialized cell types found in plant stems, leaves, roots, flowers, and fruits are organized into three tissue systems: the ground tissue system, the dermal tissue system, and the **vascular** tissue system. Each tissue system carries out a different general function: the vascular tissue system transports water and solutes over long distances within the plant, the dermal tissue system provides protection and gas exchange at the surface of the plant, and

the ground tissue system provides cells that carry out photosynthesis, storage, and support. Each tissue system has many specialized cell types, and a few cell types are found in more than one tissue system.

The different types of specialized plant cells are distinguished by cell shape and by properties of the cell wall and **protoplast**. The plant cell wall is one of the most important distinguishing features of the different kinds of specialized cells. All plant cells have a thin and flexible primary wall, made of the **polymer** cellulose and other carbohydrates. Other cell types have, in addition to a primary wall, a thick, rigid secondary wall, made of cellulose impregnated with lignin.

Cells of the Ground Tissue System

Parenchyma cells are the generalized, multipurpose cells in the plant. Most parenchyma cells have thin primary walls and range from spherical to barrel-like in shape. Parenchyma cells often store food reserves, as in the starch-storing parenchyma cells of a potato tuber or the sugar-storing parenchyma cells of an apple. The parenchyma cells of green leaves are specialized for photosynthesis; these cells contain numerous large **chloroplasts** and are called chlorenchyma cells. Other parenchyma cells called transfer

Transmission electron micrograph of a parenchyma cell.

protoplast the portion of the cell within the cell wall

polymer a large molecule made from many similar parts

chloroplast the photosynthetic organelle of plants and algae

cells are specialized for the transport of **solutes** across the cell membrane. These cells have a greatly enlarged surface area due to the highly convoluted inner surface of the cell wall. Transfer cells are found in **nectaries** where the extensive cell membrane houses transport channels that secrete sugars and other nectar components to the exterior of the cell.

Collenchyma cells function in the support of growing tissues. Individual collenchyma cells are long and narrow and have an unevenly thickened primary wall. Collenchyma cells form a long cable of thousands of cells that together can provide mechanical support while a stem or leaf elongates. Collenchyma is common in the veins of leaves and forms the strings of celery stalks.

Sclerenchyma cells function in the support of tissues that are no longer expanding. Individual sclerenchyma cells are long and narrow with a thick, hard, rigid secondary wall. Unlike parenchyma and collenchyma cells that are living cells, sclerenchyma cells are dead at maturity. The cell's function in mechanical support is carried out by the strong cell walls; a living protoplast is unnecessary. Sclerenchyma fibers make up the bulk of woody tissues and also form long strands in the leaves and stems of many plants. Natural fiber ropes such as those made from hemp or sisal plants are made up of thousands of sclerenchyma fibers. Some sclerenchyma cells called sclereids are much shorter than fibers; these form the hard layers of walnut shells and peach pits, and small clusters of sclereids form the grit in pear fruits.

Cells of the Dermal System

Epidermal cells form the surface layer of the plant, the epidermis. Typical epidermal cells are flat and form a continuous sheet with no spaces between the cells. Each epidermal cell secretes a layer of the **hydrophobic** polymer cutin on the surface, which greatly reduces the amount of water lost by evaporation. Most epidermal cells also secrete waxes on the surface of the cutin, which further reduces **transpiration**, as well as wettability of the leaf surface. When you polish an apple, you are melting these surface waxes through friction. Epidermal cells of green leaves lack pigmented chloroplasts, allowing light to penetrate to the photosynthetic tissues within. Epidermal cells of petals often contain blue or red anthocynanin pigments within the vacuole or orange carotenoid pigments within the plastids, giving rise to the bright colors of many flowers.

Guard cells are specialized epidermal cells that function to open small pores in the plant surface, allowing the carbon dioxide needed for photosynthesis to diffuse from the external atmosphere into the chlorenchyma tissue. Guard cells are usually crescent-shaped, contain green chloroplasts, and are able to rapidly change their shape in response to changes in water status. As guard cells take up water, the pore opens; as they lose water the pore closes. The two guard cells and pore are termed a stomate.

Trichomes are hairlike cells that project from the surface of the plant. They function to reduce water loss by evaporation by trapping water vapor near the plant surface. In some plants, trichomes are glandular and secrete sticky or toxic substances that repel insect **herbivores.**

Cells of the Vascular Tissue System

The vascular tissue system is composed of both xylem and phloem tissue. Xylem functions to carry water and mineral nutrients absorbed at the

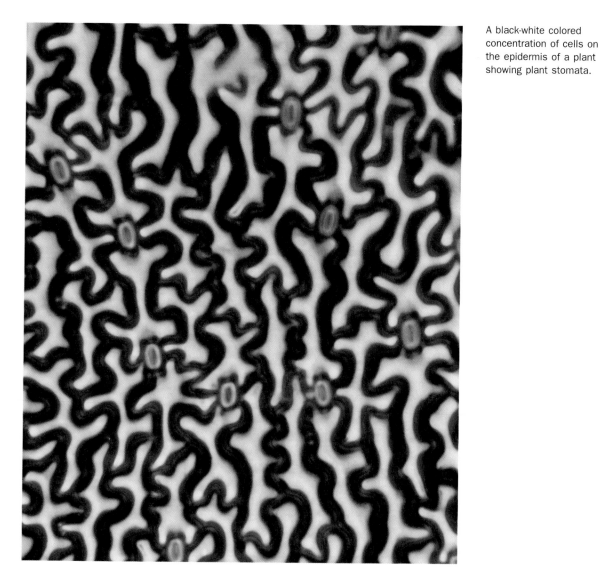

A black-white colored concentration of cells on the epidermis of a plant showing plant stomata.

root tips throughout the plants roots, stems, and leaves. Vessel elements are the major cell type involved in the transport of water and these solutes. Vessel elements are elongate cells with thick secondary walls. Xylem sap travels under a negative pressure or vacuum, and the strong rigid walls keep the vessel elements from collapsing, much like the steel coil in a vacuum-cleaner hose. Like sclerenchyma fibers, vessel elements are dead at maturity, so that each cell forms an empty tube. Before vessel elements die, however, the cell's protoplast releases **enzymes** that degrade the cell wall at both ends of the cell, forming a perforation. Individual vessel elements are joined end to end at the perforations, thus forming a long, continuous pipe, the vessel. Other xylem cells called **tracheids** also function in transport of water and solutes, but are less efficient because they lack perforations and do not form long vessels. Xylem tissue also contains sclerenchyma cells that function in support and parenchyma cells that function in storage or as transfer cells. When transfer cells are found in the xylem, they function to recover valuable solutes such as nitrogen compounds from the sap traveling in the xylem vessels.

enzyme a protein that controls a reaction in a cell

tracheid a type of cell that conducts water from root to shoot

Phloem tissue functions to transport the products of photosynthesis from green tissues to parts of the plant where energy-rich carbohydrates are required for storage or growth (a process called translocation). Sieve elements are the conducting cells of the phloem. Sieve elements are elongated cells, with a thick primary wall. Phloem sap travels under a positive pressure, and the thick, elastic cell walls allow the cells to adjust to the fluctuations in pressure over a day-night cycle. Sieve elements have large, conspicuous pores on the end walls, forming a sieve plate. The sieve plate pores allow the phloem sap to travel from cell to cell along the file of cells called a sieve tube. Each sieve element is living, with an intact plasma membrane; the differential permeability of the membrane prevents solutes from leaking out of the sieve tube. Sieve-tube elements lack a nucleus and some other components of the cytoplasm; this feature functions to keep the pores unplugged. Companion cells are small parenchyma cells associated with each sieve element. The nucleus of the companion cell must direct the metabolism of both the companion cell itself and of its sister sieve element. SEE ALSO ANATOMY OF PLANTS; CELL CYCLE; CELLS; FIBER AND FIBER PRODUCTS; TISSUES; TRANSLOCATION; TRICHOMES; VASCULAR TISSUES; WATER MOVEMENT.

Nancy G. Dengler

Bibliography

Burgess, Jeremy. *An Introduction to Plant Cell Development.* New York: Cambridge University Press, 1985.

Esau, Katherine. *Anatomy of Seed Plants,* 2nd ed. New York: John Wiley & Sons, 1977.

Gunning, Brian E. S., and Martin W. Steer. *Plant Cell Biology: Structure and Function.* Boston: Jones and Bartlett, 1996.

Raven, Peter H., Ray F. Evert, and Susan E. Eichhorn. *Biology of Plants,* 6th ed. New York: W. H. Freeman and Company, 1999.

Cellulose

Cellulose is a major structural component of the cell walls of all land plants, including trees, shrubs, and herbaceous plants. The cell wall is a complex **polysaccharide** layer that surrounds each cell within a plant. Chemically, cellulose is a polysaccharide made up of long, unbranched chains of glucose linked end to end, making a very flat chain. (Starch is also made up of glucose, but linked such that it curls, resulting in very different properties.) Many cellulose chains associate side by side to make a cellulose ribbon, or microfibril, that has exceptional mechanical strength and chemical stability. Cellulose microfibrils, which are approximately 5 to 10 **nanometers** thick and many micrometers long, make cell walls strong and able to resist large forces, such as those generated internally by **turgor** pressure or externally by the weight of the plant or by wind. Economically, cellulose is important as a major component of wood products and of fibers used to make paper and textiles, such as cotton and linen. For industry, cellulose is dissolved and spun as a thread (called rayon) or formed into a thin sheet (cellophane). Cellulose is also chemically modified to make many kinds of films (such as cellulose acetate), thickeners used in foods and paints, and coatings such as nail polish (which contains cellulose nitrate). SEE ALSO CARBOHYDRATES; CELL WALLS; FIBER AND FIBER PRODUCTS.

Daniel Cosgrove

polysaccharide a linked chain of many sugar molecules

nanometer one-millionth of a meter

turgor the internal pressure pushing outward in a plant cell

Bibliography

Brett, C. T., and K. Waldron. *Physiology and Biochemistry of Plant Cell Walls*, 2nd ed. London: Chapman and Hall, 1996.

Cell Walls

With a few notable exceptions, plant cells are encased in a complex **polymeric** wall that is synthesized and assembled by the cell during its growth and differentiation. Cell walls function as the major mechanical restraint that determines plant cell size and **morphology**. They enable cells to generate high **turgor** pressure and thus are important for the water relations of plants. Cell walls also act as a physical and chemical barrier to slow the invasion of bacteria, fungi, and other plant pests, and they also take part in a sophisticated signaling and defense system that helps plants sense **pathogen** invasion by detecting breakdown products from wall **polysaccharides**. Finally, cell walls glue plant cells together and provide the mechanical support necessary for large structures (the largest trees may reach 100 meters in height, generating tremendous compression forces due to their own weight).

Cell walls vary greatly in appearance, composition, and physical properties. In growing cells, such as those found in shoot and root **apical meristems**, cell walls are pliant and extensible (that is, they can extend in response to the expansive forces generated by cell turgor pressure). Such walls are called primary cell walls. After cells cease growth, they sometimes continue to synthesize one or more additional cell wall layers that are referred to as the secondary cell wall. Secondary cell walls are generally inextensible and may be thick and **lignified**, as in the xylem cells that make up wood.

Composition and Molecular Architecture

The primary cell wall contains three major classes of polysaccharides: cellulose, hemicellulose, and pectin. Hemicellulose and pectin collectively constitute the matrix polysaccharides of the cell wall. Cellulose is present in the form of thin microfibrils, about 5 **nanometers** in thickness and indefinite length. The cellulose microfibril is made up of many parallel chains of 1,4-β-glucan, which is a linear polymer of glucose molecules linked end-to-end through the carbon atoms numbered 1 and 4. These chains form a crystalline ribbon that makes cellulose very strong and relatively **inert** and indigestible.

Hemicellulose refers to various polysaccharides that are tightly associated with the surface of the cellulose microfibril. They are chemically similar to cellulose, except they contain short side branches or kinks that prevent close packing into a microfibril. The backbone of hemicelluloses is typically made up of long chains of glucose or xylose residues linked end to end, often ornamented with short side chains. The most abundant hemicelluloses are xyloglucans and xylans. By adhering to the surface of cellulose microfibrils, hemicelluloses prevent direct contact between microfibrils, but may link them together in a cohesive network.

Pectin constitutes the third class of wall polysaccharide. It forms a gel-like phase in between the cellulose microfibrils. Unlike cellulose and hemi-

polymer a large molecule made from many similar parts

morphology shape and form

turgor the internal pressure pushing outward in a plant cell

pathogen disease-causing organism

polysaccharide a linked chain of many sugar molecules

apical at the tip

meristem the growing tip of a plant

lignified composed of lignin, a tough and resistant plant compound

nanometer one-millionth of a meter

inert incapable of reaction

Colored transmission electron micrograph of cells in a young leaf.

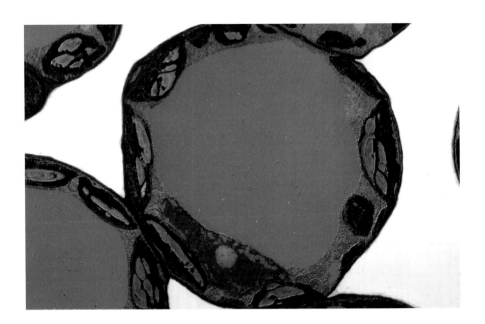

cellulose, pectin may be solubilized with relatively mild treatments such as boiling water or mildly acidic solutions. Pectin includes relatively simple polysaccharides such as polygalacturonic acid, a long chain of the acidic sugar galacturonic acid. This pectin readily forms gels in which calcium ions link adjacent chains together. Other pectin polysaccharides are more complex, with backbones made of alternating sugar residues such as galacturonic acid and rhamnose, and long side chains made up of other sugars such as arabinose or galactose. In the cell wall, pectins probably form very large aggregates of indefinite size.

In addition to these polysaccharides, primary cell walls also contain a small amount of structural proteins, such as hydroxyproline-rich glycoproteins and glycine-rich proteins.

Secondary cell walls are like primary walls except they contain more cellulose and less pectin than primary walls, and often contain hemicellulose polymers of differing composition. Many, but not all, secondary walls also contain lignin, which is a complex and irregular phenolic polymer that acts like epoxy to glue the wall polysaccharides together. Lignification greatly increases the mechanical strength of cell walls and makes them highly resistant to degradation.

Cell Wall Synthesis

The components of the cell wall are synthesized via distinct pathways and then assembled at the cell surface. Cellulose is synthesized by a large, cellulose synthase **enzyme** complex embedded in the plasma membrane. This complex is large enough to be seen in the electronic microscope and looks like a hexagonal array, called a particle rosette because of its appearance. The cellulose-synthesizing complex synthesizes thirty to forty glucan chains in parallel, using **substrates** from the cytoplasm. The growing chains are extruded to the outside of the cell via a pore in the complex and the chains then crystallize into a microfibril at the surface of the cell. In some algae the cellulose synthase complexes assume other configurations and this

enzyme a protein that controls a reaction in a cell

substrate molecules acted on by enzymes

is associated with differing sizes and structures of the microfibril. Genes encoding plant cellulose synthases were first identified in the late 1990s, and the molecular details of how these proteins synthesize cellulose is still being studied.

The matrix polysaccharides (hemicellulose and pectin) are synthesized in the Golgi apparatus by enzymes called glycosyl transferases. They are transported to the cell wall via **vesicles** that fuse with the plasma membrane and dump their contents into the wall space. The matrix polymers and newly extruded cellulose microfibrils then assemble into an organized cell wall, probably by spontaneous self-organization between the different classes of polymers.

Wall enzymes may also aid assembly by forming cross-links between wall components. For example, some enzymes remove side chains from the hemicelluloses. This enables the hemicelluloses to stick more readily to cellulose. Other enzymes cut and link polysaccharides together, forming a more intricate weave of matrix polysaccharides.

vesicle a membrane-bound cell structure with specialized contents

Economic Importance of the Cell Wall

The cell wall is unmatched in the diversity and versatility of its economic uses. Lumber, charcoal, and other wood products are obvious examples. Textiles such as cotton and linen are derived from the walls of unusually long and strong fiber cells. Paper is likewise a product of long fiber cell walls that are extracted, beaten, and dried as a uniform sheet. Cellulose can be dissolved and regenerated as a manmade fiber called rayon or in sheets called cellophane. Chemically modified cellulose is used to make plastics, membranes, coatings, adhesives, and thickeners found in a vast array of products, from photographic film to paint, nail polish to explosives. In agriculture, cell walls are important as animal fodder, whereas in the human diet, cell walls are important as dietary fiber or roughage. Pectin is used as a gelling agent in jellies, yogurt, low-fat margarines, and other foods, while powered cellulose is similarly used as a thickener in foods and as an inert filler in medicinal tablets.

SEE ALSO ANATOMY OF PLANTS; CARBOHYDRATES; CELLS; CELLULOSE.

Daniel J. Cosgrove

Bibliography

Brett, C. T., and K. Waldron. *Physiology and Biochemistry of Plant Cell Walls,* 2nd ed. London: Chapman and Hall, 1996.

Cosgrove, Daniel J. "Cell Walls: Structure, Biogenesis, and Expansion." In *Plant Physiology,* 2nd ed. Lincoln Taiz and Eduardo Zeiger, eds. Sunderland, MA: Sinauer Associates, 1998.

Lapasin, Romano, and Sabrina Pricl. *The Rheology of Industrial Polysaccharides: Theory and Applications.* London: Blackie Academic & Professional, 1995.

Chaparral

Chaparral is an evergreen shrub vegetation that dominates the rocky slopes of southern and central California. It forms a nearly continuous cover of closely spaced shrubs 6 to 12 feet (2 to 4 meters) tall, with intertwining branches that make the vegetation nearly impenetrable to humans. Herbaceous vegetation (grasses and wildflowers) is generally lacking, except after fires, which are frequent throughout the range. Because of complex patterns

Montane chaparral vegetation such as xerophytic shrubs and singleleaf piñon (*Pinus monophylla*) can survive the seasonal droughts that occur on the flanks of the Sierra Nevadas.

topographic related to the shape or contours of the land

juxtaposition contrast brought on by closeness

alluvial plain broad area formed by the deposit of river sediment at its outlet

of **topographic**, soil, and climatic variations, chaparral may form a mosaic pattern in which patches of oak woodland, grassland, or coniferous forest appear in sharp **juxtaposition**. Fire frequency and soil are major factors that determine these patterns. Chaparral is replaced by grassland on frequently burned sites, especially along the more arid borders at low elevations (where shrub recovery is more precarious due to drought) and on deeper clay soils and **alluvial plains**, and by oak woodland on more moist slopes (where fires are less frequent and often less intense).

California chaparral is distributed in a region of Mediterranean climate, which has cool (40°F), wet winters and hot (95°F), dry summers. Rainfall is 10 to 20 inches (25 to 100 centimeters) annually, two-thirds of which falls November to April in storms of several days duration.

Plants of the Chapparal

The most widely distributed chaparral shrub is chamise (*Adenostoma fasciculatum*), an adapted shrub with short needlelike leaves, which is distributed from Baja California in the south to Oregon in the north. Buckbrush (*Cean-*

othus spp.) and manzanitas (*Arctostaphylos*) are large **genera** (about seventy species each) and often form pure stands commonly referred to as manzanita chaparral or ceanothus chaparral. Some species are highly restricted in distribution, whereas others are nearly as widespread as chamise. Most species in these two genera are **endemic** to the California chaparral and have suites of characters reflecting a long association with fire. For example, many species of *Ceanothus* and *Arctostaphylos* have woody tubers at their base that sprout new stems after fire. All species in these two genera produce deeply **dormant** seeds that accumulate in the soil and require fire for germination.

At the lowest elevations throughout much of its range, chaparral is commonly replaced by a smaller and highly aromatic vegetation known as soft chaparral or coastal sage. This vegetation differs from chaparral by being summer-deciduous; this loss of leaves during drought confers a greater ability to tolerate the drier conditions at low elevations. The dominant shrubs are only 3 to 6 feet (1 to 2 meters) tall and include California sagebrush (*Artemisia californica*), black sage (*Salvia mellifera*), California buckwheat (*Eriogonum fasciculatum*), deerweed (*Lotus scoparius*), and monkeyflower (*Mimulus aurantiacus*). These smaller shrubs grow rapidly and have well-developed wind dispersal of seeds so they often **colonize** disturbed sites.

The Californian Mediterranean climate is conducive to massive wildfires. Mild, wet winters contribute to a prolonged growing season, which, coupled with moderately fertile soils, result in dense stands of contiguous fuels. Long summer droughts produce highly flammable fuels that are readily ignited by lightning from occasional thunderstorms but more commonly as the result of human carelessness. On average fire frequency for any one area is about every two to three decades, but this may be more frequent than in the past. Throughout much of its range, chaparral forms a continuous cover over great distances, and as a result, huge wildfires that cover tens of thousands of acres are common, particularly during Santa Ana wind conditions. These dry winds from the east occur every autumn and often exceed sixty miles per hour. Some scientists have suggested that massive wildfires are an artifact due to modern-day fire suppression, which causes an unnaturally heavy accumulation of plant fuel. Others dispute this conclusion, pointing to evidence that shows this vegetation has always experienced large, high-intensity fires.

The Role of Fire

Although shrubs dominate chaparral, the **community** comprises a rich diversity of growth forms, many of which are conspicuous only after fire. In addition to evergreen shrubs and trees, there are semi-deciduous subshrubs, slightly ligneous (hardened) **suffrutescents**, woody and herbaceous vines, and a rich variety of herbaceous perennials and annuals. A large number of these species arise from dormant seeds deposited into the soil decades earlier, following an earlier fire. Dormancy is broken in some seeds by heat but in many other species smoke from the fire triggers germination. In the first spring following fire, there is an abundant growth of herbaceous plants, which are relatively short-lived and are replaced by shrubs within the first five years. The postfire herbaceous flora often is dominated by annual species that live for less than one year, and species diversity is typically greatest in this first year after fire. Recovery of shrub **biomass** is from basal resprouts and seedling recruitment from a dormant soil-stored seed bank.

genera plural of genus

endemic belonging or native to a particular area or country

dormant inactive, not growing

colonize to inhabit a new area

community a group of organisms of different species living in a region

suffrutescent a shrub-like plant with a woody base

biomass the total dry weight of an organism or group of organisms

compound a substance formed from two or more elements

toxin a poisonous substance

predation the act of preying upon; consuming for food

The striking contrast between the diminished herb growth under mature chaparral and the flush of herbs after fire is thought to be caused by allelopathic (chemical) suppression of germination by the overstory shrubs. Many of the smaller shrubs, such as sage (*Salvia* spp.) or sagebrush (*Artemisia* spp.), release volatile, aromatic **compounds**, and it has been suggested that these compounds inhibit the growth of competing grasses and wildflowers. This theory holds that fire destroys these **toxins**, and that this occurs throughout the shrub land and in a zone at the border between shrub lands and grasslands, forming a meter-wide strip known as the bare zone. However, experiments in which animals have been excluded from the bare zone demonstrate that the lack of herbaceous plants in and around mature shrub lands is as much due to animal **predation** as it is to chemical inhibition. In addition, it appears that the vast majority of species that germinate after fire do so more because their dormant seeds are stimulated to germinate by fire.

Resource agencies often respond to wildfires with emergency revegetation programs, which drop grass seed on newly burned sites with the expectation that this will reduce soil erosion and eliminate the threat of mudslides and flooding. The rationale for this management is that burned sites have greatly increased surface flow of rainwater and thus high soil erosion. Emergency seeding is considered essential on sites following exceptionally intense fires because of the anticipated negative effects. Throughout the state of California the seed of choice has been the nonnative annual ryegrass (*Lolium multiflorum*). However, there is abundant evidence that this practice fails to substantially reduce threats of mudslides and flooding and competitively displaces the native flora.

senescent aging or dying

ecosystem an ecological community together with its environment

Some scientists have suggested that chaparral shrub lands become **senescent** if they are free of fire for more than a few decades. Detailed studies, however, find that these shrub land **ecosystems** can retain productive vegetation for a century or more, and in fact some shrubs require long periods without fire for successful seedling recruitment. SEE ALSO ALLELOPATHY; BIOME; ECOLOGY, FIRE.

Jon E. Keeley

Bibliography

Callaway, F. M., and F. W. Davis. "Vegetation Dynamics, Fire, and the Physical Environment in Coastal Central California." *Ecology* 74 (1993): 1567–678.

Davis, F. W., M. I. Borchert, and D. C. Odion. "Establishment of Microscale Vegetation Pattern in Maritime Chaparral After Fire." *Vegetation* 84 (1989): 53–67.

Davis, F. W., D. E. Hickson, and D. C. Odion. "Composition of Maritime Chaparral Related to Fire History and Soil, Burton Mesa, Santa Barbara County, California." *Madroño* 35 (1988): 169–95.

Davis, F. W., P. A. Stine, and D. M. Stoms. "Distribution and Conservation Status of Coastal Sage Scrub in Southwestern California." *Journal of Vegetation Science* 5 (1994): 743–56.

Davis, S. D., and H. A. Mooney. "Water Use Patterns of Four Co-occurring Chaparral Shrubs." *Oecologia* 70 (1986): 172–77.

Haidinger, T. L., and J. E. Keeley. "Role of High Fire Frequency in Destruction of Mixed Chaparral." *Madroño* 40 (1993): 141–47.

Keeley, J. E. "Chaparral." In *North American Terrestrial Vegetation*, 2nd ed. M. G. Barbour and W. D. Billings, eds. Cambridge: Cambridge University Press, 2000.

———. "Demographic Structure of California Chaparral in the Long-Term Absence of Fire." *Journal of Vegetation Science* 3 (1992): 79–90.

Tyler, C. M. "Factors Contributing to Postfire Seedling Establishment in Chaparral: Direct and Indirect Effects of Fire." *Journal of Ecology* 83 (1985): 1009–20.

Zedler, P. H. "Fire Frequency in Southern California Shrublands: Biological Effects and Management Options." In *Wildfires in California Brushlands: Ecology and Resource Management*, J. E. Keeley, and T. Scott. Fairfield, eds. Spokane, WA: International Association of Wildland Fire, Fairfield, 1995.

Chestnut Blight

The American chestnut (*Castanea dentata*) formerly was the most prevalent tree in the mountains of the eastern United States, comprising more than 25 percent of the forest. Chestnut was a fast growing, valuable tree. Its wood was used in all phases of construction, from rough timbers and telephone poles to fine furniture; its bark was a source of **tannins** for making leather; and its nuts provided nourishment for wildlife, livestock, and people.

The chestnut blight fungus (*Cryphonectria parasitica*) was introduced into North America at the beginning of the twentieth century, probably on imported Japanese chestnut seedlings. The blight fungus swept through the chestnut forests, killing approximately ten billion trees by the middle of the century. Fewer than one hundred trees within the original range survived the onslaught of blight. This level of destruction of an entire, well-established species by a disease is unparalleled in the annals of plant and animal pathology.

The blight fungus kills chestnut trees by destroying the phloem and outer layers of xylem, growing around the tree trunk at a rate of approximately 15 centimeters per year. When all the bark and underlying wood around a trunk is killed, the tree dies because it can no longer circulate water and sugar between its leaves and roots.

Millions of chestnut sprouts persist today in the Appalachian Mountains, escaping blight due to their small size (although they are still susceptible to the disease). These are being used as mother trees in an effort to backcross the blight resistance of the Chinese chestnut tree into its American cousin. Scientists also have found some viruses that attack the blight fungus, making it unable to kill trees. It is hoped that one or both of these approaches will allow the return of this noble tree. SEE ALSO INTERACTIONS, PLANT-FUNGAL; PATHOGENS.

Frederick V. Hebard

tannins compounds produced by plants that usually serve protective functions; often colored and used for "tanning" and dyeing

Bibliography

Griffin, G. J. "Blight Control and Restoration of the American Chestnut." *Journal of Forestry* 98 (2000): 22–7.

Smith, D. M. "American Chestnut: Ill-Fated Monarch of the Eastern Hardwood Forest." *Journal of Forestry* 98 (2000): 12–15

Chlorophyll

All forms of life on the surface of Earth are powered, directly or indirectly, by absorption of the energy in sunlight by chlorophyll molecules in plant cells. The subsequent processes of photosynthesis convert light energy to

The absorption spectra of chlorophyll *a* and *b* in methanol.

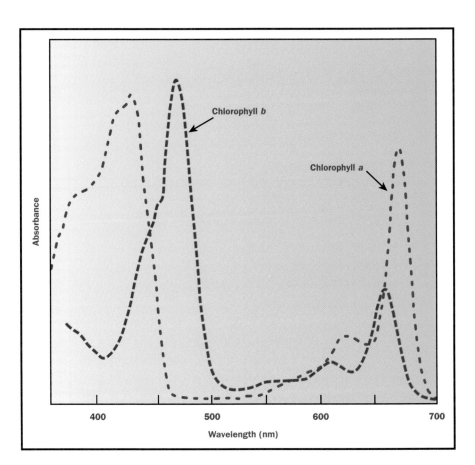

electrical and then chemical energy, which the cell uses for growth. The minimal absorption of green light by chlorophyll causes plants to have a green color (see accompanying graph).

Chlorophylls are cyclic tetrapyrroles, that is, molecules made by connecting four 5-membered pyrrole rings into a macrocycle. The initial biosynthetic precursor, 5-aminolevulinic acid (ALA), is made from the abundant amino acid glutamic acid. Condensation of two ALA molecules produces the 5-membered ring compound porphobilinogen. Four of these molecules are joined into a large ring structure, some of the side chains are modified, and the compound is oxidized to generate the fully conjugated double-bond arrangement that allows efficient absorption of light energy. At this stage, Mg^{2+} is inserted into the center of the large ring structure, and the fifth ring is formed.

The long hydrocarbon side chain causes chlorophyll to act as a lipid, allowing it to become embedded in thylakoid membranes. Chlorophyll *a* can be oxidized to chlorophyll *b*, which differs only in the presence of an aldehyde group on ring B. All chlorophyll molecules are bound to protein molecules and incorporated into complexes that allow energy absorbed by the molecules to be trapped in **reaction centers** of photosynthesis. In **eukaryotic** photosynthetic organisms, all these reactions occur in the **chloroplast**.

Other forms of chlorophyll also are found in nature. Some families of algae contain chlorophyll *c*, which does not have a long lipid tail and differs in several other respects. Chlorophyll *d*, which was found recently as the major chlorophyll in a photosynthetic **prokaryote** living inside ascidians in the Pacific Ocean, is similar to chlorophyll *b* but with the aldehyde on ring A. Bacteriochlorophylls, possibly the evolutionary ancestors of chlorophylls, occur in photosynthetic bacteria. Unlike other chlorophylls, bacteriochlorophylls absorb light in the infrared region, near 800 **nanometers** (nm). SEE ALSO CHLOROPLASTS; PHOTOSYNTHESIS, LIGHT REACTIONS AND; PIGMENTS.

J. Kenneth Hoober

Bibliography

Beale, Samuel I. "Enzymes of Chlorophyll Biosynthesis." *Photosynthesis Research* 60 (1999): 43–73.

Chloroplasts

The chloroplast is a membrane-bound organelle within a cell that conducts photosynthesis. From the molecular perspective, the chloroplast is very large and contains millions of protein molecules along with vast sheets of membranes. If we imagine an average-sized **enzyme** molecule to be the size of an automobile, a chloroplast in a plant leaf cell would be about 6 kilometers on its long axis and about 2 kilometers on its short axis. The approximately cube-shaped plant cell, 15 to 20 kilometers per side, would contain fifty to one hundred of these compartments.

Structure of Chloroplasts

The chloroplast is enclosed by two membranes, designated the outer and inner membranes of the chloroplast envelope. About one-half the volume within the chloroplast is occupied by stacks of fifty to one hundred flattened sacs called thylakoids, from the Greek word meaning "like an empty pouch." The thylakoid membrane surrounds the lumen or interior space and is the major membrane of the chloroplast. Groups of thylakoids adhere into stacks called grana. The remaining soluble phase of the chloroplast, outside thylakoids, is the stroma.

Function of Chloroplasts

The primary function of chloroplasts is photosynthesis, the light-driven fixation of carbon dioxide into organic **compounds**. The products of the photochemical reactions that occur within thylakoid membranes provide the material with which the plant cells grow and on which all forms of life on the surface of Earth depend.

Photosynthesis begins when light is absorbed by the green pigment chlorophyll, which occurs only in photosynthetic thylakoid membranes. The absorbed light energy is transferred to a **reaction center** called Photosystem II (PSII), where electrons are removed from water to release molecular oxygen. The electrons are carried through an electron transport chain in thylakoid membranes to Photosystem I (PSI) to eventually produce reduced compounds (for example, **NADPH**) that drive carbon fixation reactions. The flow of electrons through this linked set of carriers also transfers protons (H⁺) from the stroma to the thylakoid lumen, which generates a concentration gradient. These protons can only flow back to the stroma through protein channels within the thylakoid membrane. At the stromal

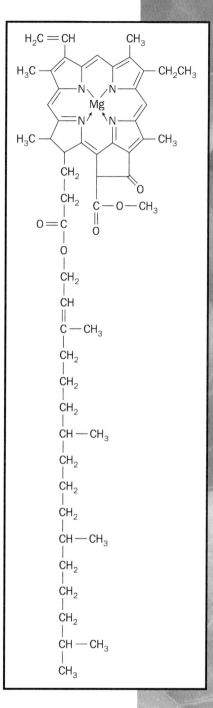

Structure of chlorophyll *a*.

compounds substances formed from two or more elements

NADPH reduced form of nicotinomide adenine dinucleotide phosphate, a small, water-soluble molecule that acts as a hydrogen carrier in biochemical reactions

Major structural compartments of a plant cell chloroplast.

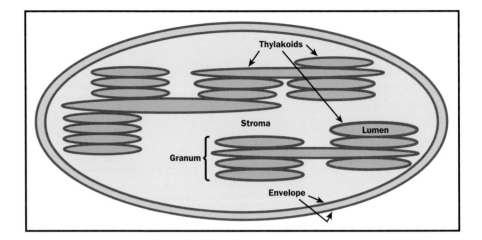

ATP adenosine triphosphate, a small, water-soluble molecule that acts as an energy currency in cells

end of the membrane channels is adenosine triphosphate (**ATP**) synthase, which uses the flow of H$^+$ to drive the synthesis of H$^+$ ATP. ATP is used as the primary energy source for biosynthetic reactions within the cell. The ATP and NADPH created are then used to produce sugars from carbon dioxide.

The most abundant enzyme in the biosphere, ribulose 1,5-bisphosphate carboxylase/oxygenase (rubisco, for short), catalyzes the reaction of carbon dioxide with ribulose 1,5-bisphosphate, a 5-carbon compound, to make glyceraldehyde 3-phosphate and 3-phosphoglycerate. These two 3-carbon compounds enter the reductive pentose-phosphate cycle (also called the Calvin-Benson cycle) and eventually are converted to a 6-carbon sugar, glucose 6-phosphate, the ultimate product. Glucose 6-phosphate is the precursor of many of the storage products in the plant cell, such as starch, sucrose, and lipids, and is also the starting point for biosynthesis of most of the cellular material. All fatty acids and most amino acids used by the cell are also synthesized in the chloroplast.

saturate containing as much dissolved substance as possible

Rubisco is a large enzyme—containing eight large (molecular weight 52,000) and eight small (molecular weight 14,000) subunits—that is also very sluggish, catalyzing a reaction only three times per second even when **saturated** with carbon dioxide. The usual concentration of carbon dioxide in the watery cell interior is sufficient for only one-half this rate. Perhaps these are the reasons why plants developed mechanisms to achieve a high concentration of the enzyme in the stroma to catalyze this reaction that is essential to maintenance of life. Approximately two million molecules of rubisco are present in each chloroplast.

Development of Chloroplasts

vesicle a membrane-bound cell structure with specialized contents

Germination of a seed results in growth of a shoot, in which the initial plastids exist with the cells as simple, double-membrane-enclosed **vesicles** that contain deoxyribonucleic acid (DNA), ribosomes, and a set of enzymes needed for expression of the DNA. These structures, only about 20 percent of the size of a mature chloroplast, are called proplastids. When the shoot reaches the light, the plastid begins the synthesis of chlorophyll, which is required for nearly all remaining aspects of development. Synthesis of lipids, which form the framework of thylakoid membranes, is stimulated within the inner membrane of the envelope.

Proteins are also imported into the chloroplasts after synthesis on cytosolic ribosomes as precursor molecules. Such proteins contain an extension at their amino-terminal end, designated the transit sequence, that serves as a targeting signal for import into the chloroplast. As soon as the protein reaches the stroma, the transit sequence is removed by a specific protease. The chloroplast envelope contains an elaborate apparatus made of numerous protein molecules that function to guide proteins through the membranes into the interior. While some proteins remain embedded in the membrane, others pass through the envelope into the stroma. Of these, a relative few are also transported across thylakoid membranes into the thylakoid lumen. The two major proteins that are imported are the precursor of the small subunit of rubisco, which is released into the stroma, and the chlorophyll-binding proteins, which are integrated into large light-harvesting antenna complexes within the envelope inner membrane. These complexes absorb and funnel light energy to reaction centers to drive the light reactions of photosynthesis. The addition of lipids, pigments, and proteins causes expansion of this membrane, which pinches off into vesicles that subsequently fuse to construct the large thylakoid structure in the interior of the organelle.

Chloroplasts grow and divide along with the cell they reside in as the plant grows. Nearly one hundred copies of the chloroplast **genome**, a circular, rather small molecule of DNA, are present in each chloroplast. The genes are expressed by transcription to make messenger ribonucleic acid

genome the genetic material of an organism

False color transmission electron micrograph of a developing chloroplast in a tobacco leaf.

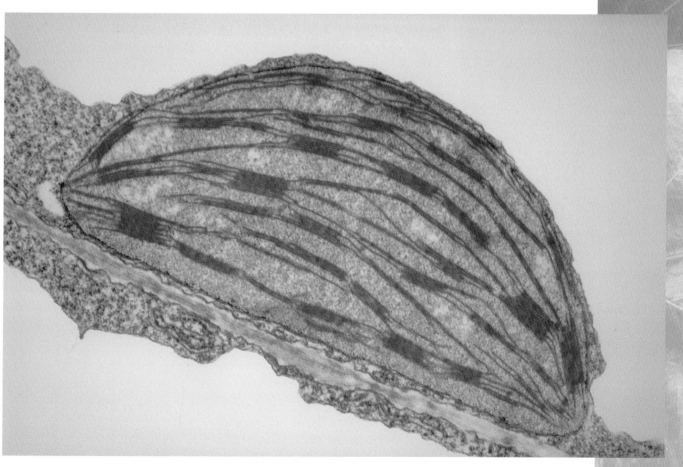

(mRNA), which is translated on chloroplast ribosomes. These ribosomes, about one million in total number per chloroplast, are synthesized inside the chloroplast and are slightly smaller than the cytosolic ribosomes that are encoded by nuclear DNA. Therefore, chloroplasts are able to synthesize their own proteins, but in fact make only about 10 percent of the proteins they contain. Although a chloroplast may contain 500 to 1,000 different proteins, the chloroplast genome contains only 70 to 80 genes for proteins among its total of about 150 genes. The remainder of the proteins are encoded in nuclear DNA and imported.

Evolution of Chloroplasts

The presence of a separate genome, along with similarities between the structures of the chloroplast and photosynthetic **cyanobacteria**, prompted scientists to propose that chloroplasts originated as the result of an early **eukaryotic** cell engulfing a **prokaryotic** cyanobacterium. This proposal has recently received nearly unequivocal support in view of the remarkable similarities in sequences in genes that occur within chloroplasts and cyanobacteria. The evidence suggests that this event, called endosymbiosis, happened once, or a few times, about one billion years ago and that chloroplasts in all photosynthetic eukaryotic organisms are descendants of this event. Shortly after the cyanobacterium became resident within the host cell, much of the genetic information in the bacterium was transferred to the nucleus of the host. Following this endosymbiosis event, as photosynthetic organisms evolved, their chloroplasts diverged as well.

The divergent evolutionary heritages of chloroplasts in various organisms has led to a collection of unique properties. Most of the variety occurs among the algae. Light-harvesting complexes in green algae (Chlorophyceae) contain chlorophylls *a* and *b* bound to proteins within the membrane that are very similar to higher plants. The red algae (Rhodophyceae) are similar to green algae except that they contain phycobilisomes as major light-harvesting complexes attached to the surface of thylakoid membranes and do not contain chlorophyll *b*, which is similar to cyanobacteria. Brown algae (Phaeophyceae), yellow-green algae (Chrysophyceae), **diatoms** (Bacillariophyceae), and dinoflagellates (Dinophyceae) contain proteins similar to those in light-harvesting complexes in green algae; they differ in that they contain chlorophyll *c* instead of chlorophyll *b*. These latter algal families contain an additional pair of membranes surrounding the chloroplast. These extra membranes are thought to have originated when a second eukaryotic cell engulfed an entire chloroplast-containing eukaryotic alga. SEE ALSO CELLS; CHLOROPHYLL; ENDOSYMBIOSIS; PHOTOSYNTHESIS, CARBON FIXATION AND; PHOTOSYNTHESIS, LIGHT REACTIONS AND; PLASTIDS.

J. Kenneth Hoober

cyanobacteria photosynthetic prokaryotic bacteria formerly known as blue-green algae

eukaryotic a cell with a nucleus (*eu* means "true" and *karyo* means "nucleus"); includes protists, plants, animals, and fungi

prokaryotes single-celled organisms without nuclei, including Eubacteria and Archaea

diatoms hard-shelled single-celled marine organisms; a type of algae

Bibliography

Hoober, J. Kenneth, and Laura L. Eggink. "Assembly of Light-Harvesting Complex II and Biogenesis of Thylakoid Membranes in Chloroplasts." *Photosynthesis Research* 61 (1999): 197–215.

Raghavendra, A. S., ed. *Photosynthesis. A Comprehensive Treatise.* Cambridge, UK: Cambridge University Press, 1998.

Tomitani, Akiko, Kiyotaka Okada, Hideaki Miyashita, Hans C. P. Matthijs, Terufumi Ohno, and Ayumi Tanaka. "Chlorophyll *b* and Phycobilins in the Common Ancestor of Cyanobacteria and Chloroplasts." *Nature* 400 (1999): 159–62.

Chocolate   *See Cacao.*

Chromosomes

The genetic material in plants, animals, and fungi is called deoxyribonucleic acid (DNA), a long, linear **polymer** that is physically organized at the microscopic level into chromosomes. Chromosomes are threadlike cellular structures made up of elaborately packaged DNA complexed with proteins. When a cell reproduces itself to make two identical daughter cells, the chromosomes are replicated and divided so that each daughter cell has the same genetic and DNA content. The chromosome division process is called mitosis. During mitosis the individual chromosomes can be stained and seen under a microscope.

Genes code for the production of structural proteins and **enzymes** and are located at specific sites along the DNA. These sites are called loci (singular: locus) and represent a sort of chromosomal street address for the basic units of heredity, the genes. Genetic loci number in the tens of thousands for most plant species, and they are physically linked if they reside on the same chromosome.

Plant chromosomes replicate and divide in a typical fashion. They are also subject to a type of molecular infection by small, self-replicating, or mobile, pieces of DNA called transposable DNA elements (or transposons), which can hop from one chromosome to another, as described below.

Historically, some important basic principles of genetics and heredity have come from the scientific study of plants. In his classic work on the transmission of traits (such as wrinkled seed) in peas, Gregor Mendel discovered the basic rules of heredity. Mendel showed that both mother (egg) and father (pollen sperm) contribute genetic factors to the next generation by cell union at fertilization. Similarly, the discovery of the existence of jumping genes (described below) was made by Barbara McClintock in her work on corn (*Zea mays*).

Plant chromosome research has come full circle in the new millenium with the ability to relate molecular structure to whole plant function. For instance, the wrinkled seed trait studied by Mendel was recently discovered to have been caused by a transposon that hopped into and broke a gene involved in filling the pea seed with starch. Mendel was able to track the broken gene through multiple generations by observing the inheritance of the wrinkled seed trait. Understanding plant chromosome structure and function helps bridge the gap between molecular biology and whole plant biology.

Physical Description

DNA does not exist in the cell as an isolated chemical, but rather as an elaborately packaged and microscopically visible structure called a chromosome. All chromosomes are comprised of both DNA and proteins, although only the DNA contains the genetic code. Each chromosome carries thousands of genes, and each time a cell divides all of the cell's chromosomes are replicated, divided, and sorted into two pools, one for each new daugh-

polymer a large molecule made from many similar parts

enzyme a protein that controls a reaction in a cell

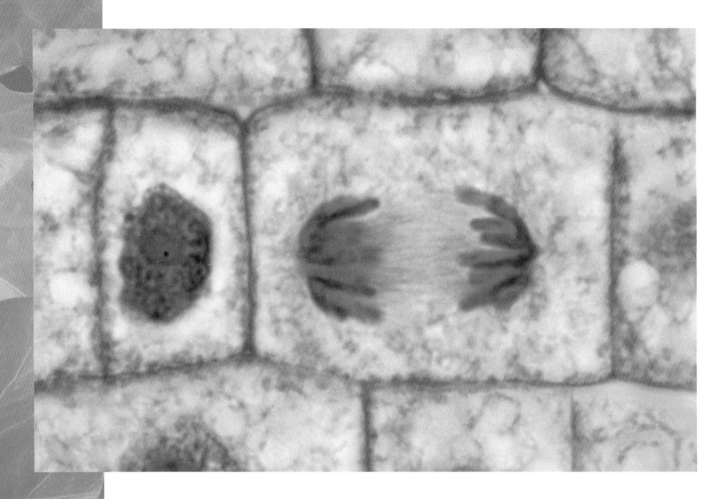

The anaphase stage of mitosis in the cell of an allium root. The chromosomes, replicated and condensed into chromatids, are lined up along an axis.

ter cell. Each chromosome has a centromere (the site on the chromosome where the spindle attaches), which functions as a "luggage handle" for the genetic cargo. This attachment provides the mechanical basis for movement of chromosomes toward one of the two pointed ends (poles) of the football-shaped spindle apparatus.

The entire complement of chromosomes in a given cell or for a given species is referred to as the genome. Plant genomes vary in total DNA content from one species to the next, yet they all have a similar number of functional genes (between fifty and one hundred thousand per individual) required to support the life cycle of a typical plant.

Chromosome Pairing and Segregation

Because most plant species reproduce sexually, they have genomes consisting of two complete sets of genetic instructions, one from each parent, just like humanoids. Most cells of the plant body (stems, roots, leaves) carry this duplicate set, which makes them **diploid**.

diploid having two sets of chromosomes, versus having one (haploid)

haploid having one set of chromosomes, versus having two (diploid)

During meiosis, the genome content gets reduced to one complete set of chromosomes per cell, producing gamete cells that are said to be **haploid**. The male haploid cells in flowering plants give rise to the pollen grains (sperm) whereas the female haploid cells give rise to eggs. As with animals, the diploid state is restored at fertilization by the union of DNA from the sperm and egg cells. Thus the plant life cycle is frequently divided into two major stages: the diploid stage (2N), which occurs after fertilization; and the haploid stage (1N), which occurs after meiosis.

A replicated chromosome consists of two identical sister chromatids that remain connected by a centromere. At mitosis, all the chromosomes attach their replicated and connected centromeres to a bipolar spindle apparatus. For each replicated chromosome, the two centromeres become attached to spindle fibers pointing in opposite directions (the metaphase stage of mitosis). Moving along the spindle fibers (the anaphase stage of mitosis), the sister chromatids of each replicated chromosome separate and move to opposite poles. Thus mitosis ensures that when a single cell divides into two, each new daughter cell is equipped with a complete and equal set of genetic instructions. After fertilization, the **zygote** grows into an embryo and then an adult by using mitosis until the time for sexual reproduction (flowering).

zygote the egg immediately after it has been fertilized; the one-cell stage of a new individual

When producing sperm and egg cells for sexual reproduction, the genetic content must first be reduced from diploid to haploid. This reduction is accomplished by meiosis, a specialized process involving two sequential nuclear DNA divisions without an intervening DNA replication step. The first division requires the matching diploid chromosomes to pair, two-by-two, then segregate away from each other to reduce the genome from diploid to haploid. This chromosome pairing is necessary for proper chromosome segregation and much of the genetic shuffling that takes place from one generation to the next. The second meiotic division is like mitosis and divides replicated chromosomes into the haploid gamete-producing cells. Plant pollen mother cells that undergo meiosis provide excellent cytogenetic **specimens** to study because the cells and chromosomes are easy to see under the microscope.

specimen object or organism under consideration

Transposable Elements

Transposable DNA elements are sometimes called "jumping genes" because they can move around within the genome. The earliest evidence for the existence of these transposons came from analysis of certain strains of corn by McClintock. At the time in the 1940s, the idea that some parts of the chromosome could be mobile contradicted the notion that the chromosome was a stable, single structure. McClintock's pioneering work on transposons was formally recognized in 1983 when she was awarded a Nobel Prize. The activity of transposons sometimes causes visible features such as stripes and speckles on seeds (such as maize or beans) or flowers (such as petunias).

Transposons are active in most species of plants and animals, and their hopping around can change or even break individual genes. Thus transposons are thought to provide a source of genetic variation within the gene pool of a breeding population. In recent years, many plant transposons have been isolated molecularly (cloned) and used as tools to study plant genetics and create new genetic variations (mutations) by a technique called transposon mutagenesis. SEE ALSO CELL CYCLE; FLOWERS; GENETIC ENGINEERING; MCCLINTOCK, BARBARA; REPRODUCTION, SEXUAL.

Hank W. Bass

Bibliography

John, Bernard. *Meiosis.* New York: Cambridge University Press, 1990.

Fedoroff, Nina, and David Botstein. *The Dynamic Genome: Barbara McClintock's Ideas in the Century of Genetics.* Plainview, NY: Cold Spring Harbor Laboratory Press, 1992.

Classification *See Taxonomy.*

Clements, Frederic

American Botanist
1874–1945

More than any scientist of his time, Frederic Clements (1874–1945) developed the methods and ideas that helped ecologists unravel nature's complexity. Indeed, ecology is arguably the most complex of all the sciences. The natural world that ecologists seek to understand is in constant flux. The weather and hundreds of other variables in the environment change from day to day, month to month, and from year to year. In any given habitat thousands of species and millions of individual plants and animals interact in a bewildering array of intricate associations.

When Clements arrived at the University of Nebraska in 1892 to begin studies in botany, the science of ecology was just beginning to crystallize from its diverse origins in plant **physiology**, plant geography, and plant **morphology**. Clements had been influenced by several European botanists, especially the German plant geographer Oscar Drude. Drawing on the ideas of Alexander von Humboldt, Drude had stressed the **holistic** nature of the plant community and the need for general theories of plant distribution rather than static descriptions of where different species lived. While studying at Nebraska, Clements began to formulate his own theory of plant associations. He soon became the leading ecologist in America during the early part of the twentieth century.

Despite his stature, little has been written about Clements's life outside of his contributions to ecology and the plant sciences. We know that he received his doctoral degree from Nebraska in 1898 and married another Nebraska Ph.D. student, Edith Schwartz. The two collaborated on research and published numerous scientific books throughout their lives. After his studies at Nebraska, Clements joined the biology department at the University of Minnesota. In 1913, the Carnegie Institution of Washington helped Clements move his field studies to the Alpine Laboratory near Pikes Peak in Colorado. There Clements and his wife conducted detailed studies of environmental influences on plant associations, including the effects of temperature, humidity, light levels, and evaporation.

Early in his career, Clements set out to bring order to what was thought of as the chaotic and unsystematized state of ecology. Over a period of forty years, Clements developed a dynamic theory of plant communities that viewed plant associations as constantly changing rather than static, fixed entities. One of the major ideas that Clements used to understand ecological systems was the concept of vegetation as a super organism. To Clements, plant communities, like an animal's body, are comprised of interrelated parts, each vital to the functioning of the entire organism. Just like an individual organism, communities are born, grow, and mature, and then die.

physiology the biochemical processes carried out by an organism

morphology shape and form

holistic including all the parts or factors that relate to an object or idea

Clements is best known for his theory of ecological succession. Building on the studies of Johannes Warming and Henry Chandler Cowles, Clements stated as a universal law that "all bare places give rise to new communities except those which present the most extreme conditions." Clements spent a lifetime studying vegetational changes in "bare places" such as ploughed fields or forests destroyed by fire. One of his major conclusions was that, in a given climatic area, all ecological successions lead to the same stable association of plant species. Clements called this final stage in a series of changes in plant communities the "climax state." While modern ecologists have rejected the theory of stable climax associations, Clements's pioneering ideas continue to influence our efforts to understand change and complexity in the natural world. SEE ALSO HUMBOLDT, ALEXANDER VON; WARMING, JOHANNES.

Bradford Carlton Lister

Bibliography

Clements, F. E. "Nature and Structure of the Climax." *Journal of Ecology* 24 (1936): 252–84.

Kingsland, S. E. *Modeling Nature Episodes in the History of Population Ecology.* Chicago: University of Chicago Press, 1985.

McIntosh, R. P. *The Background of Ecology: Concept and Theory.* Cambridge: Cambridge University Press, 1985.

Clines and Ecotypes

Clines and ecotypes are variants of a particular species adapted to a specific locale or set of environmental conditions. Charles Darwin (1809–1882) put forth his concept of evolution by natural selection to explain patterns of within species variation in 1859. Early-twentieth-century plant ecologists and **systematists** such as Frederic Clements (1874–1945) and Gote Turesson (1892–1970) recognized the usefulness of Darwin's theory and built on it. These plant biologists reasoned that variation within species reflects adaptations to specific environmental conditions.

Different **populations** of the same species often grow across a range of environmental conditions, encompassing variation in moisture levels, soil composition, length of growing season, types and amounts of **herbivores**, and, for animal-pollinated species, even variation in the composition of the pollinators. These differences in environmental conditions may generate different selection pressures across the species range, resulting in genetic divergence among populations. For example, studies of Northern Hemisphere native plants often reveal that populations from more southern latitudes require shorter day length to flower than higher latitude populations of the same species. Natural selection has favored individuals found at higher latitudes to flower later, when conditions are more favorable for growth and when pollinators are abundant. In many examples researchers have conducted transplant experiments, taking plants from one locale and growing them in the site of another population of the same species. Often the transplants perform less successfully than plants from the home locale, demonstrating that the two populations are genetically diverged in terms of their adaptation to local environmental conditions (see Briggs and Walters, 1984, for examples).

systematists scientists who study systematics, the classification of species to reflect evolutionary relationships

population a group of organisms of a single species that exist in the same region and interbreed

herbivore an organism that feeds on plant parts

Sand verbena and dune evening primrose bloom at night, adapted to the desert conditions of Joshua Tree National Monument in California.

These genetically based adaptations to the environment were first termed "ecotypes" by Turesson. The ecotype concept integrates the type concept of systematists, who group organisms that are most similar to the type specimen (the "ideal" representative of the species) with the realization that within-species variation has important ecological significance. The ecotype concept suggests that variation is discrete or discontinuous and early critics noted that important environmental variation, such as the day length example, is continuous and graded. Thus to the ecotype concept was added the notion of clinal variation, such that continuous variation of traits would reflect responses by populations to environmental selective agents. The demonstration of ecotypes and clines was very important to the confirmation of Darwin's theory of evolution by natural selection and continues to provide insight into the mechanisms of evolution of biological variation.

The recognition of ecotypic and clinal variation has also figured prominently in the development of conservation and restoration policy of biodiversity. The primary concerns are the permanent loss of adaptive genetic variation as rare plants become reduced to few populations, deciding which populations to save based on strategies to maximize the species range, and the adaptation of captive populations (in zoos or botanical gardens) to their captive environment at the cost of their ability to survive in their native wild environment. Most of the current questions in the study of biodiversity revolve around our limited understanding of the genetics of adaptations, in particular how rapidly populations can evolve ecotypes. This, in turn, depends on the amount of genetic variation maintained within populations and the ability of new mutations to contribute to adaptive change. SEE ALSO BIOGEOGRAPHY; BIOME; CLEMENTS, FREDERIC; DARWIN, CHARLES.

Charles B. Fenster and Hans K. Stenøien

Bibliography

Briggs, D., and S. M. Walters. *Plant Variation and Evolution.* Cambridge: Cambridge University Press, 1984.

Clements, F. E. "An Ecological View of the Species Concept." *American Naturalist* 42 (1908): 253.

Darwin, Charles. *On the Origins of Species by Natural Selection, or the Preservation of Favored Races in the Struggle for Life.* Cambridge, MA: Harvard University Press, 1859.

Turesson, G. "The Species and Variety as Ecological Units." *Hereditas* 3 (1922): 100–13.

Photo and Illustration Credits

The illustrations and tables featured in Plant Sciences *were created by GGS Information Services. The photographs appearing in the text were reproduced by permission of the following sources:*

Volume 1

Ted Spiegel/Corbis: **2, 17, 96;** JLM Visuals: **4, 107;** Bojan Brecelj/Corbis: **6;** Tom Bean/Corbis: **9, 49;** Thomas Del Brase/The Stock Market: **11;** Chinch Gryniewicz; Ecoscene/Corbis: **13;** Charles O'Rear/Corbis: **19;** Steve Raymer/Corbis: **21;** Alex Rakoey/Custom Medical Stock Photo, Inc.: **28;** Wolfgang Kaehler/Corbis: **30, 100;** Field Mark Publications: **44;** Lester V. Bergman/Corbis: **50, 158;** Julie Meech; Ecoscene/Corbis: **53;** Raymond Gehman/Corbis: **55;** Dr. Kari Lounatmaa; Science Photo Library/Photo Researchers, Inc: **57;** Roger Tidman/Corbis: **58;** The Purcell Team/Corbis: **60;** David Muench/Corbis: **63, 114;** Adrian Arbib/Corbis: **67;** Barry Griffiths; National Audubon Society Collection/Photo Researchers, Inc.: **76;** Kopp Illustration, 81; Prof. Jim Watson; Science Photo Library/Photo Researchers, Inc: **85;** Michael S. Yamashita/Corbis: **87;** Pallava Bagla/Corbis: **88;** Bettmann/Corbis: **90, 116;** Richard T. Nowitz/Corbis: **92, 94;** UPI/Corbis–Bettmann: **109;** Owen Franken/Corbis: **112;** Bill Lisenby/Corbis: **119;** Hans & Cassady: **124, 136;** Fritz Polking; Frank Lane Picture Agency/Corbis: **128;** Ron Watts/Corbis: **130;** UPI/Bettmann Newsphotos: **131;** David Spears; Science Pictures Limited/Corbis: **138, 143;** Dr. Dennis Kunkel/Phototake NYC: **141;** Dr. Jeremy Burgess/Photo Researchers, Inc.: **146, 155;** Andrew Brown; Ecoscene/Corbis: **148;** Richard Cummins/Corbis: **162.**

Volume 2

Arne Hodalic/Corbis: **2;** Gregory G. Dimijian/Photo Researchers, Inc.: **5;** Michael & Patricia Fogden/Corbis: **9;** Dean Conger/Corbis: **11, 76;** Joseph Sohm; ChromoSohm, Inc./Corbis: **16;** Darrell Gulin/Corbis: **18, 61;** Galen Rowell/Corbis: **23;** Courtesy of the Library of Congress: **24, 40, 143;** Charles O'Rear/Corbis: **26, 157;** Liba Taylor/Corbis: **29;** Richard Hamilton Smith/Corbis: **31, 32;** Bojan Brecelj/Corbis: **35;** Lester V. Bergman/Corbis: **39, 119, 166, 175;** Robert Estall/Corbis: **48;** William A. Bake/Corbis: **52;** Rosemary Mayer/Photo Researchers, Inc.: **54;** George Lepp/Corbis: **56;** Michael S. Yamashita/Corbis: **58, 114;** Raymond Gehman/Corbis: **62, 93;** Wayne Lawler; Ecoscene/Corbis: **64;** Dr. William M. Harlow/Photo Researchers, Inc.: **66;** William Boyce/Corbis: **74;** David Spears; Science Pictures Limited/Corbis: **82;** Roger Tidman/Corbis: **84;** Hans & Cassady: **86;** Roger Ressmeyer/Corbis: **103;** Susan Middleton and David Liitschwager/Corbis: **107;** Robin Foster/Conservation International: **108;** John Durham/Photo Researchers, Inc.: **112;** Jaime Razuri; AFP/Corbis: **116;** Courtesy of Linda E. Graham: **122, 125;** Buddy Mays/Corbis: **136;** Michael Freeman/Corbis: **142;** Field Mark Publications: **146, 186;** David Cumming; Eye Ubiquitous/Corbis: **149;** Bob Krist/Corbis: **152;** Gunter Marx/Corbis: **154;** Jim Sugar Photography/Corbis: **156;** Courtesy of Dr. Orson K. Miller, Jr.: **162, 163, 164;** Lowell Georgia/Corbis: **167, 170;** William James Warren/Corbis: **169;** Patrick Johns/Corbis: **178;** Eric and David Hosking/Corbis: **180;** Thomas Bettge,

National Center for Atmospheric Research/ University Corporation for Atmospheric Research/National Science Foundation: **182, 183**; Philip Gould/Corbis: **184**; Roy Morsch/ The Stock Market: **188**; Tom Bean/Corbis: **190**; Archive Photos, Inc.: **194**; JLM Visuals: **199, 200**.

Volume 3

Courtesy of the Library of Congress: **1, 30, 61, 73**; JLM Visuals: **3, 49, 106**; Corbis: **4**; Anthony Cooper; Ecoscene/Corbis: **9**; Photo Researchers, Inc.: **11**; Archive Photos, Inc.: **12**; Ed Young/Corbis: **23, 147**; Kansas Division of Travel and Tourism: **26**; Asa Thoresen/Photo Researchers, Inc.: **28**; Ted Streshinsky/Corbis: **32**; Michael S. Yamashita/Corbis: **35**; Patrick Johns/Corbis: **38, 96, 104, 125, 187**; Cumego/Corbis/ Bettmann: **39**; David Spears; Science Pictures Limited/Corbis: **41, 54, 114, 129**; W. Wayne Lockwood, M.D./Corbis: **42**; Field Mark Publications: **44, 57, 71, 169, 171, 175**; Michael & Patricia Fogden/Corbis: **46**; Phil Schermeister/Corbis: **52**; Judyth Platt; Ecoscene/Corbis: **59**; Courtesy of Hunt Institute for Botanical Documentation, Carnegie Mellon University, Pittsburgh, PA: **62**; UPI/Bettmann: **66**; Eric Crichton/Corbis: **72**; Biophoto Associates; National Audubon Society Collection/Photo Researchers, Inc.: **88**; Adam Hart-Davis/Photo Researchers, Inc.: **92**; Lester V. Bergman/Corbis: **94, 108, 167**; Patrick Field; Eye Ubiquitous/Corbis: **103**; Michael Boys/Corbis: **105**; Sally A. Morgan; Ecoscene/Corbis: **110**; Kevin Schafer/Corbis: **112**; Jim Zipp; National Audubon Society Collection/Photo Researchers, Inc.: **117**; Richard T. Nowitz/ Corbis: **120**; Wayne Lawler; Ecoscene/ Corbis: **122**; Bob Krist/Corbis: **123**; Tom and

Pat Lesson/Photo Researchers, Inc.: **158**; Raymond Gehman/Corbis: **164**; George Lepp/Corbis: **177**; Richard Hamilton Smith/Corbis: **181**; Nigel Cattlin; Holt Studios International/Photo Researchers, Inc.: **185**; Owen Franken/Corbis: **189**; Alison Wright/Corbis: **193**.

Volume 4

Kevin Schafer/Corbis: **2, 42**; Wolfgang Kaehler/Corbis: **5, 7**; E. S. Ross: **9**; Galen Rowell/Corbis: **14, 127**; David Spears; Science Pictures Limited/Corbis: **17, 20, 79, 120, 161, 172**; Robert Pickett/Corbis: **19, 101**; Dr. Jeremy Burgess/Photo Researchers, Inc.: **21, 159**; Biophoto Associates/Photo Researchers, Inc.: **22, 142**; JLM Visuals: **25, 26, 40, 140, 155, 169**; Owen Franken/ Corbis: **27**; Philip Gould/Corbis: **30, 70**; Corbis: **39, 152**; Steve Raymer/Corbis: **49**; Mark Gibson/Corbis: **57**; James Lee Sikkema: **58**; Field Mark Publications: **62, 130, 167**; Wayne Lawler/Corbis: **63**; Richard T. Nowitz/Corbis: **66**; Photo Researchers, Inc.: **68**; Karen Tweedy-Holmes/Corbis: **73**; Lester V. Bergman/Corbis: **77, 147**; Craig Aurness/Corbis: **83**; John Holmes; Frank Lane Picture Agency/Corbis: **86**; Archivo Iconografico, S.A./Corbis: **92**; Paul Almasy/Corbis: **98**; Tiziana and Gianni Baldizzone/Corbis: **105**; Darrell Gulin/ Corbis: **108**; Lynda Richardson/Corbis: **110**; Courtesy of Thomas L. Rost and Deborah K. Canington: **112, 113, 114**; Laure Communications: **115**; Archive Photos, Inc.: **116**; Jim Sugar Photography/Corbis: **132**; Hugh Clark; Frank Lane Picture Agency/Corbis: **136, 137**; Ron Boardman; Frank Lane Picture Agency/ Corbis: **148**; Richard Hamilton Smith/Corbis: **165**; Joseph Sohm; ChromoSohm, Inc./ Corbis: **175**; Dave G. Houser/Corbis: **176**.

Glossary

abiotic nonliving

abrade to wear away through contact

abrasive tending to wear away through contact

abscission dropping off or separating

accession a plant that has been acquired and catalogued

achene a small, dry, thin-walled type of fruit

actinomycetes common name for a group of Gram-positive bacteria that are filamentous and superficially similar to fungi

addictive capable of causing addiction or chemical dependence

adhesion sticking to the surface of

adventitious arising from secondary buds, or arising in an unusual position

aeration the introduction of air

albuminous gelatinous, or composed of the protein albumin

alkali chemically basic; the opposite of acidic

alkalinization increase in basicity or reduction in acidity

alkaloid bitter secondary plant compound, often used for defense

allele one form of a gene

allelopathy harmful action by one plant against another

allopolyploidy a polyploid organism formed by hybridization between two different species or varieties (*allo* = other)

alluvial plain broad area formed by the deposit of river sediment at its outlet

amended soils soils to which fertilizers or other growth aids have been added

amendment additive

anaerobic without oxygen

analgesic pain-relieving

analog a structure or thing, especially a chemical, similar to something else

angiosperm a flowering plant

anomalous unusual or out of place

anoxic without oxygen

antenna system a collection of protein complexes that harvests light energy and converts it to excitation energy that can migrate to a reaction center; the light is absorbed by pigment molecules (e.g., chlorophyll, carotenoids, phycobilin) that are attached to the protein

anthropogenic human-made; related to or produced by the influence of humans on nature

antibodies proteins produced to fight infection

antioxidant a substance that prevents damage from oxygen or other reactive substances

apical meristem region of dividing cells at the tips of growing plants

apical at the tip

apomixis asexual reproduction that may mimic sexual reproduction

appendages parts that are attached to a central stalk or axis

arable able to be cultivated for crops

Arcto-Tertiary geoflora the fossil flora discovered in Arctic areas dating back to the Tertiary period; this group contains magnolias (*Magnolia*), tulip trees (*Liriodendron*), maples (*Acer*), beech (*Fagus*), black gum (*Nyssa*), sweet gum (*Liquidambar*), dawn redwood (*Metasequoia*), cypress (*Taxodium*), and many other species

artifacts pots, tools, or other cultural objects

assayer one who performs chemical tests to determine the composition of a substance

ATP adenosine triphosphate, a small, water-soluble molecule that acts as an energy currency in cells

attractant something that attracts

autotroph "self-feeder"; any organism that uses sunlight or chemical energy

auxin a plant hormone

avian related to birds

axil the angle or crotch where a leaf stalk meets the stem

axillary bud the bud that forms in the angle between the stem and leaf

basipetal toward the base

belladonna the source of atropine; means "beautiful woman," and is so named because dilated pupils were thought to enhance a woman's beauty

binomial two-part

biodirected assays tests that examine some biological property

biodiversity degree of variety of life

biogeography the study of the reasons for the geographic distribution of organisms

biomass the total dry weight of an organism or group of organisms

biosphere the region of the Earth in which life exists

biosynthesis creation through biological pathways

biota the sum total of living organisms in a region of a given size

biotic involving or related to life

bryologist someone who studies bryophytes, a division of nonflowering plants

campanulate bell-shaped

capitulum the head of a compound flower, such as a dandelion

cardiotonic changing the contraction properties of the heart

carotenoid a yellow-colored molecule made by plants

carpels the innermost whorl of flower parts, including the egg-bearing ovules, plus the style and stigma attached to the ovules

catastrophism the geologic doctrine that sudden, violent changes mark the geologic history of Earth

cation positively charged particle

catkin a flowering structure used for wind pollination

centrifugation spinning at high speed in a centrifuge to separate components

chitin a cellulose-like molecule found in the cell wall of many fungi and arthropods

chloroplast the photosynthetic organelle of plants and algae

circadian "about a day"; related to a day

circumscription the definition of the boundaries surrounding an object or an idea

cisterna a fluid-containing sac or space

clade a group of organisms composed of an ancestor and all of its descendants

cladode a modified stem having the appearance and function of a leaf

coalescing roots roots that grow together

coleoptile the growing tip of a monocot seedling

collenchyma one of three cell types in ground tissue

colonize to inhabit a new area

colony a group of organisms inhabiting a particular area, especially organisms descended from a common ancestor

commensalism a symbiotic association in which one organism benefits while the other is unaffected

commodities goods that are traded, especially agricultural goods

community a group of organisms of different species living in a region

compaction compacting of soil, leading to the loss of air spaces

complex hybrid hybridized plant having more than two parent plants

compound a substance formed from two or more elements

concentration gradient a difference in concentration between two areas

continental drift the movement of continental land masses due to plate tectonics

contractile capable of contracting

convective uplift the movement of air upwards due to heating from the sun

coppice growth the growth of many stems from a single trunk or root, following the removal of the main stem

cortical relating to the cortex of a plant

covalent held together by electron-sharing bonds

crassulacean acid metabolism water-conserving strategy used by several types of plants

crop rotation alternating crops from year to year in a particular field

cultivation growth of plants, or turning the soil for growth of crop plants

crystallography the use of x-rays on crystals to determine molecular structure

cuticle the waxy outer coating of a leaf or other structure, which provides protection against predators, infection, and water loss

cyanide heap leach gold mining a technique used to extract gold by treating ore with cyanide

cyanobacteria photosynthetic prokaryotic bacteria formerly known as blue-green algae

cyanogenic giving rise to cyanide

cytologist a scientist who studies cells

cytology the microscopic study of cells and cell structure

cytosol the fluid portion of a cell

cytostatic inhibiting cell division

deductive reasoning from facts to conclusion

dendrochronologist a scientist who uses tree rings to determine climate or other features of the past

dermatophytes fungi that cause skin diseases

desertification degradation of dry lands, reducing productivity

desiccation drying out

detritus material from decaying organisms

diatoms hard-shelled, single-celled marine organisms; a type of algae

dictyosome any one of the membranous or vesicular structures making up the Golgi apparatus

dioicous having male and female sexual parts on different plants

diploid having two sets of chromosomes, versus having one set (haploid)

dissipate to reduce by spreading out or scattering

distal further away from

diurnal daily, or by day

domestication the taming of an organism to live with and be of use to humans

dormant inactive, not growing

drupe a fruit with a leathery or stone-like seed

dynamical system theory the mathematical theory of change within a system

ecophysiological related to how an organism's physiology affects its function in an ecosystem

ecosystem an ecological community and its environment

elater an elongated, thickened filament

empirical formula the simplest whole number ratio of atoms in a compound

emulsifier a chemical used to suspend oils in water

encroachment moving in on

endemic belonging or native to a particular area or country

endophyte a fungus that lives within a plant

endoplasmic reticulum the membrane network inside a cell

endosperm the nutritive tissue in a seed, formed by the fertilization of a diploid egg tissue by a sperm from pollen

endosporic the formation of a gametophyte inside the spore wall

endosymbiosis a symbiosis in which one organism lives inside the other

Enlightenment eighteenth-century philosophical movement stressing rational critique of previously accepted doctrines in all areas of thought

entomologist a scientist who studies insects

enzyme a protein that controls a reaction in a cell

ephemeral short-lived

epicuticle the waxy outer covering of a plant, produced by the epidermis

epidermis outer layer of cells

epiphytes plants that grow on other plants

escarpment a steep slope or cliff resulting from erosion

ethnobotanist a scientist who interacts with native peoples to learn more about the plants of a region

ethnobotany the study of traditional uses of plants within a culture

euglossine bees a group of bees that pollinate orchids and other rain-forest plants

eukaryotic a cell with a nucleus (*eu* means "true" and *karyo* means "nucleus"); includes protists, plants, animals, and fungi

extrafloral outside the flower

exudation the release of a liquid substance; oozing

facultative capable of but not obligated to

fertigation application of small amounts of fertilizer while irrigating

filament a threadlike extension

filamentous thin and long

flagella threadlike extension of the cell membrane, used for movement

flavonoids aromatic compounds occurring in both seeds and young roots and involved in host-pathogen and host-symbiont interactions

florigen a substance that promotes flowering

floristic related to plants

follicle sac or pouch

forbs broad-leaved, herbaceous plants

free radicals toxic molecular fragments

frugivous feeding on fruits

gametangia structure where gametes are formed

gametophyte the haploid organism in the life cycle

gel electrophoresis a technique for separating molecules based on size and electrical charge

genera plural of genus; a taxonomic level above species

genome the genetic material of an organism

genotype the genetic makeup of an organism

germplasm hereditary material, especially stored seed or other embryonic forms

globose rounded and swollen; globe-shaped

gradient difference in concentration between two places

green manure crop planted to be plowed under to nourish the soil, especially with nitrogen

gymnosperm a major group of plants that includes the conifers

gynoecium the female reproductive organs as a whole

gypsipherous containing the mineral gypsum

hallucinogenic capable of inducing hallucinations

haploid having one set of chromosomes, versus having two (diploid)

haustorial related to a haustorium, or food-absorbing organ

hemiterpene a half terpene

herbivore an organism that feeds on plant parts

heterocyclic a chemical ring structure composed of more than one type of atom, for instance carbon and nitrogen

heterosporous bearing spores of two types, large megaspores and small microspores

heterostylous having styles (female flower parts) of different lengths, to aid cross-pollination

heterotroph an organism that derives its energy from consuming other organisms or their body parts

holistic including all the parts or factors that relate to an object or idea

homeotic relating to or being a gene that produces a shift in structural development

homology a similarity in structure between anatomical parts due to descent from a common ancestor

humus the organic material in soil formed from decaying organisms

hybrid a mix of two varieties or species

hybridization formation of a new individual from parents of different species or varieties

hydrological cycle the movement of water through the biosphere

hydrophobic water repellent

hydroponic growing without soil, in a watery medium

hydroxyl the chemical group -OH

hyphae the threadlike body mass of a fungus

illicit illegal

impede to slow down or inhibit

inert incapable of reaction

inflorescence a group of flowers or arrangement of flowers in a flower head

infrastructure roads, phone lines, and other utilities that allow commerce

insectivorous insect-eating

intercalary inserted; between

interspecific hybridization hybridization between two species

intertidal between the lines of high and low tide

intracellular bacteria bacteria that live inside other cells

intraspecific taxa levels of classification below the species level

intuiting using intuition

ionic present as a charged particle

ions charged particles

irreversible unable to be reversed

juxtaposition contrast brought on by close positioning

lacerate cut

Lamarckian inheritance the hypothesis that acquired characteristics can be inherited

lamellae thin layers or plate-like structure

land-grant university a state university given land by the federal government on the condition that it offer courses in agriculture

landrace a variety of a cultivated plant, occurring in a particular region

lateral to the side of

legume beans and other members of the Fabaceae family

lignified composed of lignin, a tough and resistant plant compound

lineage ancestry; the line of evolutionary descent of an organism

loci (singular: locus) sites or locations

lodging falling over while still growing

lytic breaking apart by the action of enzymes

macromolecule a large molecule such as a protein, fat, nucleic acid, or carbohydrate

macroscopic large, visible

medulla middle part

megaphylls large leaves having many veins or a highly branched vein system

meiosis the division of chromosomes in which the resulting cells have half the original number of chromosomes

meristem the growing tip of a plant

mesic of medium wetness

microfibrils microscopic fibers in a cell

micron one millionth of a meter; also called micrometer

microphylls small leaves having a single unbranched vein

mitigation reduction of amount or effect

mitochondria cell organelles that produce adenosine triphosphate (ATP) to power cell reactions

mitosis the part of the cell cycle in which chromosomes are separated to give each daughter cell an identical chromosome set

molecular systematics the analysis of DNA and other molecules to determine evolutionary relationships

monoculture a large stand of a single crop species

monomer a single unit of a multi-unit structure

monophyletic a group that includes an ancestral species and all its descendants

montane growing in a mountainous region

morphology shape and form

motile capable of movement

mucilaginous sticky or gummy

murein a peptidoglycan, a molecule made up of sugar derivatives and amino acids

mutualism a symbiosis between two organisms in which both benefit

mycelium the vegetative body of a fungus, made up of threadlike hyphae

NADP⁺ oxidized form of nicotinamide adenine dinucleotide phosphate

NADPH reduced form of nicotinamide adenine dinucleotide phosphate, a small, water-soluble molecule that acts as a hydrogen carrier in biochemical reactions

nanometer one billionth of a meter

nectaries organs in flowers that secrete nectar

negative feedback a process by which an increase in some variable causes a response that leads to a decrease in that variable

neuromuscular junction the place on the muscle surface where the muscle receives stimulus from the nervous system

neurotransmitter a chemical that passes messages between nerve cells

node branching site on a stem

nomenclature a naming system

nonmotile not moving

nonpolar not directed along the root-shoot axis, or not marked by separation of charge (unlike water and other polar substances)

nonsecretory not involved in secretion, or the release of materials

Northern Blot a technique for separating RNA molecules by electrophoresis and then identifying a target fragment with a DNA probe

nucleolar related to the nucleolus, a distinct region in the nucleus

nurseryman a worker in a plant nursery

obligate required, without another option

obligate parasite a parasite without a free-living stage in the life cycle

odorant a molecule with an odor

organelle a membrane-bound structure within a cell

osmosis the movement of water across a membrane to a region of high solute concentration

oviposition egg-laying

oxidation reaction with oxygen, or loss of electrons in a chemical reaction

paleobotany the study of ancient plants and plant communities

pangenesis the belief that acquired traits can be inherited by bodily influences on the reproductive cells

panicle a type of inflorescence (flower cluster) that is loosely packed and irregularly branched

paraphyletic group a taxonomic group that excludes one or more descendants of a common ancestor

parenchyma one of three types of cells found in ground tissue

pastoralists farming people who keep animal flocks

pathogen disease-causing organism

pedicel a plant stalk that supports a fruiting or spore-bearing organ

pentamerous composed of five parts

percolate to move through, as a fluid through a solid

peribacteroid a membrane surrounding individual or groups of rhizobia bacteria within the root cells of their host; in such situations the bacteria have frequently undergone some change in surface chemistry and are referred to as bacteroids

pericycle cell layer between the conducting tissue and the endodermis

permeability the property of being permeable, or open to the passage of other substances

petiole the stalk of a leaf, by which it attaches to the stem

pH a measure of acidity or alkalinity; the pH scale ranges from 0 to 14, with 7 being neutral. Low pH numbers indicate high acidity while high numbers indicate alkalinity

pharmacognosy the study of drugs derived from natural products

pharmacopeia a group of medicines

phenology seasonal or other time-related aspects of an organism's life

pheromone a chemical released by one organism to influence the behavior of another

photooxidize to react with oxygen under the influence of sunlight

photoperiod the period in which an organism is exposed to light or is sensitive to light exposure, causing flowering or other light-sensitive changes

photoprotectant molecules that protect against damage by sunlight

phylogenetic related to phylogeny, the evolutionary development of a species

physiology the biochemical processes carried out by an organism

phytogeographer a scientist who studies the distribution of plants

pigments colored molecules

pistil the female reproductive organ of a flower

plasmodesmata cell-cell junctions that allow passage of small molecules between cells

polyculture mixed species

polyhedral in the form of a polyhedron, a solid whose sides are polygons

polymer a large molecule made from many similar parts

polynomial "many-named"; a name composed of several individual parts

polyploidy having multiple sets of chromosomes

polysaccharide a linked chain of many sugar molecules

population a group of organisms of a single species that exist in the same region and interbreed

porosity openness

positive feedback a process by which an increase in some variable causes a response that leads to a further increase in that variable

precipitation rainfall; or the process of a substance separating from a solution

pre-Columbian before Columbus

precursor a substance from which another is made

predation the act of preying upon; consuming for food

primordial primitive or early

progenitor parent or ancestor

prokaryotes single-celled organisms without nuclei, including Eubacteria and Archaea

propagate to create more of through sexual or asexual reproduction

protist a usually single-celled organism with a cell nucleus, of the kingdom Protista

protoplasmic related to the protoplasm, cell material within the cell wall

protoplast the portion of a cell within the cell wall

psychoactive causing an effect on the brain

pubescence covered with short hairs

pyruvic acid a three-carbon compound that forms an important intermediate in many cellular processes

quadruple hybrid hybridized plant with four parents

quantitative numerical, especially as derived from measurement

quid a wad for chewing

quinone chemical compound found in plants, often used in making dyes

radii distance across, especially across a circle (singular = radius)

radioisotopes radioactive forms of an element

rambling habit growing without obvious intended direction

reaction center a protein complex that uses light energy to create a stable charge separation by transferring a single electron energetically uphill from a donor molecule to an acceptor molecule, both of which are located in the reaction center

redox oxidation and reduction

regurgitant material brought up from the stomach

Renaissance a period of artistic and intellectual expansion in Europe from the fourteenth to the sixteenth century

salinization increase in salt content

samara a winged seed

saprophytes plants that feed on decaying parts of other plants

saturated containing as much dissolved substance as possible

sclerenchyma one of three cell types in ground tissue

sedimentation deposit of mud, sand, shell, or other material

semidwarf a variety that is intermediate in size between dwarf and full-size varieties

senescent aging or dying

sepals the outermost whorl of flower parts; usually green and leaf-like, they protect the inner parts of the flower

sequester to remove from circulation; lock up

serology the study of serum, the liquid, noncellular portion of blood

seta a stiff hair or bristle

silage livestock food produced by fermentation in a silo

siliceous composed of silica, a mineral

silicified composed of silicate minerals

soil horizon distinct layers of soil

solute a substance dissolved in a solution

Southern blot a technique for separating DNA fragments by electrophoresis and then identifying a target fragment with a DNA probe

spasticity abnormal muscle activity caused by damage to the nerve pathways controlling movement

speciation the creation of new species

specimen an object or organism under consideration

speciose marked by many species

sporophyte the diploid, spore-producing individual in the plant life cycle

sporulate to produce or release spores

sterile not capable or involved in reproduction, or unable to support life

sterols chemicals related to steroid hormones

stolons underground stems that may sprout and form new individuals

stomata openings between guard cells on the underside of leaves that allow gas exchange

stratification layering, or separation in space

stratigraphic geology the study of rock layers

stratigraphy the analysis of strata (layered rock)

strobili cone-like reproductive structures

subalpine a region less cold or elevated than alpine (mountaintop)

substrate the physical structure to which an organism attaches, or a molecule acted on by enzymes

succession the pattern of changes in plant species that occurs after a soil disturbance

succulent fleshy, moist

suckers naturally occuring adventitious shoots

suffrutescent a shrub-like plant with a woody base

sulfate a negatively charged particle combining sulfur and oxygen

surfaced smoothed for examination

susceptibility vulnerability

suture line of attachment

swidden agriculture the practice of farming an area until the soil has been depleted and then moving on

symbiont one member of a symbiotic association

symbiosis a relationship between organisms of two different species in which at least one benefits

systematists scientists who study systematics, the classification of species to reflect evolutionary relationships

systemic spread throughout the plant

tannins compounds produced by plants that usually serve protective functions, often colored and used for "tanning" and dyeing

taxa a type of organism, or a level of classification of organisms

tensile forces forces causing tension, or pulling apart; the opposite of compression

tepal an undifferentiated sepal or petal

Tertiary period geologic period from sixty-five to five million years ago

tetraploid having four sets of chromosomes; a form of polyploidy

thallus simple, flattened, nonleafy plant body

tilth soil structure characterized by open air spaces and high water storage capacity due to high levels of organic matter

tonoplast the membrane of the vacuole

topographic related to the shape or contours of the land

totipotent capable of forming entire plants from individual cells

toxin a poisonous substance

tracheid a type of xylem cell that conducts water from root to shoot

transcription factors proteins that bind to a specific DNA sequence called the promoter to regulate the expression of a nearby gene

translocate to move materials from one region to another

translucent allowing the passage of light

transmutation to change from one form to another

transpiration movement of water from soil to atmosphere through a plant

transverse across, or side to side

tribe a group of closely related genera

trophic related to feeding

turgor pressure the outward pressure exerted on the cell wall by the fluid within

twining twisting around while climbing

ultrastructural the level of structure visible with the electron microscope; very small details of structure

uniformitarian the geologic doctrine that formative processes on earth have proceeded at the same rate through time since earth's beginning

uplift raising up of rock layers, a geologic process caused by plate tectonics

urbanization increase in size or number of cities

vacuole the large fluid-filled sac that occupies most of the space in a plant cell. Used for storage and maintaining internal pressure

vascular plants plants with specialized transport cells; plants other than bryophytes

vascular related to the transport of nutrients, or related to blood vessels

vector a carrier, usually one that is not affected by the thing carried

vernal related to the spring season

vesicle a membrane-bound cell structure with specialized contents

viable able to live or to function

volatile easily released as a gas

volatilization the release of a gaseous substance

water table the level of water in the soil

whorl a ring

wort an old English term for plant; also an intermediate liquid in beer making

xenobiotics biomolecules from outside the plant, especially molecules that are potentially harmful

xeromorphic a form adapted for dry conditions

xerophytes plants adapted for growth in dry areas

zonation division into zones having different properties

zoospore a swimming spore

zygote the egg immediately after it has been fertilized; the one-cell stage of a new individual

Topic Outline

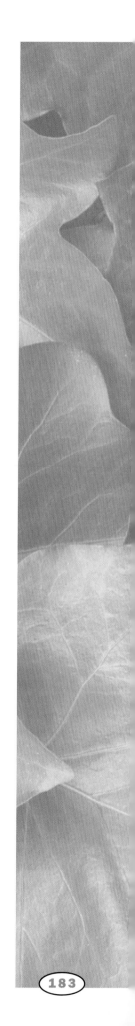

ADAPTATIONS

Alkaloids
Allelopathy
Cacti
Cells, Specialized Types
Clines and Ecotypes
Defenses, Chemical
Defenses, Physical
Halophytes
Lichens
Mycorrhizae
Nitrogen Fixation
Poisonous Plants
Seed Dispersal
Shape and Form of Plants
Symbiosis
Translocation
Trichomes

AGRICULTURE

Agriculture, History of
Agriculture, Modern
Agriculture, Organic
Agricultural Ecosystems
Agronomist
Alliaceae
Asteraceae
Biofuels
Borlaug, Norman
Breeder
Breeding
Burbank, Luther
Cacao
Carver, George W.
Coffee
Compost
Cork

Corn
Cotton
Economic Importance of Plants
Ethnobotany
Fertilizer
Fiber and Fiber Products
Food Scientist
Fruits
Fruits, Seedless
Genetic Engineer
Genetic Engineering
Grains
Grasslands
Green Revolution
Halophytes
Herbs and Spices
Herbicides
Horticulture
Horticulturist
Hydroponics
Native Food Crops
Nitrogen Fixation
Oils, Plant-Derived
Pathogens
Pathologist
Polyploidy
Potato
Potato Blight
Quantitative Trait Loci
Rice
Seed Preservation
Soil, Chemistry of
Soil, Physical Characteristics
Solanaceae
Soybeans
Sugar
Tea
Tissue Culture

Tobacco
Transgenic Plants
Vavilov, N. I.
Vegetables
Weeds
Wheat
Wine and Beer Industry

ANATOMY

Anatomy of Plants
Bark
Botanical and Scientific Illustrator
Cell Walls
Cells
Cells, Specialized Types
Cork
Differentiation and Development
Fiber and Fiber Products
Flowers
Fruits
Inflorescence
Leaves
Meristems
Mycorrhizae
Phyllotaxis
Plants
Roots
Seeds
Shape and Form of Plants
Stems
Tissues
Tree Architecture
Trichomes
Vascular Tissues
Vegetables
Wood Anatomy

BIOCHEMISTRY/PHYSIOLOGY

Alcoholic Beverage Industry
Alkaloids
Anthocyanins
Biofuels
Biogeochemical Cycles
Bioremediation
Carbohydrates
Carbon Cycle
Cells
Cellulose
Chlorophyll
Chloroplasts

Cytokinins
Defenses, Chemical
Ecology, Energy Flow
Fertilizer
Flavonoids
Flavor and Fragrance Chemist
Halophytes
Herbicides
Hormones
Lipids
Medicinal Plants
Nitrogen Fixation
Nutrients
Oils, Plant-Derived
Pharmaceutical Scientist
Photoperiodism
Photosynthesis, Carbon Fixation
Photosynthesis, Light Reactions
Physiologist
Pigments
Poisonous Plants
Psychoactive Plants
Soil, Chemistry of
Terpenes
Translocation
Vacuoles
Water Movement

BIODIVERSITY

Agricultural Ecosystems
Aquatic Ecosystems
Biodiversity
Biogeography
Biome
Botanical Gardens and Arboreta
Chapparal
Clines and Ecotypes
Coastal Ecosystems
Coniferous Forests
Curator of a Botanical Garden
Curator of an Herbarium
Deciduous Forests
Deforestation
Desertification
Deserts
Ecology
Ethnobotany
Global Warning
Herbaria
Human Impacts
Invasive Species

EVOLUTION

FOODS

HORTICULTURE

Alliaceae
Asteraceae
Bonsai
Botanical Gardens and Arboreta
Breeder
Breeding
Cacti
Curator of a Botanical Garden
Horticulture
Horticulturist
Hybrids and Hybridization
Hydroponics
Landscape Architect
Ornamental Plants
Polyploidy
Propagation
Turf Management

INDIVIDUAL PLANTS AND PLANT FAMILIES

Alliaceae
Asteraceae
Bamboo
Cacao
Cacti
Cannabis
Coca
Coffee
Corn
Cotton
Dioscorea
Fabaceae
Ginkgo
Grasses
Kudzu
Opium Poppy
Orchidaceae
Palms
Poison Ivy
Potato
Rice
Rosaceae
Sequoia
Solanaceae
Soybeans
Tobacco
Wheat

LIFE CYCLE

Breeder
Breeding Systems
Cell Cycle
Differentiation and Development
Embryogenesis
Flowers
Fruits
Gametophyte
Genetic Mechanisms and Development
Germination
Germination and Growth
Hormonal Control and Development
Meristems
Pollination Biology
Reproduction, Alternation of Generations
Reproduction, Asexual
Reproduction, Fertilization
Reproduction, Sexual
Rhythms in Plant Life
Seed Dispersal
Seed Preservation
Seeds
Senescence
Sporophyte
Tissue Culture

NUTRITION

Acid Rain
Biogeochemical Cycles
Carbon Cycle
Carnivorous Plants
Compost
Decomposers
Ecology, Fire
Epiphytes
Fertilizer
Germination and Growth
Hydroponics
Mycorrhizae
Nitrogen Fixation
Nutrients
Peat Bogs
Physiologist
Roots
Soil, Chemistry of
Soil, Physical Characteristics
Translocation
Water Movement

Volume 1 Index

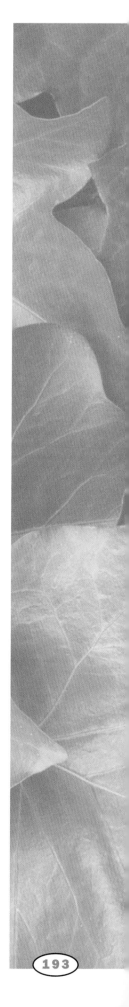

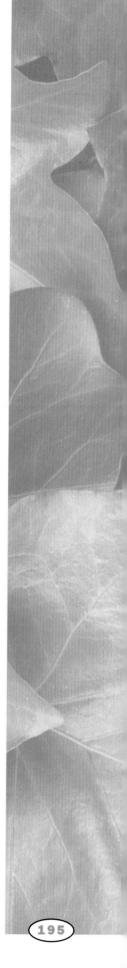